SugarCRM For Dumm

S0-AKC-624

Sugar Modules Explained

Here's what all modules have in common:

- ✔ A Home page listing all the records you've added to that module.
- ✔ Basic and Advanced searching capability for a record within a module.
- ✔ Sub-panels that contain related information.
- ✔ A Shortcuts menu.
- ✔ A Quick Entry form.
- ✔ The ability to mass update the records in the module.
- ✔ The ability to export a list of the module records.

The Most Frequently Used Modules

- ✔ **Accounts:** Companies that you do business with.
- ✔ **Contacts:** People that you do business with.
- ✔ **Leads:** People or companies that you hope you do business with in the future.
- ✔ **Campaigns:** An organized structure for keeping track of your marketing efforts; hopefully you'll attract new customers — and retain the ones you already have.
- ✔ **Opportunities:** Identifies the various chances you have for selling your goods or services.
- ✔ **Projects:** Your mega-tasks that generally require lots of steps — and lots of people to help you out.
- ✔ **Cases:** The customer service issues that your company is currently dealing with.

In addition to the basic SugarCRM modules, you can download more modules at www.sugarexchange.com/ or www.sugarforge.org/. If you still can't find just what you're looking for create your own using Sugar's module builder.

Breaking Down the SugarCRM Editions

Function	Community Edition	Professional Edition	Enterprise Edition
Contact Management			
Leads	X	X	X
Contacts	X	X	X
Accounts	X	X	X
Team Management		X	X
Offline Client			X
View Your Data			
Personal Home Page	X	X	X
Dashboards	X	X	X
Reporting		X	X
Advanced Charts & Dashboards		X	X
Advanced SQL Reporting			X

SugarCRM For Dummies®

Cheat Sheet

Function	Community Edition	Professional Edition	Enterprise Edition
Marketing			
Campaigns	X	X	X
E-mail marketing	X	X	X
E-mail Client	X	X	X
Web to Lead Forms	X	X	X
E-mail Templates	X	X	X
Outlook Integration		X	X
Word Templates		X	X
Scheduling			
Activity Management	X	X	X
Shared Calendar	X	X	X
Project Management	X	X	X
Advanced Project Management		X	X
Workflow		X	X
Sales			
Opportunities	X	X	X
Sales Forecasting		X	X
Product Catalog		X	X
Quotes & Contracts		X	X
Customer Support			
Cases	X	X	X
Bug Tracking	X	X	X
Knowledge Base		X	X
Customer Portals			X
Customizations			
Layout Editor	X	X	X
Module Builder	X	X	X
Custom Modules & Fields	X	X	X
Available in over 70 languages	X	X	X
Windows, Mac & Linux compatible	X	X	X
Access Control		X	X
Oracle Support			X

For Dummies: Bestselling Book Series for Beginners

by Karen S. Fredricks

Wiley Publishing, Inc.

SugarCRM® For Dummies®

Published by
Wiley Publishing, Inc.
111 River Street
Hoboken, NJ 07030-5774
www.wiley.com

For general information on our other products and services, please contact our Customer Care Department within the U.S. at 800-762-2974, outside the U.S. at 317-572-3993, or fax 317-572-4002.

For technical support, please visit www.wiley.com/techsupport.

Wiley also publishes its books in a variety of electronic formats. Some content that appears in print may not be available in electronic books.

Library of Congress Control Number: 2008939702

ISBN: 978-0-470-38462-6

Manufactured in the United States of America

10 9 8 7 6 5 4 3 2 1

WILEY

About the Author

Karen S. Fredricks began her life rather non-technically, growing up in Kenya. She attended high school in Beirut, Lebanon, where she developed her sense of humor while dodging bombs. After traveling all over the world, Karen ended up at the University of Florida and has been an ardent Gator fan ever since. In addition to undergraduate studies in English and accounting, Karen has a Master's degree in psycholinguistics. Beginning her career teaching high school English and theatre, Karen switched to working with the PC during its inception in the early '80s and has worked as a full-time consultant and trainer ever since.

Karen holds certifications in ACT!, QuickBooks, and Microsoft Office. This is the tenth For Dummies book that she has written. Specializing in CRM and contact management software, she has written titles on ACT!, Outlook 2007, Outlook 2007 with Business Contact Manager, and Microsoft Office Live. She is a frequent guest on several syndicated computer radio talk shows and has frequent public speaking engagements.

Karen resides in Boca Raton, Florida. Her company, Tech Benders, specializes in CRM software and provides computer consulting, support, and training services. Karen particularly enjoys helping her clients increase their bottom line through their marketing efforts and improved sales processes. In her spare time, Karen loves to spend time with family and friends, play tennis, work out, ride bikes, and write schlocky poetry.

Feel free to send your comments about the book to www.dummies@tech benders.com.

Dedication

This book is dedicated to new and existing CRM users. I know that you'll be able to use this book to take your business to "the next level." I hope you enjoy reading it as much as enjoyed writing it!

Acknowledgments

The people at Wiley Publishing are fantastic to work with and have made writing this book a pleasure! My acquisitions editor, Kyle Looper, is a joy to work with. This is the third book I've done with my project editor, Blair Pottenger; I know when to stick with a good thing! Brian Walls, my copy editor, made sure that all "T's" were crossed and the "I's" dotted; Brian, your edits were always right on!

Family, friends, and fun go together, and fortunately for me I have lots of all three. Special recognition goes to my daughter, Alyssa, on her graduation from that "other" Florida school and to my mother for still going strong in her nineties. Boca's Swim and Racquet Club has the friendliest group anywhere; hellos go out to my various "games" and especially to my "Almost Champions" team mates on the USTA 4.0 league.

Writing a book is not easy, but having someone special in your life certainly makes it a lot more fun! Gary Kahn has loved and supported me during the writing of my last 9 books. You're the best — I couldn't have done it without you. Can't wait to see where the next Bruce concert will be!

Publisher's Acknowledgments

We're proud of this book; please send us your comments through our online registration form located at www.dummies.com/register/.

Some of the people who helped bring this book to market include the following:

Acquisitions and Editorial

Project Editor: Blair J. Pottenger

Acquisitions Editor: Kyle Looper

Copy Editor: Brian Walls

Technical Editors: Michael Lonski, Sujata Pamidi

Editorial Manager: Kevin Kirschner

Editorial Assistant: Amanda Foxworth

Sr. Editorial Assistant: Cherie Case

Cartoons: Rich Tennant (www.the5thwave.com)

Composition Services

Project Coordinator: Katie Key

Layout and Graphics: Reuben W. Davis, Sarah E. Philippart, Christine Williams

Proofreaders: Joni Heredia, Amanda Steiner

Indexer: Potomac Indexing, LLC

Special Help: Chris Harrick (Senior Director of Product Marketing, SugarCRM)

Publishing and Editorial for Technology Dummies

Richard Swadley, Vice President and Executive Group Publisher

Andy Cummings, Vice President and Publisher

Mary Bednarek, Executive Acquisitions Director

Mary C. Corder, Editorial Director

Publishing for Consumer Dummies

Diane Graves Steele, Vice President and Publisher

Joyce Pepple, Acquisitions Director

Composition Services

Gerry Fahey, Vice President of Production Services

Debbie Stailey, Director of Composition Services

Table of Contents

Introduction

You just have to love any product with the word *sugar* in its name. *SugarCRM* is one of the best-selling customer relationship management (CRM) software products on the market today. For many users, SugarCRM represents their first foray into the area of CRM. CRM software is a little more complex to understand than other types of software. With a word processor, each document that you create is totally separate; if you make a mistake, you need only to delete your current document and start fresh. CRM, however, builds its way into a final product; if you don't give a bit of thought as to what goal you wish to achieve, you could end up with a muddled mess.

I'm excited about the product and know that by the time you discover how to unleash the power of SugarCRM, you'll be excited, too. You can use SugarCRM at work. You can use SugarCRM on the road. You can use SugarCRM at home. Most importantly, you can use SugarCRM to grow your business.

So what am I so excited about? I've seen firsthand how SugarCRM can save you time and make you more efficient. To me, accomplishing more in less time is an exciting thought — it allows more time for the fun things in life. Best of all, SugarCRM is a program that's very easy to get up and running in a very short time. You'll be amazed at not only how quickly you can set up a database but also at how easily you can put that database to work.

About This Book

SugarCRM For Dummies is a reference book. As such, each chapter can be read independently in the order you want. Each chapter focuses on a specific topic, so you can dive right in and head straight for the chapter that interests you most. I must say, however, that I've tried to put the chapters into a logical sequence so that those of you who are new to Sugar can just follow the bouncing ball from chapter to chapter. More experienced users can use the Table of Contents and the index to simply navigate from topic to topic as needed.

Essentially, this book is a nuts-and-bolts how-to guide for accomplishing various tasks. Drawing on many of my own experiences as a full-time CRM consultant and trainer, I also include specific situations to give you a feel for the full power of Sugar.

Sugar is Open Source software which means that programmer types can access the most inner parts of the software and make modifications. It also means that many Sugar users are very verbal when it comes to the changes that want to see in the software. Fortunately, the nice folks at Sugar are extremely responsive to the requests they receive so you'll find that your version of Sugar will constantly update itself. This book is based on version 5.0, although most of the functionality covered applies to earlier versions as well.

Conventions Used in This Book

Like in most Windows-based software programs, you often have several different ways to accomplish a task in SugarCRM.

For the most part, I show you how to perform a function by using the SugarCRM menus. If I say to "click the Accounts tab," you must click the word *Accounts* located on the Module bar that runs along the top of every Sugar window. When an instruction reads, "click the Create Contact shortcut," you must click the words *Create Contact* (located at the left side of the SugarCRM screen). In most cases, you can access these commands from anywhere within Sugar, but I generally advise new users to always start a task from the Home page, which is the first window you see when Sugar opens. If you must be in a particular area to complete a task otherwise, I tell you where.

What You Should Read

Of course, I hope that you're going to sit down and read this entire book from cover to cover. Then again, this book isn't The Great American Novel. You're probably finding yourself with too much to do and too little time in which to do it. So, like a kid in the candy store, you'll want to race from one area to another as quickly as possible so that you can reach your final goal as quickly as possible.

For the time being, I'm going to let you get away with reading just the parts that interest you most. You can read the last chapter first and the first chapter last if you like because this book is designed to allow you to read each chapter independently. However, when you find yourself floating in a swimming pool, soaking up the sun, and wondering what to do with all your spare time, you might want to go back and read some of those chapters you skipped. You just might discover something!

What You Don't Have to Read

This book is intended for both new and existing SugarCRM users. Most of the instructions apply to both groups of readers. Occasionally, I include some information that might be of special interest to more advanced readers. Newbies, feel free to skip these sections! Also, any information tagged with a Technical Stuff icon is there for the truly technically inclined. Everyone else can just skip this info.

Foolish Assumptions

One of my least favorite words in the English language is the word *assume,* but I have to admit that I've made a few foolish — albeit necessary — assumptions when writing this book. First, I assume that you own a computer and have Internet browser software. Second, I assume that you have a basic knowledge of how to use your computer, keyboard, and mouse, and that SugarCRM isn't the very first application that you're trying to master.

I also assume that you have a genuine desire to organize your life and grow your business and have determined that SugarCRM is the way to go. Finally (and I feel quite comfortable with this assumption), I assume that you'll grow to love SugarCRM.

How This Book Is Organized

I organized this book into six parts. Each part contains several chapters covering related topics. The following is a brief description of each part, with chapter references directing you where to go for particular information.

Part 1: Adding Sugar to Your Life

In Part I, you get an introduction to the concepts of CRM and Open Source software and find out why SugarCRM has become such a popular choice of CRM users (Chapter 1). In this part, you read about how to install Sugar and how to tweak some of your user preferences (Chapter 2). You discover how to navigate your way around Sugar (Chapter 3) and then start sweetening the pot by adding a few Contacts, Accounts, and Leads to Sugar (Chapter 4).

Part 11: Cooking with Sugar

Part II focuses on helping you keep your business day organized and productive. You start by scheduling appointments, finding your way around the Sugar calendars, and taking a few notes (Chapter 5). You might find that your activities evolve into major projects (Chapter 6), or that you need help organizing your sales opportunities (Chapter 7). If you have trouble organizing your filing system, you might benefit from the Sugar library (Chapter 8), where you can store your customer-related documents. And, after you've filled your Sugar bowl with lots of information, you'll need ways to get to that data quickly and easily (Chapter 9).

Part 111: A Spoonful of Sugar Keeps Your Customers Happy

CRM stands for *customer relationship management,* and that's exactly the focus of Part III. The customer is always right and if he's not happy, you'll want to create a case to resolve his issues (Chapter 10). If you are a manufacturer, Sugar can come to the rescue of your quality control issues by helping you report bugs in your products and perhaps create a Knowledge Base (KB) to help you find the proper solution (Chapter 11).

Part IV: Sharing the Sugar Bowl

One of the best features of SugarCRM is the ability to communicate easily with the outside world. Part IV shows you how to set up your e-mail and work with e-mail templates to automate routine communications (Chapter 12). If you're serious about expanding your business, you'll want to set up a campaign — and track its success — by creating lead forms, sending newsletters or other templates, and then analyzing the success of the campaign (Chapter 13).

Part V: Working with Extra-Strength Sugar

We're all different and often like to do things in our own unique way. SugarCRM understands that concept, and Part V helps you customize Sugar to your heart's content. SugarCRM comes in three flavors, and you'll want to make sure you're using the right one (Chapter 14). At first glance, SugarCRM might seem to include everything you need to organize and grow your business, but by adding fields and modules, and placing them on customized layouts (Chapter 15), you'll be able to transform Sugar into your own unique software application.

Every CRM product needs an Administrator. If you're elected to the job, you need to know how to take control of your users and perform administrative tasks, such as performing routine maintenance, backing up your database, and troubleshoot problems if they arise (Chapter 16).

Part VI: The Part of Tens

With apologies to David Letterman, Part VI gives you a few of my favorite SugarCRM lists. First, I list the features that are found only in the Professional and Enterprise editions of SugarCRM (Chapter 17). SugarCRM is Open Source software, which makes it easy for developers to create products that give Sugar even more power and functionality; I highlight a few of these products in Chapter 18. Finally, I give you ten ways to help you understand everything there is to know about SugarCRM — and then some (Chapter 19)!

Icons Used in This Book

A Tip icon indicates a special timesaving tip or a related thought that might help you use SugarCRM to its full advantage. Try it; you might like it!

A Warning icon alerts you to the danger of proceeding without caution. *Do not* attempt to try something that you're warned not to do!

Remember icons alert you to important pieces of information that you don't want to forget.

A Technical Stuff icon indicates tidbits of advanced knowledge that might be of interest to IT specialists but might just bore the heck out of the average reader. Skip these at will.

Where to Go from Here

For those of you who are Sugar old-timers, you might want to skim the entire contents of this book before hunkering down to read the sections that seem the most relevant to you. My experience is that the average Sugar user probably employs only a portion of the program and might not even be aware of some of the really cool features of SugarCRM. You might be surprised to discover all that SugarCRM has to offer!

For the SugarCRM newbie, I recommend heading straight for Part I, where you can acquaint yourself with Sugar before moving on to other parts of the book and the Sugar program.

Part I
Adding Sugar to Your Life

"Look, you've got Product Manager, Sales Manager, and Account Manager, but Sucking Up to the Manager just isn't a field the program comes with."

In this part . . .

1 know that you're excited about all the possibilities SugarCRM has to offer and that you want to dive into the program as soon as possible. Here's where you find an overview of some of the cool features that you find in Sugar. You also become familiar with the many faces of Sugar; after all, you wouldn't want to get lost along the way. But first, you have to do a bit of homework and whip Sugar into shape by fiddling with a few preference settings to ensure that Sugar produces the type of results you're looking for. Finally, you add in a dash of Contacts records, sprinkle in a few Accounts records, and top it off with a few Leads records.

Chapter 1

Adding Sugar to Your Life

So what is SugarCRM, anyway? I find that one of the hardest things that I have to do with SugarCRM is to explain exactly what it is. In this chapter, I give you a bit of background into the company and explain some of the terms that you're likely to hear bantered around. I also give you a few ideas on the types of folks who are using Sugar, and give you a few ground rules that I've established over the years after watching new users wrestle with certain aspects of CRM. I even point out the various flavors of Sugar.

The History of Sugar

It's not imperative that you commit the history of SugarCRM to memory, but I do think it can give you a bit more of an understanding as to why the software is so functional — and why it will work so well for your business.

Once upon a time, there were three young men. I could refer to them as the three Musketeers, but actually, they were John, Jacob, and Clint. They had brains. They were tech-savvy. They had a vision. Unfortunately, they didn't have a lot of money.

Our three heroes soon found that their one edition of Microsoft Office (Student Edition) wasn't sufficient to run a business, so they sought out low-cost alternatives. As their coffers were limited — okay, they were empty — they discovered Open Office, a free alternative to the more expensive Microsoft Office software. Like Scarlet O'Hara, they vowed never to go software hungry again and to purchase the more robust Office when their business expanded.

If this were a big budget Hollywood movie, the seas would part and the music would crescendo; a light bulb went off in their collective heads. "What if," they wondered, "we built a really great piece of software and *gave it away free* in the hope that businesses would upgrade to something pricier when they could afford it?" Thus, SugarCRM was born.

As in most Hollywood movies, this story has a happy ending. Since its inception in 2004, over 4 million users have downloaded SugarCRM Community Edition (CE) — it's available in 75 different languages and over 3,000 companies (representing approximately 150,000 users) have actually purchased the software. And yes, our heroes are now using Microsoft Office as are several hundred of their employees.

Getting Started with a Few Basic Concepts

Nobody likes technical jargon, but in the course of showing you how to use SugarCRM I might lapse into Geek Speak and use a handful of somewhat technical terms; I just can't avoid it. Becoming familiar with them now is less painful in the long run.

What in the world is Open Source?

SugarCRM is *Open Source* software, which means the underlying source code is available to programmer- and developer-types who want to totally transform the software. I like to explain SugarCRM initially by using very politically correct terminology:

- **Free redistribution:** Open Source software is free; as in, it doesn't cost you anything.

- **Includes the source code:** The *source code* is the actual language that the programmer used to create the product. By making the source code available, users can change the software at will — and continue to embellish it.

- **Derived works:** Once downloaded, you can share the software legally with any of your friends, neighbors, and relatives.

- **License must not restrict other software:** When you download Open Source software, any tools that you need to run it are included free — there are no hidden charges.

- **License must be technology-neutral:** Many software programs will only work with specific operating systems; Open Source products, such as Sugar, will work on virtually *any* operating system.

By now, you might be scratching your head and wondering, "Why in the world would anyone want to go to the bother of creating software and giving it away for free?" I'm glad you asked because there's a bit of method to what you might consider madness:

- ✔ By giving a version of the software away free, you're able to put your software in the hands of a lot of users who will try it, hopefully like it, and eventually buy a fee-based version if the need arises.

- ✔ Companies like SugarCRM spend very little money on marketing; free distribution leads to a great deal of "word of mouth" advertising.

- ✔ Companies like SugarCRM spend very little money on a sales force because most users that want to upgrade to a fee-based product have already tried the free version for a while and just want to add a little extra functionality.

- ✔ Manufacturers of Open Source receive lots of free feedback on their products, which helps them to both identify any bugs or problems in the software and increase the functionality of the software.

What in the world is CRM?

Just in case you feel like your drowning in a vat of alphabet soup, I'd like to give you a bit more of a feel for *customer relationship management* (CRM). In a nutshell, CRM can help you manage any interaction a company has with its customers — or potential customers. CRM can

- ✔ **Provide you with a unified database to house the contact details for all of your prospects and customers.**

- ✔ **Allow you to associate notes, histories, appointments, and even documents with a specific contact record.**

- ✔ **Give you automated methods to improve your marketing effectiveness.**

- ✔ **Improve your relationship with your current customers by providing you with customer service tools.**

- ✔ **Provide executives with tools to track their sales performance.**

In addition, really good CRM software can:

- ✔ **Be easily customized by adding fields and changing layouts based on your company's requirements.**

- ✔ **Offer a variety of deployment options so that it can be used by businesses ranging from single owners to mammoth corporations.**

A few other terms to know

SugarCRM is a database program. A *database* is a collection of information organized in such a way that the user of the database can quickly find desired pieces of information. Think of a database as an electronic filing system. Although most Sugar users create a database of contacts, some users develop Sugar databases to collect information about things other than contacts. For example, you might create a Sugar database to track the serial numbers of the products you've sold or the properties that you manage.

Traditional databases are organized by *fields, records,* and *instances:*

- ✔ **Field:** A *field* is a single piece of information. In databases, fields are the smallest units of information. A tax form, for example, contains a number of fields: one for your name, one for your Social Security number, one for your income, and so on. In SugarCRM, you start with numerous fields for Contact, Accounts, and Leads to hold information such as name, address and shoe size.

  You find out how to add information into these fields in Chapter 4. And, in Chapter 15, I show you how to change the attributes of existing fields and how to add new fields to your database if you're the database administrator.

- ✔ **Record:** A *record* is one complete set of fields. In SugarCRM, all the information you collect that pertains to one individual Contact, Account, or Lead is a *record.*

- ✔ **Instance:** An *instance* is the entire collection of data or information. Each database that you create in SugarCRM is given a unique MySQL instance. You can create more than one instance or database in SugarCRM — head to Chapter 2 to find out how.

Sugar, Sugar!

Fortunately for you, you can't hear me singing my somewhat off-key rendition of *Sugar, Sugar.* I have to admit that I start to hum a few bars every time I think about some of the cool feature of SugarCRM. In this section, I've put together a little shopping list of features so that you can see all that SugarCRM can do for you, too. In parentheses after each item, I include a chapter reference where you can find more information about a particular feature (if you're so inclined).

One of the things you might find interesting is that the folks at SugarCRM "eat their own dog food." What I mean by that is everyone from the top-level executives and the folks at tech support to the marketing gurus, administrative staff,

SUGARCRM®

www.sugarcrm.com

s use Sugar. By doing so, they see firsthand
vith all the tools they need to run a successful

isiness management tool that

**information, including name, company,
addresses, and e-mail addresses.** (Chapter 4)

lefined fields to get you rolling. If you want to
modules to meet your specific needs, go right

**umber of dated notes, histories, and activities
s so that you can easily keep track of impor-
events.** This feature is particularly useful for
our friend, the elephant) do forget things on

es that your customers are having. Create
k bugs in your product line (Chapter 11), or
produce individualized customer portals that offer customers access to
your company's Knowledge Base and FAQ's (Chapter 10).

✔ **Allows you to stay in front of your customers and prospects.** Merge
your contact information into a template that you create, and then send
merged documents via e-mail (Chapter 12), snail mail, or as part of a full-
scale marketing campaign (Chapter 13).

✔ **Manages your sales pipeline.** Create sales opportunities, track their
progress, and analyze the results (Chapter 7).

✔ **Shares your data with remote users.** If you have other SugarCRM users
in remote locations, they can view database changes online, offline, or
even via the browser of their PDA.

✔ **Automates your follow-up, assuring that none of your contacts "fall
through the cracks."** Sugar's Workflow feature assures that you contact
your customers and prospects automatically by relying on a schedule
and method that you design (Chapter 14).

Identifying the Typical SugarCRM User

Who is the typical SugarCRM user? Well, with more than 4 million user down-
loads of the free SugarCRM Community Edition (CE) and over 3,000 businesses currently using a subscription edition of Sugar, you're safe to assume
that nearly every industry is represented among its user base.

I think it's only fair to warn you that once you develop a sweet tooth, you'll soon find that Sugar is indispensible. You'll become addicted to SugarCRM and eventually use it to manage all facets of your business. You might just become a Sugar junkie. (Quite simply, a *Sugar junkie* is a SugarCRM user who has become addicted to using SugarCRM.)

So, just who is using SugarCRM? Everyone!

- **A CEO or sales manager** uses SugarCRM because they want to know what the salespeople are doing and how successful their efforts are.

- **An administrative assistant** uses SugarCRM to automate routine tasks and to keep a schedule of various tasks and activities.

- **A salesperson** uses SugarCRM to make sure that she's following up on all her prospects.

- **Customer Service representatives** use Sugar to make sure that all customers are *happy* customers.

- **The IT department** uses Sugar to help prioritize — and resolve — any computer-related issues that the staff might encounter.

- **Tech Support** uses Sugar to track and follow through on customer problems.

- **The Marketing department** uses SugarCRM to send mailings and marketing campaigns — and to measure their success.

So what kinds of businesses use SugarCRM? All kinds!

- **Manufacturers** who need to organize any problems that their customers might encounter, and keep track of any known product defects.

- **Financial planners** who need to track very detailed information on each of their clients.

- **Businesses in any industry** looking for software that can automate their business and make them more productive in less time.

- **Large businesses** that want to improve communication among employees, track their leads, and keep their customers happy.

- **Small businesses** that have to rely on a small staff to complete a multitude of tasks.

Knowing the Basic SugarCRM Ground Rules

Sometimes you just need to figure out things the hard way. After all, experience is the best teacher. Luckily for you, however, I've compiled a list of rules based on a few mistakes that I see other Sugar users commit. You're not going to find these rules written down anywhere else, and they might not even make a whole lot of sense to you. However, as you become more and more familiar with Sugar, these rules will make all the sense in the world. You might even want to refer to them from time to time.

Karen's Four Rules of Always:

- ✔ **Always log in to SugarCRM as yourself.**

- ✔ **Always strive for standardization in your database by entering your data in a consistent manner.**

- ✔ **Always input as much information into your database as possible.**

- ✔ **Always have a well-trained administrator who will be able to upgrade Sugar when necessary, perform required maintenance, and make sure your administrator is backing-up your database routinely!**

Looking at the Three Versions of SugarCRM

SugarCRM comes in three separate editions, which are

- ✔ **SugarCRM Community Edition (CE):** This is the free version of Sugar. As the saying goes, the best things in life are free and that just might be the case with Sugar CE. Typically used by businesses with 1–10 users, it is possible to use CE with businesses of virtually any size; in fact, one business with over 2,000 users is currently using Sugar CE.

- ✔ **SugarCRM Professional:** This version is generally used by larger organizations wanting additional "team" functionality, improved quoting and forecasting, and reporting capabilities. However, smaller organizations also use the Professional version to take advantage of other features, including integration with Microsoft Office products and wireless PDA access. Professional will cost you $275 per user per year.

✔ **SugarCRM Enterprise:** Enterprise is generally the version of choice for companies with one hundred or more users. In addition to having all the features found in the CE and Professional versions, Enterprise throws Oracle support, Advanced SQL Reporting, and an offline client into the mix. Enterprise costs $449 per user per year.

Every feature found in SugarCRM Community Edition is found in the other versions of SugarCRM as well. In fact, you'll find that 85% of the content of the Professional and Enterprise versions is identical to the content of Sugar Community Edition. However, from time to time, I point out a feature that is found only in the Professional or Enterprise (Pro and Ent, respectively) versions. You might want to look at Chapter 14, which highlights features that you find only in Pro and Ent, or at Chapter 17 for a full list of some of the cooler Pro and Ent features. Figure 1-1 is a visual comparison of the three versions.

Both the Professional and Enterprise versions of Sugar include the addition of phone-based support. For other support options, take a gander at Chapter 19.

Not ready to bite the bullet and start paying for your Sugar rush? You might consider one other option — Sugar Network. Sugar Network, which runs $119 per user per year, supplies you with the plug-ins to the Microsoft Office products (Word, Outlook, and Excel) and gives you access to phone-based support. Such a deal!

So what are you waiting for? Boot up your computer, grab this book, and get going. After all, it's time to satisfy your sweet tooth!

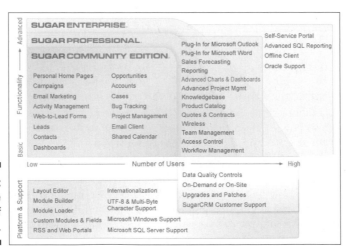

Figure 1-1: The three flavors of SugarCRM.

Chapter 2

Acquiring a Sweet Tooth

*B*efore you start using SugarCRM, you need to install it. You have a couple of options for doing this and I show you what they are. I show you how to set up a second database as well. You also discover how to log in — and how to change some of the preference settings after you do.

Taking the Sugarland Express

In Chapter 1, you find out about the various flavors of SugarCRM. In this chapter, I discuss the three deployment options available to you.

Ultimately, the deployment option you choose rests on two important factors:

- ✔ **Your comfort level in knowing that another company is managing — and has full access to — your company data.**
- ✔ **The amount of IT expertise that resides within your company.**

If you require a bit of handholding you might want to check out `www.sugar crm.com/crm/crmquiz` which offers a nifty little deployment calculator. You'll also find a white paper link there explaining the various deployment options in even greater detal.

Hosting SugarCRM On-Site

Quite simply, the On-Site deployment option means that your SugarCRM is kept in your very own location — or at a data center that you selected. At first glance, this may seem like a logical approach. However, before you decide this is the way to go, you might want to weigh the pros and cons.

Hosting your own SugarCRM installation has a number of benefits:

✔ **You don't have to pay anyone a monthly fee to host Sugar for you.**

✔ **Your data is on your very own site, which means you don't have to worry that the host might possibly abscond with your data.**

✔ **You're in compliance if your company prohibits letting customer information outside your firewall.**

✔ **You can integrate your data with other applications, such as Web or accounting data, that you may have on-site.**

Now you're wondering why someone *wouldn't* want to host his own database. Although it's very easy to host a Sugar database, you need to consider a few details before proceeding:

✔ **You have a static IP address or dynamic DNS service if you want other remote users to be able to access your database using a web address via the Internet.**

✔ **Your IT infrastructure must meet the demand of housing — and hosting — a database. You need to make sure that your server and bandwidth are up to the challenge.**

✔ **Your IT department understands what running a Web server entails.**

✔ **Your IT department is responsible for any data loss you might experience through improper maintenance procedures.**

Demanding to have your Sugar hosted

The folks at SugarCRM aim to please. Want free software? Not a problem — just download the CE version. Want to host it yourself? SugarCRM makes the process so easy that even a Dummy can do it — as you can see later on in this chapter. But how about you folks who are feeling a bit intimidated by thoughts of Web servers, IP addresses, and the responsibility of being the administrator of the whole enchilada? Not to worry, SugarCRM has your back.

Sugar offers "hosted" solutions for both its Professional and Enterprise editions. The fees include both the Sugar software and a server to host it on. Best of all, these solutions include all the IT expertise needed to ensure that your database remains alive and kicking.

- ✔ **Sugar Professional On-Demand:** For $480 per year per user, Sugar will have you and your company up and running on one of their servers quicker than you can say, "Show me the Sugar!" When you consider that this works out to be approximately $17 per user per month more than just purchasing Professional, this is a great bargain!

- ✔ **Sugar Enterprise On-Demand:** For those of you who want every sugary bell and whistle — and want someone else to worry about all the gory details — this might just be the way for you to go. Although this solution will set you back $75 per user per month, the hosting portion works out to be less than $40 per month, which is considerably less than the typical server rental cost. In exchange, you'll have every feature that Sugar has to offer — and you'll sleep well at night knowing that your data is in good hands.

Although SugarCRM doesn't offer hosting for the Sugar Community Edition, a number of companies out there do specialize in Sugar hosting. In addition, some companies lease servers so that all you have to do is install Sugar — they do all the rest!

Building a Sugar Cube

By now, you might feel that your beloved author has had so much sugar that it's gone to her head. Fear not; with a name like Sugar, it's only natural that some form of the product be named Sugar Cube.

Sugar Cube — or appliance — deployment is the icing on the cake, the cherry on the top — okay, it's a turn-key system that includes a server that's already configured for Sugar. This is an ideal solution for companies who don't want to have a third-party vendor control their data, but don't have the IT expertise to set up a Web browser. Plug in the server, open your Web browser, and you're ready to go.

Sugar Cube deployment offers the following benefits:

- ✔ **A Web-based CRM solution — without having a full-time IT department.**
- ✔ **Fast deployment — Sugar has already configured your hardware and software.**
- ✔ **Data security — your data is located on your premises, safely behind your firewall.**

The folks at Sugar tell me that Sugar Cube deployment is mostly used by governmental agencies who want to make sure that their data is totally secure, but it certainly seems like a viable option for many other companies as well.

Preparing for Your Sugar Installation

After you've made the decision to host your own Sugar, you can literally be up and running in about 15 minutes if you do a bit of homework first. On paper — or at least on the side of the software box — placing a database on the Web sounds easy. However, you'll want to check out a few things *before* you start installing — you don't want to install the software first and then find out that your system isn't up to the task.

Compatibility is always an issue when it comes to integrating new software into your current mix. However, the basic rule of thumb is that if your existing component runs PHP 4.4 or higher, it will work with Sugar.

Adding Sugar to your Web server

All you need to put your database on the Internet for all the world (or at least your company) to see is a Web server. Sugar isn't picky and will give you two Web server options:

- ✔ Apache
- ✔ Windows Internet Information Server (IIS)

What's in an IP name?

Although you and I might name our computers with endearing names, such as *Hal* or *Son of a Pitchfork,* programmers think in terms of numbers and name their computers with names like 192.168.2.38. Guess that has a ring to it, if you're a computer. This name/number is a computer's *internal IP address.* A computer's internal IP address identifies it from the other computers in your internal network: hence, the modifier *internal.* Within your network, you can assign IP addresses at random as long as each one is unique.

When you connect to the outside world, you have an *external IP address.* This number identifies you to the great big world outside your internal network. Your external IP also has a cute name, such as 67.87.243.62.

External IP addresses come in two flavors: dynamic and static. A *dynamic* IP address is like a cute little toddler — it bounces around all over the place. A dynamic external IP address is assigned to you by your ISP (Internet service provider) on a round-robin, first-come-first-served basis. Consequently, one day, your name is 67.87.243.62; the next day, it's 1.160.10.240.

Your remote users log in to your Web server via your Web server's external IP address. The trouble is that remote users might feel like they're playing a giant game of keep-away if they have to use a different IP address every time they want to get into Sugar. Enter the static IP address. A *static* IP address doesn't change, making life much easier for your remote users.

If you have a dynamic IP address, you have to get a static one or risk having your remote users being unable to access the database. This is the hardest part of the entire procedure: You have to check with your ISP to get one. Surprisingly enough, if you pay your ISP a little extra money each month, most are happy to accommodate you.

If you really want to get fancy, consider registering a domain name. You can substitute it for your external IP address number so that you can go to your Web site by using mywebsite.com instead of 12.34.567.89.

Operating under the right operating system

The neat thing about Sugar is that it plays nicely with most of the other kids in the technology playground.

Sugar works with most any operating system (OS) including:

- ✔ Linux
- ✔ Windows
- ✔ Mac
- ✔ Solaris

BYOD (Bring Your Own Database)

Sugar needs a database and, unlike many other CRM programs, will work with many different flavors. You don't need to go out and purchase one, however, because Sugar works with MySQL, which is free. If you already have a pricey database on hand, Sugar also works with

- ✔ SQL Server 2005
- ✔ Oracle

No browser, no Sugar

Sugar is *browser-based software,* which means that your information opens in a browser window. Therefore, it only stands to reason that you'll need a browser if you're going to be using Sugar. If you can surf the Internet, you can most likely surf Sugar because it works on any of the popular browsers:

- ✔ Mozilla
- ✔ Firefox
- ✔ Internet Explorer

Just to be safe, you'll want to make sure that you are in the latest and greatest version of your browser.

Plugging in to a Plug-In

Sugar plug-Ins connect Sugar to Word for purposes of mail merge, and to either Outlook or Thunderbird for purposes of e-mail. Make sure you have one of the following versions:

- ✔ Microsoft Office 2003, Office XP, or Office 2007
- ✔ Thunderbird 1.5 or 2.0

The plug-ins are available with the Professional or Enterprise versions of Sugar, or can be purchased as part of the Sugar Network support plan.

Ready, Set, Install!

Now that your homework is done, it's time to move on to the fun stuff — installing Sugar! Okay, you might not think this is the most fun you've ever had, but it's certainly going to be one of the easiest things you've done.

How does this stack up for you?

SugarCRM features *FastStack* installers, which means all the software you need to get up and running is included in one easy file. You can download it from www.sugarcrm.com/crm/download/sugar-suite.html. Like pancakes at IHOP, you can get your stack in a number of flavors; regardless of the flavor, all stacks include the following elements:

- ✔ **The newest version of PHP.**
- ✔ **Web server software:** You can use your existing Windows IIS or install the free Apache software.
- ✔ **A database engine:** You can choose a stack that includes the free MySQL, or you can bring your own SQL Server or Oracle database to the party.
- ✔ **Sugar software:** You can pick your favorite flavor of Sugar including Windows, Linux, and Mac. Sorry, blueberry and apple aren't yet available.

.NET 2.0 must be installed on your system before you attempt to install Sugar FastStack, so make sure that your Windows operating system is up to date and loaded with the latest patches.

Feel a bit overwhelmed? Try using the Download Wizard if you're unsure about which stack to download. Figure 2-1 shows you exactly what the download page looks like.

Downloading a file is half the fun. The other half is remembering exactly *where* you downloaded that file. You might want to jot down the location.

The Download Wizard link

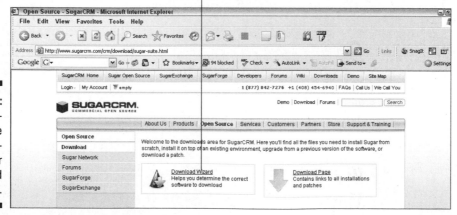

Figure 2-1: Downloading the appropriate Sugar download file.

It's typical to use the Typical install

After you download the appropriate FastStack file, you need to run it. Fortunately, Sugar has removed the guesswork and made the installation process extremely easy. Follow these steps:

1. **Double-click the file that you downloaded and then click Run.**

   After a moment of silence, the first screen of the FastStack Setup Wizard appears (see Figure 2-2).

Figure 2-2:
Starting the
FastStack
Setup
Wizard.

2. **Click Next, accept the EULA (End User License Agreement), and then click Next to continue.**

   Like most software, if you don't agree to play by the rules you don't get to play the game!

3. **Select your installation directory and then click Next to continue.**

   Sugar very nicely suggests an appropriate installation directory with a clever name like `SugarCRM_5.0B` (if you're installing the 5.0B version of Sugar).

4. **Select the components that you want to install and then click Next to continue.**

   As you see in Figure 2-3, this isn't an earth-shattering decision; it's a given that you're installing Sugar. Optionally, you can install phpMyAdmin, which will come in handy if you want to do a bit of the advanced maintenance I mention in Chapter 16.

Figure 2-3:
Selecting
the com-
ponents
you want to
install.

5. **Select Typical install and then click Next to continue.**

   Unless you are very conversant in the language of Apache and PHP, I
   recommend that you go with the Typical installation and let Sugar do all
   the thinking. If IIS is installed on your system, the Sugar Installer will use
   it instead of Apache Web Server; if IIS isn't installed, the Sugar Installer
   will install Apache.

6. **Type a System Name and then click Next to Continue.**

   This name will appear in the title of the browser that your users use to
   access the Sugar database. As shown in Figure 2-4, you want to choose a
   name with some semblance of logic.

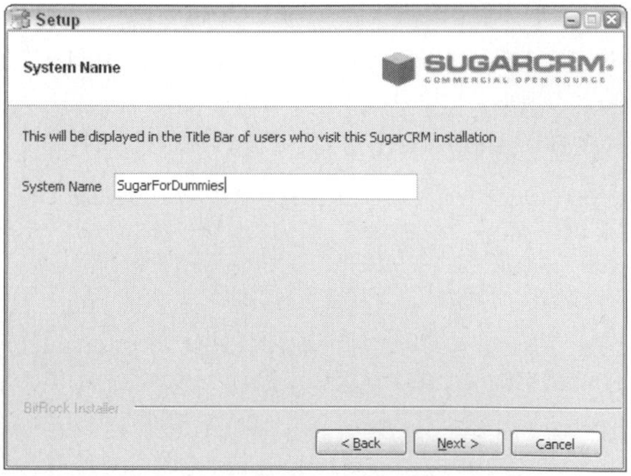

Figure 2-4:
Assigning
a System
Name.

7. **Assign a password for the SugarCRM administrator, type it a second time to make sure you got it right the first time, and then click Next to continue.**

   Sugar automatically names your administrator `Admin`. Suffice it to say, you'll want to remember that password because you'll need it to open up your database!

8. **Indicate whether you'd like to install the demo database and then click Next to continue.**

   If you are a Sugar newbie, you just might want to install the demo database.

   You can install as many databases as you'd like on your Web server, as I show you in the next section.

9. **Select Yes to install Sugar as a Service and then click Next to continue.**

   This means that Sugar will automatically run every time you fire up your computer — and that any remote users will be able to see your database.

10. **Enter the port number Sugar will use to listen for visitors and then click Next to continue.**

    By default, Sugar cheerfully suggests that you use port 80, which is a great choice unless another program on your Web server is also using port 80. In that case, Sugar politely informs you that the port is already being used; you can then suggest another port number — such as 81 or 82.

11. **Enter the SSL Port number and then click Next to continue.**

    Again, Sugar recommends the port wine, er, port number of 443. If it's being used, feel free to choose 444 or 445.

12. **Enter your Web server domain and then click Next.**

    Here's where you add your static IP address or your domain name (see Figure 2-5), if you registered one.

13. **Type the MySQL port number and then click Next.**

    In case you're feeling dazed and confused in the maze of port numbers, don't worry. Once again, Sugar will come to the rescue, providing you with a suggested port number. If that one doesn't work, just type the next sequential number until you hit a winner.

14. **Assign a password for the MySQL user, type it a second time to make sure you got it right the first time, and then click Next to continue.**

    Previously you entered the *Sugar* password; now you're entering the *MySQL* password.

15. **Assign a password for the phpMyAdmin tool user, type it a second time to make sure you got it right the first time, and then click Next to continue.**

Here's where you type the third — and last — password. This one allows you to access the phpMyAdmin tool that installs with Sugar.

If you have a mind like a steel trap, you might want to use three separate passwords. However, if you occasionally suffer from "senior moments," you might consider using the same password for all three instances. You might also want to write down this information — and put it in a safe spot — just in case you need to use those passwords again.

16. **Click Next to complete the installation.**

You see an indicator bar scroll across your computer screen while Sugar installs.

Figure 2-5:
Assigning
the Web
server
domain.

Creating a second database

After you install Sugar, you might want to peruse the file structure of your computer to get a feel for what was actually installed, especially if you want to install a second database.

In the previous section, you install Sugar using the FastStack installer. When installing a second database, it's only necessary to install an additional instance of Sugar. The other elements — PHP, MySQL, and Apache — do not need to be installed again.

Here's what you'll do to get that second database up and running:

1. **Download the Sugar install file from** www.sugarcrm.com/crm/ download/sugar-suite.html.

This time, make sure that you're *not* installing a FastStack.

2. **Extract the contents of the downloaded file to the Htdocs folder.**

    You'll find that folder lurking under the SugarCRM folder in the Program Files area of your computer. If you look inside the Htdocs folder, you see a subfolder that corresponds to the name you gave your database in Step 6 of the previous section.

    To make life easier, you might want to give the folder that will hold your extracted files a moniker that corresponds to the name of your new database.

3. **Open your Web browser and navigate to the section of your Web server that holds the newly downloaded files.**

    This takes a little more explaining, Lucy. Say your IP address is 65.7.123.456 and you extracted your Sugar files to a subfolder of Htdocs that you named Dummy. Let's also assume that you opened Port 81 in Step 10 of the previous section. You would be typing in `http://65.7.123.456:81/dummy/install.php`.

4. **The Installation Wizard opens.**

    At this point, you're free to follow the Installation Wizard — or the steps in the previous section.

    For the sake of simplicity, give the System Name the same name as the Htdocs folder that is holding the extracted Sugar files.

Logging in to SugarCRM

Whew! The hard part is over and you're now free to share your Sugar database with all your friends and enemies — or at least your co-workers.

Finding your database requires three components:

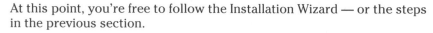

- ✔ **The static IP or domain name.**
- ✔ **The Web server port.**
- ✔ **The name of the folder containing your database.**

So, using the example in the previous section, you'd access your database by typing `http://65.7.123.456:81/dummy`.

After you've navigated to the Sugar database, feel free to save the URL in your Internet Favorites folder because this is bound to become one of your favorite sites!

SugarCRM presents you with a login screen each time you attempt to open your database. Essentially, the login screen (shown in Figure 2-6) asks you for your user name and your password. You need to make sure that you correctly enter your user name and password information. For example, if your user name includes your middle initial with a period, you must type that middle initial — including the period — to gain access to your database.

Your user name is not case sensitive (that is, you can enter your name by typing either lowercase or UPPERCASE letters). However, your password *is* case sensitive, so make sure you're not typing WITH THE CAPS LOCK ON.

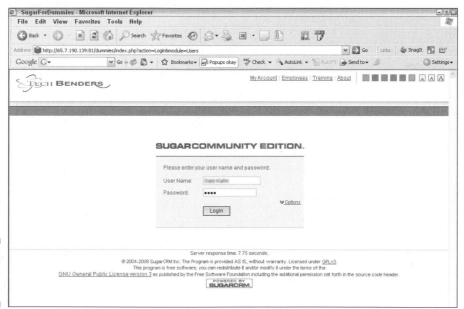

Figure 2-6:
Logging in to
SugarCRM.

Generally, the administrator of your database determines your password. The *database administrator* is the person responsible for making major changes to the database and for performing routine database maintenance. (For more information, see Chapter 16.)

Notice that dots appear while you type your password. That's normal. Just like when you type your ATM card PIN, your SugarCRM database password is hidden while you type to prevent any lurking spies from discovering your password.

The Importance of Being Yourself

The first thing that you see when you log in to a SugarCRM database is your Home page. The Home page contains all the information pertaining to you — Contacts, Leads, Appointments — so if you log in to Sugar as someone else, you just might find yourself sending a birthday card to someone's Aunt Bertha.

Logging in as yourself allows you to use a few other important SugarCRM features:

- ✔ **Permission to perform various functions is based on the security level of each user.**

- ✔ **Every time you enter a new Contact, Account, or Lead record, your name appears as the creator.**

- ✔ **When you edit a Contact, Account, or Lead record, your name appears in the log file.**

- ✔ **Every time you add a note, history, or activity to a Contact record, your name appears as the Record Creator.**

Chapter 3

Finding Your Way Around Sugar

In This Chapter
▶ The Sugar Home page
▶ Working with User Preferences
▶ Changing passwords

*A*fter getting the hang of maneuvering in SugarCRM, you'll find that it's an amazingly easy program to master. The key is to become familiar with the lay of the land *before* you start building your database. By doing so, you avoid playing hide-and-seek *later*. Although initially getting around in SugarCRM is pretty easy, you might become lost in the maze of views and tabs that Sugar is divided into. I help you navigate through that maze by taking you on a Sugar tour so that you can become familiar with the various sweet screens.

There's No Place Like Home

The purpose of this book is to serve as a reference for both new and existing SugarCRM users. I certainly don't want to lose anyone along the way. New Sugar users might be somewhat intimidated when they encounter Sugar for the first time. Be assured that this experience is akin to the first time you drive a new car at night in the rain — momentary panic sets in. After you've driven the car for a week or so, the location of the light and windshield wiper controls becomes second nature. I guarantee you'll have the same experience with Sugar.

Navigating through Sugar is fairly easy. However, to make the navigating even easier, I highlight throughout this section a number of pitfalls that you want to avoid.

When you first open your Sugar Web site, you land smack in the middle of the Home page. The Home page is divided into separate areas, or *dashlets;* Chapter 9 shows you how to make changes to your Home page. You can see the Home page, along with other key elements of Sugar, in Figure 3-1.

Although you'll be accessing the various Sugar modules, most of the modules have the same common elements.

You can go Home again

The best way to learn about a new piece of software is to try it out. Go ahead: kick the tires, click the buttons, and try those hyperlinks. However, don't panic if you start to feel slightly lost. You can always return to your Home page by using one of the two following cures for the "I'm lost!" blues:

- ✔ **Click the back button on your browser until you reach your Home page.**
- ✔ **Click the Home tab.**

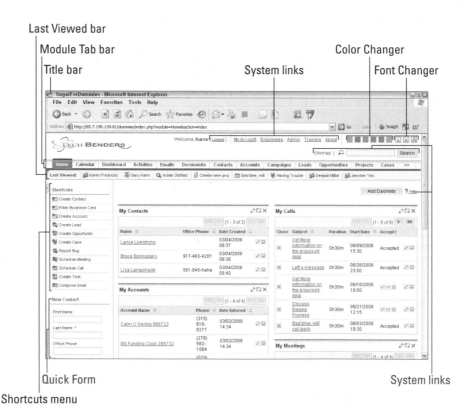

Figure 3-1:
The
SugarCRM
Home page.

Treading on the title bar

You must view Sugar in your Web browser. The title bar at the top of the browser (refer to Figure 3-1) shows you the System Name you indicate when installing Sugar (refer to Chapter 2). Don't overlook the importance of this piece of information! If your title bar reads Google, you've stumbled into the wrong Web site.

Chapter 16 shows you some of the neat things that your administrator can do to customize Sugar. You might consider replacing the SugarCRM logo with your company's logo to make it even easier to identify your database.

System links

The system links are located near the top of just about any module you happen to stumble in to (refer to Figure 3-1). They are designed to help you customize Sugar to your liking and have easy access to system information. The system links include

- ✔ **Logout:** You'll notice that Sugar cheerfully greets you by name. If, however, Sugar greets you by a name that doesn't happen to be yours, you might want to click the Logout link and log in as yourself!

- ✔ **My Account:** Allows you to add your contact information to the Sugar database, as well as change the user-defined preferences.

- ✔ **Employees:** Where you find a company directory like the one you see in Figure 3-2. You can click the name of an employee to see more detailed contact information, or you can click an e-mail address to send an e-mail to that employee.

  Every user in your database has an attached Employee Record. However, you can also add employees to your database who are not users of the Sugar database.

- ✔ **Admin:** This link is only visible to database administrators; you find a bit more about the Administrative settings in Chapter 16.

- ✔ **Training:** This link takes you to the Sugar University Web site where you can download documentation, take a recorded learning session, or sign up for a more extensive workshop.

- ✔ **About:** Click here to find out which version and release of Sugar your company is using.

- ✔ **Sitemap:** Although maps have pretty much fallen by the wayside with the advent of the GPS, the sitemap is alive and kicking — at least in Sugar country. The sitemap, tastefully displayed in Figure 3-3, shows you virtually all the elements of SugarCRM. Click any link and you're magically transported to your desired destination.

- ✔ **Search field:** The amount of information that you can store in Sugar might seem overwhelming at times. However, the Search field helps you to find any of your information at the click of a button. Type in a name and Sugar will scour your database looking for any possible matches. Figure 3-4 shows you the results of a search.

> ✔ **Print:** Although it doesn't appear on the Home page, you'll see the Print link on all the other Sugar modules (refer to Figure 3-4 for an example). As its name implies, clicking Print sends a copy of the current module to your printer.
>
> ✔ **Help:** Context-sensitive help is always right at your fingertips — if you click the Help link!

Working with Colored Sugar

If nothing else, Sugar aims to please. There are three tweaks you can make to Sugar that, although not imperative, make working with Sugar a bit more fun:

> ✔ **Color Changer:** Click one of the colored boxes (refer to Figure 3-1) and watch as the font colors and borders change right before your eyes!
>
> ✔ **Font Changer:** You young'ens in the crowd might not have to worry about this, but you old geezers might want to use a larger font (refer to Figure 3-1).
>
> ✔ **Theme Changer:** For those of you who are artistically inclined, you might want to try some of the themes that come packaged with SugarCRM. Located on the very bottom of the screen, a theme can change the entire look and feel of Sugar at the click of a button.

> Changing a theme also changes various other elements of Sugar. For example, the different themes display different shortcuts, module tabs, and system links. You'll also notice that a few of the more "graphically intensive" themes will take a bit longer to appear on your screen.

The Module tabs

The Sugar Community Edition comes with 22 *modules* or elements of the program. By default, Sugar displays 12 of these elements as tabs across the top of the screen. In addition, the rest of the modules can be accessed by clicking the double right-pointing arrows on the right side of the Module Tab bar (refer to Figure 3-1). Later in this chapter, you'll see how to decide which tabs to display — and in what order. The object of the game is to click a tab to display the corresponding module. By changing modules, other elements (including the Shortcuts menu and the Quick Form) will change as well.

The main purpose of a module is to add new information, view existing information, and change that information if the need arises. Each module contains anywhere from 15–50 fields of information pertaining to that specific module. For example, the Contact module gives you fields to input basic contact information including name, address, and phone numbers. Chapter 15 shows you how to add custom fields to a module.

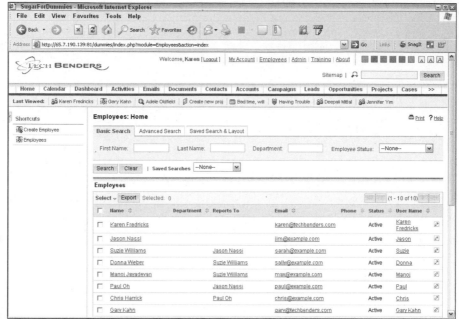

Figure 3-2:
The
Employees
directory.

Figure 3-3:
Sugar's
sitemap.

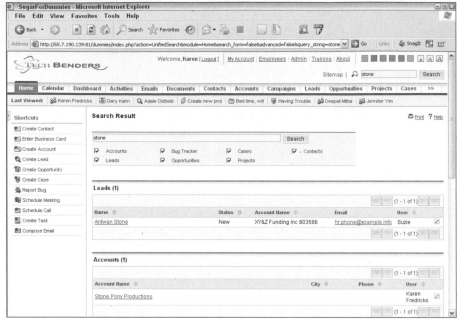

Figure 3-4:
Finding
information
quickly with
the Search
field.

The basic Sugar modules are:

- ✔ **Home:** Provides a quick snapshot of your most pressing information.

- ✔ **My Portal:** Gives you a quick way to access your favorite Web sites from within Sugar.

- ✔ **Calendar:** Where you can view your activities by day, week, or month.

- ✔ **Activities:** Here's where you create new activities including:

    - • Calls

    - • Meetings

    - • Tasks

    - • Notes

    Although theoretically separate modules, there aren't separate tabs for Calls, Meetings, Tasks, and Notes. They can only be accessed from within the Activities tab.

- ✔ **Contacts:** You can add and keep track of the contacts you keep in Sugar.

- ✔ **Accounts:** Your accounts are the businesses that you work with. In Chapter 4, you discover how to associate numerous contacts with the same Account.

- ✔ **Leads:** Here's where you add all of your *potential* customers!

Although not a module, Sugar also allows you to enter Targets or Prospects (Sugar uses the terms interchangeably) into the mix. A *target* is the coldest of contacts and is entered through the Campaign module; you read more about Targets in Chapter 13.

- **Opportunities:** Most companies are in business to make money and here's the place to keep track of all the money you hope to make.

- **Cases:** You use this module to help you manage problems or support issues your customers are experiencing, or any inquiries they might have.

- **Emails:** Here's where you can send and receive e-mail as well as create personalized e-mail templates.

- **Bug Tracker:** If you're a manufacturer, this module can help you keep track of any product defects although, hopefully, you won't find too many bugs in the sugar!

- **Documents:** This is a great module to use if you have a need to share documents among your employees. It works particularly well if several people are editing the same document — and you need to keep track of the various versions.

- **Campaigns:** You use this module to track and manage your telemarketing, mail, or e-mail marketing efforts.

- **Projects:** You might want to bundle related tasks into a project so that you can assign the various tasks to different members of your team, and track the progress.

- **RSS:** If you're into RSS (RDF Site Summary) feeds, you can add them here and peruse the headlines of your favorite ones.

- **Dashboard:** If a picture is worth a thousand words, a dashboard must be worth a million. Dashboards give you a graphical view of your sales opportunities.

- **Forums:** You won't find this module listed unless your administrator installs it for your organization. Here's where you can create internal forums to discuss anything from technical and sales topics to this year's holiday party.

The Last Viewed bar

SugarCRM is designed for busy people; and as a busy person, you probably do a lot of multi-tasking. The Last Viewed bar gives you a quick way of returning to the last eight records that you were viewing. The most recent item appears on the left edge of the menu, and the oldest item appears on the right. You'll see a little icon to the left of each item that corresponds to the module of the item (refer to Figure 3-1).

For example, you might be looking up the address of one of your employees when one of your major accounts calls with a new order. You create an opportunity but before you can act on it, one of your best customers calls with a problem. The Last Viewed bar automatically captures each of these records so that you can return to them at a click of a button.

The Shortcuts menu

The SugarCRM Shortcuts menu is located along the left side of the program. The Shortcuts menu allows you to move quickly between the various areas in Sugar. The Shortcuts menu changes depending on which Sugar module you're in. From the Home page, you see shortcuts for the most common tasks, including creating Contacts, Accounts, and Leads, and scheduling calls and meetings (refer to Figure 3-1). Switching to the Campaign module will result in options that are more "campaign-centric," including creating target lists and e-mail templates.

Want a bit more room to spread out? You can hide the shortcuts menu by clicking the left pointing arrow at the top of the shortcuts menu. Need to get them back again? Click the right pointing arrow.

Quick Form

SugarCRM is the ideal tool for busy people. One of the Sugar tools you might like the best is a Quick Form. Using a Quick Form, you can create a new record for the module that you're in. The Quick Form only requires you to add two or three fields of information; required fields are marked with an asterisk. For example, the New Contact Quick Form (refer to Figure 3-1) only requires that you add a last name and the user responsible for the contact. Once entered, you can go back to the main module and edit the new record to fill in any gaps you might have missed.

Giving Sugar the Preferential Treatment

Although the Sugar administrator is responsible for changing system-wide default settings, a number of preference settings are available to the Sugar end-user.

Follow these steps to modify your preference settings:

1. **Click the My Account system link near the top of the Home page.**

   The User Preferences window opens. Feel free to scroll down this window to see all your preference settings.

2. Click the Edit button.

You edit your preference settings in the window you see in Figure 3-5. Notice that the settings are arranged in a number of panels.

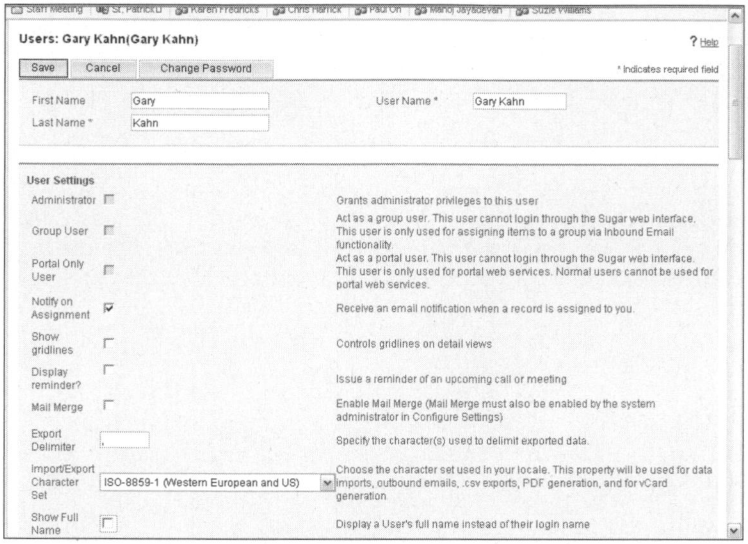

Figure 3-5: Changing the User Preferences.

(screenshot)

Users: Gary Kahn(Gary Kahn)   ? Help

| Save | Cancel | Change Password | * Indicates required field

First Name   Gary   User Name *   Gary Kahn
Last Name *   Kahn

User Settings

Administrator ☐   Grants administrator privileges to this user

Group User ☐   Act as a group user. This user cannot login through the Sugar web interface. This user is only used for assigning items to a group via Inbound Email functionality.

Portal Only User ☐   Act as a portal user. This user cannot login through the Sugar web interface. This user is only used for portal web services. Normal users cannot be used for portal web services.

Notify on Assignment ☑ Receive an email notification when a record is assigned to you.

Show gridlines ☐   Controls gridlines on detail views

Display reminder? ☐   Issue a reminder of an upcoming call or meeting

Mail Merge ☐   Enable Mail Merge (Mail Merge must also be enabled by the system administrator in Configure Settings)

Export Delimiter   Specify the character(s) used to delimit exported data.

Import/Export Character Set   ISO-8859-1 (Western European and US)   Choose the character set used in your locale. This property will be used for data imports, outbound emails, .csv exports, PDF generation, and for vCard generation.

Show Full Name ☐   Display a User's full name instead of their login name

3. (Optional) Supply your first, last, or user name.

You probably won't have to change this unless you've recently gotten married — or the administrator misspelled your name.

4. Change any applicable User Settings.

This panel shows you the privileges and system settings that the administrator has configured. You can change only some of these settings, such as whether you want to receive an alarm for upcoming meetings or be able to perform mail merges. The options that you can't change are grayed-out.

5. Tinker with the Locale Settings.

This is where you can specify your time zone, how dates are formatted, and even the currency you're using (see Figure 3-6).

Preference settings are specific to the user, which means you might be in the good old US of A playing with dollars while your counterpart might be in Japan counting his yen.

6. Edit your User Information.

As shown in Figure 3-7, here's the spot where you enter tidbits of info, including your title and phone numbers.

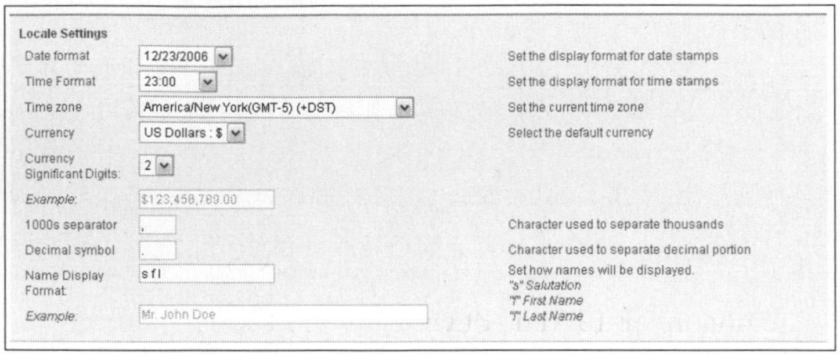

Figure 3-6:
Changing
the Locale
Settings.

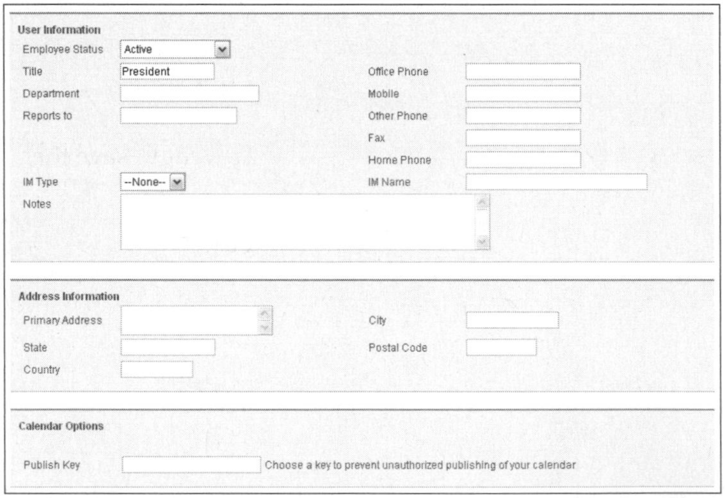

Figure 3-7:
Changing
User
Information,
Address
Information,
and
Calendar
Options.

7. Add your Address Information.

There's nothing like one-stop shopping. The administrator sets up users —
and creates an employee directory in the bargain. Here's where you enter
your home address if you want to make sure you're invited to the next
party.

8. Tweak your Calendar Options.

A Sugar database — including the calendar — is meant to be shared. If
you don't want public access to your calendar, assign it a Publish key;
only those with the key will be able to see your calendar.

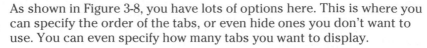

9. **Change the Layout Options.**

As shown in Figure 3-8, you have lots of options here. This is where you can specify the order of the tabs, or even hide ones you don't want to use. You can even specify how many tabs you want to display.

Hiding some modules can have unexpected consequences and make other modules not work as expected. You might consider moving unused modules to the far right end of the display order instead.

If the Administrator did not give you access to a module, you won't be able to see it here.

10. **Set your Email Options**

As shown in Figure 3-9, this is where you indicate your e-mail address, an additional Reply to address if you have one, and the default e-mail client.

11. **Click Save to save your preferences.**

Making changes is only half the fun. You'll want to save them so you can actually use them!

Not happy with the fruits of your labors? Click the My Account system link to return to the scene of the crime. Notice the Reset to Default area on the right side. Click the User Preferences button and you will be back to the default settings. Whew!

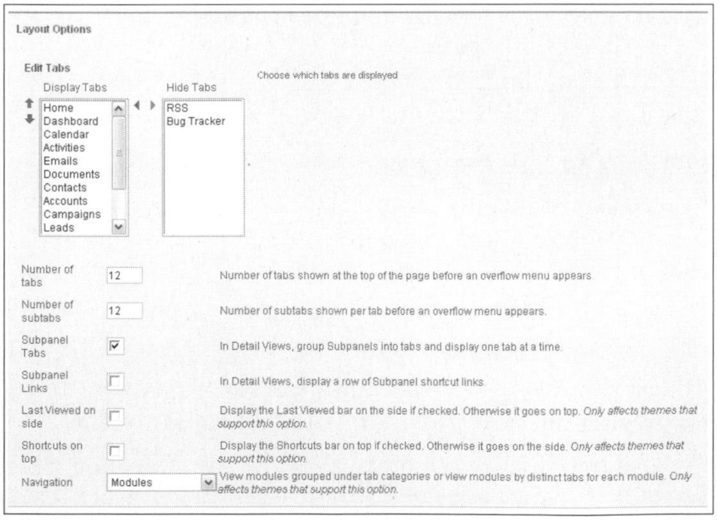

Figure 3-8:
Changing the Layout Options.

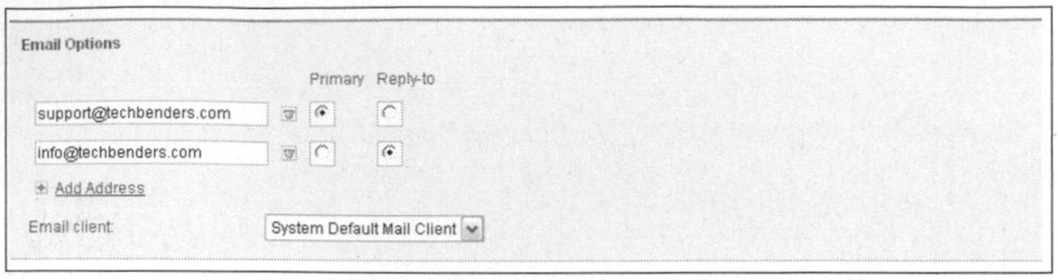

Figure 3-9:
Changing
the Email
Options.

Working with Passwords

When you start Sugar, it prompts you for a user name and password. The database administrator is required to assign a password to each new user.

The individual database user can reset his password after he logs in to the database. The theory for this is that the individual can pick a password that has some meaning to him — and so, hopefully, he doesn't forget it. If a user does forget his password, however, the administrator can reset it; you see how to do this in Chapter 16.

Here's how you reset your individual password:

1. **From any of the Sugar screens, click the My Account system link and then click the Change Password button.**

   The Set Password dialog box appears, as shown in Figure 3-10.

Figure 3-10:
Changing
your
password.

2. **Fill in your old password in the Old Password text box.**

3. **Type your new password in the New Password text box. Then, for added excitement, type it once more in the Confirm Password text box.**

4. **Click Save to save your password.**

Chapter 4

Working with Accounts, Contacts, and Leads

A database is only as good as the records it contains. In SugarCRM, adding, deleting, and editing the records in your database is easy. In this chapter, I show you how to do all three of these tasks to maintain an organized, working database. Because your business — and your database — expands, I show you how to link Contact records to Account records, as well as promote Leads to Contacts. For the overly zealous members in the audience, I show you how to get rid of any duplicates — just in case you manage to get the same record in there twice. And, if you change your mind about how records are added, I show you how to update all the information with the click of a button.

Having a Record Is a Good Thing

In this chapter, I show you how to add Accounts, Contacts, and Leads records. Before you can add any of these new records, you need to know the differences among them.

An *Accounts* record is basically a company. Generally, your business does business with other businesses — unless of course you mind your business and don't do business with anyone else!

A *Contacts* record is a person. You'll probably find that most of your Contacts work at a company, so you might want to associate a Contacts record with an Accounts record. Sound confusing? You'll know how to navigate this maze after you read this chapter.

A *Leads* record is a person with whom you are hoping to do business. Like the Contacts record, you can associate Leads with Accounts, or you can convert a Leads record to a Contacts record.

Looking at the List View

There's a lot of uniformity among Sugar modules, which means that when you master *one* module, you're well on the way to becoming a master chef in *all* modules. You create, view, and edit all records the same way. Rather than repeating myself — and probably putting you to sleep in the process — I take you through the areas that are similar for all three record types, pointing out any differences along the way.

The List view is the view you land in when you click on the Accounts, Contacts, or Leads tab. The List view displays all the records in a table format. Each record is represented by a line in the table; you click a name to drill down to the Detail view. The Account List view is shown in Figure 4-1.

All List views contain the following elements:

- ✔ **An indicator on the top-right corner of the List view lets you know how many records you have.** Only 20 display at a time. To view the next 20 records, click the right-pointing arrow.

- ✔ **You can sort the List view by clicking the appropriate column heading.**

  One interesting thing to note is that the when you click the Name column in the Contact List view, your Contacts records sort alphabetically by *last* name. However, in the Leads view, clicking the Name column sorts your Leads records alphabetically by *first* name. Go figure!

- ✔ **The List view contains both a Basic and Advanced Search tab.** Chapter 9 explains these tabs in more detail.

- ✔ **You can select records by selecting the check box to the left of a record.** Alternatively, you can click the Select drop-down button and choose This Page, to select only those records that you are currently viewing, or All Records, to select all of your records.

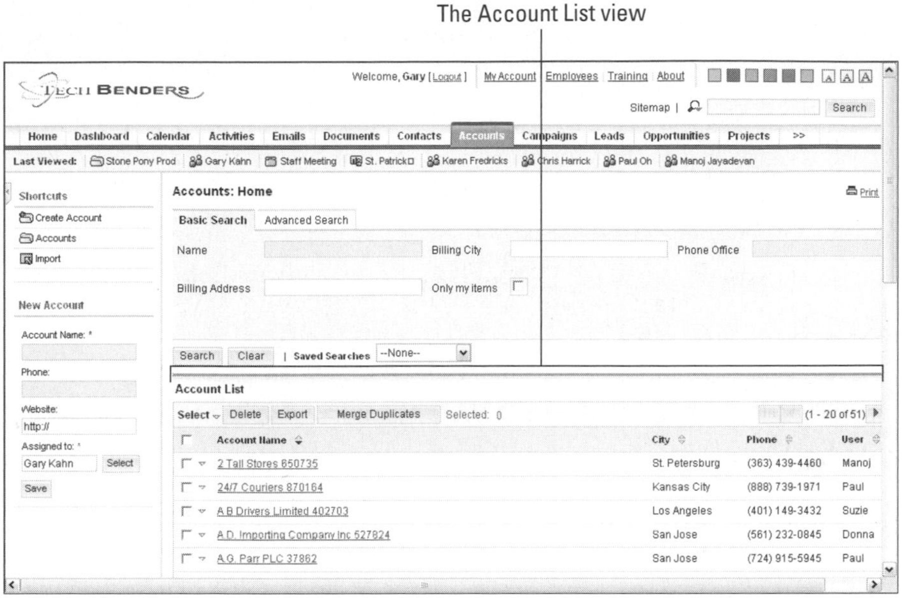

The Account List view

Figure 4-1:
The
Account
List view.

Accounting for Your Accounts

There's an old adage that asks which comes first — the account or the contact? Okay, maybe that's not *exactly* the way the saying goes, but you might wonder which type of records you should add to your database first. You might want to start by adding in your Accounts records; you'll be able to associate any new Contacts or Leads records to them as you enter them.

Adding a new Accounts record

Adding an Accounts record is simple if you follow these steps:

1. **If you aren't already in the Account List view, go there by clicking the Accounts tab on the Module Tab bar.**

   Don't know about the Module Tab bar? Check out Chapter 3, where you find out all you need to know about accessing a module and then some.

2. **Click Create Account from the Shortcuts menu to add a new account to your database.**

   The Accounts window (shown in Figure 4-2) opens.

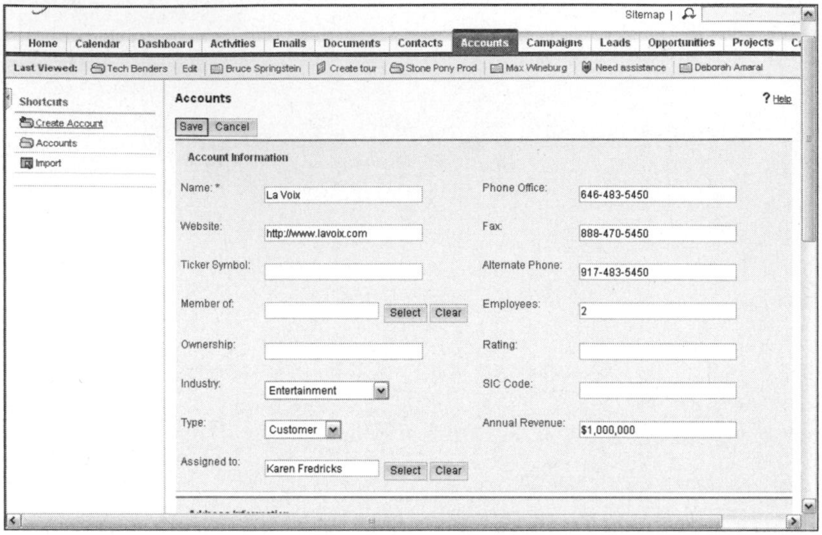

Figure 4-2:
Adding
a new
Accounts
record.

3. **Add the company's name in the Name field.**

   This is the only required field — the rest of the fields are optional but important never the less.

   Alternatively, you can fill in the account's name, who it's assigned to, and (optionally) a phone number and Web site in the Quick Form fields. However, it's well worth the effort to fill in as much information as possible.

4. **Click the next field you want to add information to and start typing.**

   You can also use the Tab key to advance to the next field. As I mention in Chapter 2, SugarCRM comes with the typical preprogrammed fields that are needed by most users. Many of the fields are fairly self-explanatory (and reflect the type of information that you probably expect to garner for any company): Ticker Symbol, Industry, Annual Revenue, and so forth.

   Not seeing the field you want? Chapter 15 takes you on a tour of the Sugar Studio where you can add fields to your heart's content!

   You can always go back to a record and delete, add, or change any information in any field, so don't worry if you leave a field blank.

5. **Scroll down.**

   Seek and ye shall find a few *more* fields to fill in, such as the ones shown in Figure 4-3.

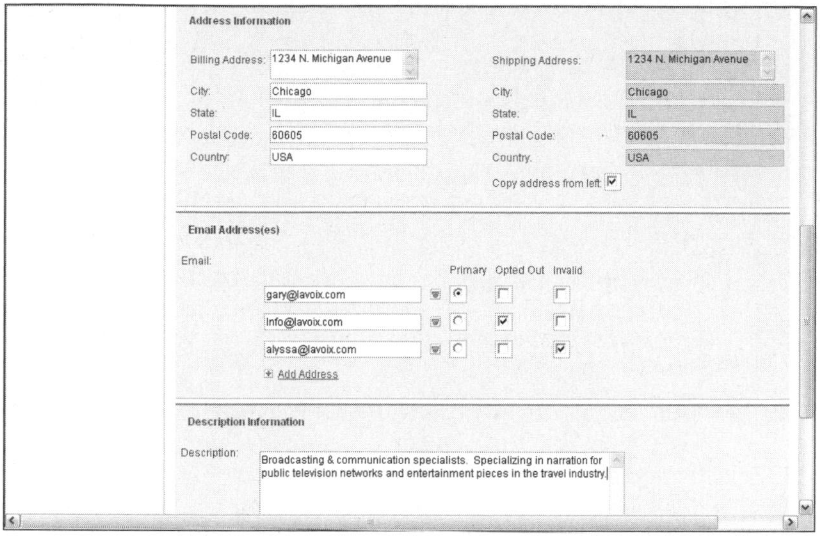

Figure 4-3:
Make sure
you find
all of the
account's
fields.

A few features are particularly noteworthy:

- Select the Copy Address From Left check box to copy the Billing Address information into the Shipping Address if the two addresses are the same.

- The Email Address(es) area allows you to enter multiple e-mail addresses so you can keep track of old addresses that you might want to mark as Opted Out or Invalid.

6. **Click the Save button at the bottom of the screen and, like magic, your new Account will be saved for posterity.**

Accessing an existing Accounts record

After you enter an Accounts record, you'll want to view the fruit of your labor. Chapter 9 shows you several search options, but for now, you can simply click an account name from the Account List view; the Accounts record will come to life in all of its glorious detail, as shown in Figure 4-4.

You'll notice five buttons running across the top of the Accounts Detail view (refer to Figure 4-4):

- **Edit:** Give this baby a click and you're able to make any necessary changes.

✔ **Duplicate:** This will start you on your way to adding a new Accounts record; however, certain key pieces of information (including the Accounts record's name, phone numbers, and Web site) will already be filled in. Tweak the Accounts record's name and *voilà!* — you have another division at the same company.

✔ **Delete:** This is the button you click to delete the record. Fortunately, you'll receive a warning notice before Sugar bids adieu to the record permanently.

✔ **Find Duplicates:** You find out how to merge duplicates from the List view later in this chapter in the "Checking for Duplicate Records" section; click this button if you prefer to merge your duplicates from the Details view.

✔ **View Change Log:** If you work in a large company, you're probably used to playing "Point the Finger." For those of you who aren't familiar with the game, this is where information changes — and everyone places the blame on someone else. Figure 4-5 shows you the Change Log, which tracks every time a user changes information in any of the fields for which the Administrator has turned on the auditing property in the Sugar Studio.

The Accounts Detail view

Figure 4-4:
Viewing an
Accounts
record.

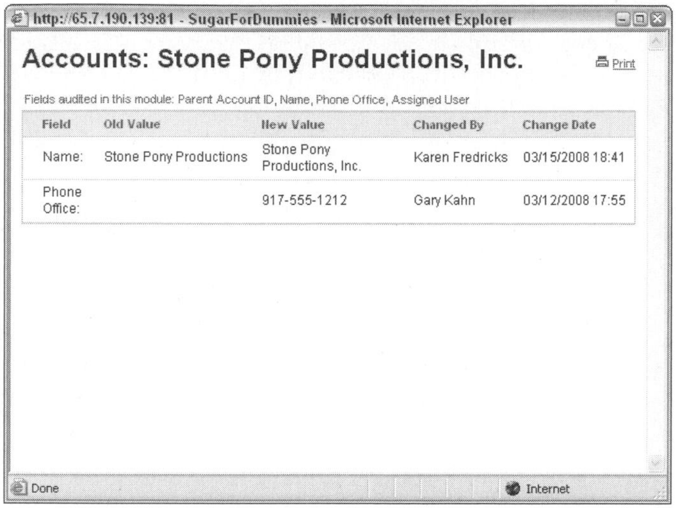
http://65.7.190.139:81 - SugarForDummies - Microsoft Internet Explorer
Accounts: Stone Pony Productions, Inc.
Print
Fields audited in this module: Parent Account ID, Name, Phone Office, Assigned User
Field
Old Value
New Value
Changed By
Change Date
Name:
Stone Pony Productions
Stone Pony Productions, Inc.
Karen Fredricks
03/15/2008 18:41
Phone Office:
917-555-1212
Gary Kahn
03/12/2008 17:55
Done
Internet

Figure 4-5: Viewing the Change Log.

Accounting for an Accounts record's subpanels

By definition, CRM software helps you track *all* of your interactions with your customers. By scrolling down an Accounts record, you're able to view subpanels with all the associated records linked to the current Accounts record. Talk about one-stop shopping.

Knowing the subpanels

The subpanels offer a wealth of information related to the Accounts record, including:

- **Activities:** See all the Tasks, Meetings, and Calls for an Accounts record.
- **History:** View the notes, documents, and e-mail attached to the Accounts record.
- **Contacts:** Here's where you can see a list of all the Contacts records that are associated with the Accounts record.
- **Opportunities:** This subpanel shows you the money — or at least all the deals that will (you hope) close and lead to big bucks.
- **Leads:** Gaze at your list of leads, cross your fingers, and hope that these people will soon become Contacts and/or Accounts records.
- **Cases:** Shows you a list of all the customer service issues that have been opened on the account's behalf — along with their status.

- **Member Organizations:** This is a fancy moniker for *Division*. You can link Accounts records to each other so that you can see the various departments from within the Accounts record.

- **Bugs:** If you're a manufacturer, you might want to cross-reference any product defects to the Accounts record that was being bugged by the bug.

- **Projects:** If you're in the service industry, you'll find this panel particularly effective; here's where you can view all the projects assigned to an Accounts record — and check their status.

Feeling a bit overwhelmed by the various subpanels? Like a good fast food restaurant, Sugar lets you have things your way. Notice the tabs running across the top of Figure 4-6; you can break the subpanels into bite-sized pieces by clicking the appropriate tab so that only the corresponding subpanels display.

Figure 4-6:
The Accounts record subpanels.

Want to get rid of a panel entirely? You can click the double up arrows at the top of each subpanel to close the panel. Need to get the panel back? Click the double down arrows to open the panel again.

More subpanel fun and games

Sugar's subpanels are more than just pretty faces. In addition to viewing account-related information, they also let you *create* new information and *edit* existing information. Talk about a time saver!

Any changes that you make are forever preserved in the Change Log, so be careful what you change — others will be able to see a record of those changes!

As you saw in Figure 4-6, the subpanels offer lots of functionality:

- ✔ **Create:** You can create a new record directly from the corresponding subpanel. Need to add another Contacts record? Want to create a note? Clicking the Create button at the top of a subpanel takes you to the corresponding new record view.

- ✔ **Select:** You might find yourself in a situation where you've added a record but forgot to associate it with the main Accounts record. For example, you might have added Max Wineburg as a contact but failed to mention that he worked at Stone Pony Productions. By clicking the Select button, you can navigate to Max's Contacts record and link him to the Accounts record for Stone Pony Productions.

- ✔ **Edit:** Sugar aims to make your life easy as pie and here's a great example. If you notice an error while you peruse the subpanels, feel free to click the Edit link to correct the entry on the fly.

- ✔ **Rem:** Short for *remove,* this link allows you to *unlink* a record from the master Accounts record if you feel it's linked in error.

Contacting Your Contacts

On the very simplest level, the main purpose of SugarCRM is to serve as a place to store all your contacts. You can add and edit your contacts from the Contacts Detail view — it contains all the information that pertains to one particular record and allows you to see all your contact's fields.

Adding a Contacts record

You probably have lots of contacts that you're dying to enter into your database, so what are you waiting for? Jump right in and follow these steps:

1. **If you aren't already in the Contact List view, click the Contacts tab on the Module Tab bar.**

2. **Click Create Contact from the Shortcuts menu to add a new contact to your database.**

   A blank contact record screen opens like the one you see in Figure 4-7; you're now ready to enter the new contact's information.

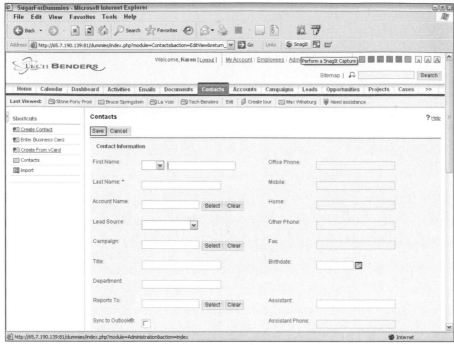

Figure 4-7:
Adding
a new
Contacts
record to
Sugar.

Alternatively, you can fill in the contact's first and last name, office phone number, and e-mail address in the Quick Form fields. However, it's well worth the effort to fill in as much information as possible.

A very nice Sugar feature is the ability to import vCards (virtual/electronic business cards). Should a potential contact send you one, you can import it by clicking the Create From vCard option in the Contacts Detail Shortcuts menu.

3. Click the Last Name field and enter the Contact's last name.

This is the only required field.

4. Click the next field you want to add information to and start typing.

Every time you add a new contact, SugarCRM automatically fills in information to the Assigned To and Date Created fields. When you add a new contact, Sugar inserts your name into the Assigned To field and your name and the current date into the Date Created field. The Date Created field serves as a permanent record; you can't change it. However, you can override the contents of the Assigned to field if you desire.

5. Continue filling in fields.

Most of these are conveniently located in the top half of the Contacts Detail view. A few of the fields are a little less obvious:

- *Account Name*: This is where you can associate a contact with an Accounts record. If you type in the first few letters of an Accounts record name, Sugar will suggest an existing Accounts record name. Alternatively, you can click the Select button and search for an Accounts record name.

  You can associate as many Contacts records as you like with the same Accounts record.

- *Lead Source:* If you're paying for advertising in two newspapers or putting a lot of time and effort into your Web site optimization, it's nice to know whether your efforts result in any new business. Here's where you enter just such information.

- *Campaign*: Chapter 13 shows you how to create a marketing campaign, but I give you a bit of a sneak preview here. A *campaign* targets a large group of individuals or organizations. Here's where you can associate a specific Contacts record with a marketing campaign to help you measure the success rate of those campaigns.

- *Reports To:* Corporate food chains are alive and kicking. Because it's not always easy to identify the key players without a scorecard, you can associate this contact with his direct superior from the same company.

- *Assigned To:* By default, your name appears in the Assigned To field. However, feel free to place the name of one of your co-workers here instead if she is responsible for this contact.

6. **Scroll down and continue adding new contact information.**

   Many cool contact fields are just waiting for data, and you don't want to miss any of them.

   - *E-mail addresses:* Feel free to add as many as you like.

   - *Address:* Out of the box, Sugar comes equipped with both *Primary* and *Other* address fields. If they are the same, select the Copy Address from Left check box to copy the Primary address information to the Other address field.

7. **Add your data as uniformly as possible.**

   One sure-fire way to sabotage your database is to develop new and creative ways to say the same thing. In Florida, users often vacillate between *Fort, Ft,* and *Ft.* Lauderdale, resulting in a bad sunburn and the inability to find all their contacts correctly. Notice that several of the SugarCRM fields contain drop-down lists. In these fields, you can choose an item in the list or you can type the first few letters of an item; the field then automatically fills with the item that matches what you typed or clicked. Chapter 15 shows you how to add — and modify — drop-down lists.

8. **Click the Save button to save the new contact information.**

The contacts they are a changing

As I mention earlier, there's a lot of similarity among Accounts, Contacts, and Leads records. When you click on a Contacts record from the Contact List view, you end up in the Contacts Detail view that you see in Figure 4-8.

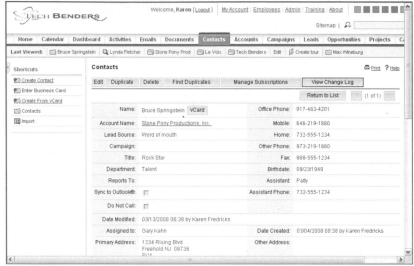

Figure 4-8:
The
Contacts
Detail view.

From here, you can edit, duplicate, delete, find duplicates, and view the Change Log exactly as you do for an Accounts record. Not wanting to bore you, you can read the earlier section, "Accessing an existing Accounts record," substituting contacts for accounts.

Managing subscriptions

One difference you'll notice between a Contacts and Accounts record is the ability to manage subscriptions directly from the Contacts Detail view. In Sugar, a *subscription* refers to a newsletter that you are producing. Chapter 13 shows you how to create marketing campaigns — including newsletters — but for now, here's how to make sure your contact is set to receive your literary work.

1. **Click the Manage Subscriptions button on the Contacts Detail view.**

    The Manage Subscriptions window (shown in Figure 4-9) springs to life.

    The Newsletters Subscribed To box gives you a list of the newsletters that the contact is receiving; the Available Newsletters box shows you other newsletters that are available to the Contacts record.

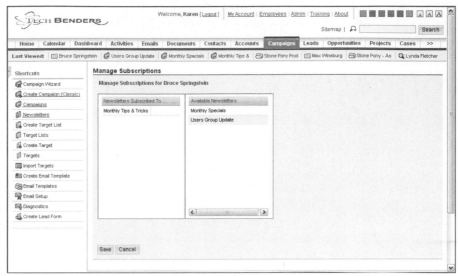

Figure 4-9:
Adding a
Contacts
record to a
newsletter
subscription
list.

2. **Drag a newsletter from the Available Newsletters box to the Newsletters Subscribed To box.**

   Alternatively, if you want to remove someone from your mailing list, you can drag in the reverse direction.

3. **Click Save to save your changes.**

   The Contacts record becomes a part of the Target List that Sugar associates with a marketing campaign.

   It would seem logical that after hitting the Save button to associate a Contacts record with a newsletter you'd return to the Contacts Detail view where you started. Wrong. However, you'll notice that the Contacts record's name now appears on the Last Viewed bar; click the name and you'll end up right where you started.

Leads Lead to Bigger Things

Sugar makes a distinction between a Leads and a Contacts record. In Sugar-speak, a *lead* is someone that has icicles hanging from his forehead — or at least hasn't started speaking with you in a warm and fuzzy manner about purchasing your products or services. A *contact*, on the other hand, is some-one you feel you have a great shot at closing — or maybe they're someone you've already had some dealings with. In any case, you can always promote a lead to a contact when the ice starts to melt from his checkbook.

Adding a few Leads records to sweeten the deal

If you've already noted the similarities between Accounts and Contacts records, you're going to feel a very strong sense of déjà vu when it comes to working with Leads records. I'll try not to bore you with any ABC (already been covered) information, but I want to point out a few of the subtle differences between the record types:

1. **Click the Leads tab on the Module Tab bar.**

   One interesting thing to note is that the Lead List view alphabetizes by first name rather than by last name.

2. **Click Create Lead from the Shortcuts menu to add a new lead to your database.**

   On cue, a blank Leads record opens and you can commence entering your new lead into the window that you see in Figure 4-10.

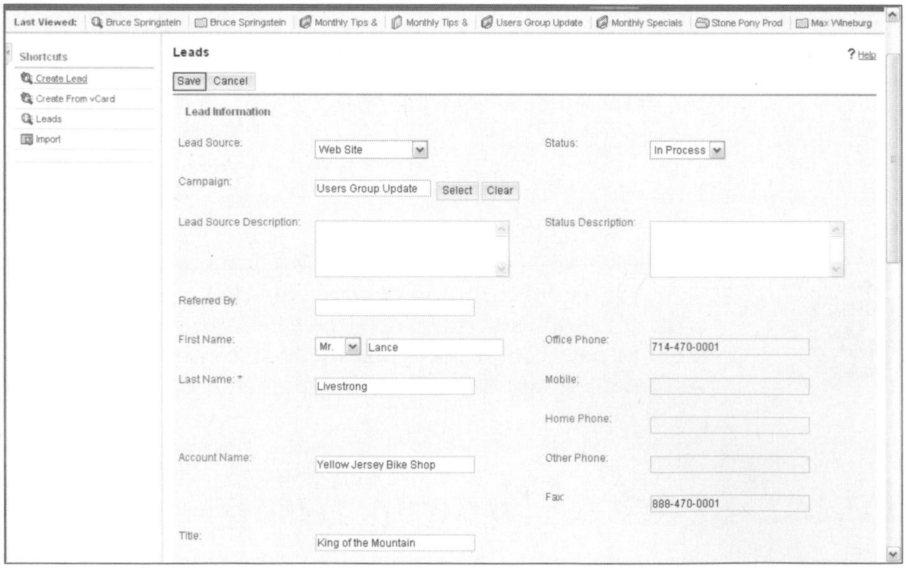

Figure 4-10: Adding a new Leads record to Sugar.

You probably already know the drill by now, but you can also use the Quick Form and fill in the lead's last name to add a bare-bones Leads record.

Sugar will not warn you if you're adding a new Leads record that's identical to an existing Contacts record. Nor can you merge the two records together when you see the error of your way. You have to either delete the Leads record or promote her to a Contacts record and then merge the two Contacts records together.

3. **Click the Lead Source drop-down field and indicate the source of the new lead.**

4. **Click the next field you want to add information to and start typing.**

   Just like a Contacts record, the only Leads record field that is required is the Last Name field. And, just like a Contacts record, every time you add a new contact, SugarCRM automatically fills your name into the Assigned To field and the date into the Date Created field. Feel free to change the contents of the Assigned To field.

5. **Continue filling in fields.**

   One difference you might notice is that the Account Name field is not linked to the Accounts module, as it is when you enter a new Contacts record. The theory here is that if the Leads record is ice-cold, it's not worth adding his company permanently to the Accounts list.

6. **Scroll down and continue adding new contact information.**

   Your mantra is consistency!

7. **Click the Save button to save the new Leads record information.**

A promotion is a very sweet thing!

By now, you might be tired of hearing about all the timesaving features that are incorporated into SugarCRM. Personally, I don't think you can ever get too much of a good thing.

Converting a Leads record to a Contacts record is ridiculously easy — and saves you having to enter all that information a second time. Here's all you need to do:

1. **Click the name of the lead from the Lead List view.**

   The Leads record opens in the Leads Detail view.

   Having trouble finding the lead you're looking for? Chapter 9 shows you a couple of ways to find just the record you need.

2. **Click the Convert Lead button.**

   The Leads Detail window changes slightly. The top half of the screen allows you to edit or add basic contact information including name, address, and phone numbers.

3. **(Optional) Click the Create Note or Attachment link to add a note or attachment to the new Contacts record.**

   Figure 4-11 shows you the expanded window, which allows you to include fields to add a note subject and body, and attach an attachment if you so desire.

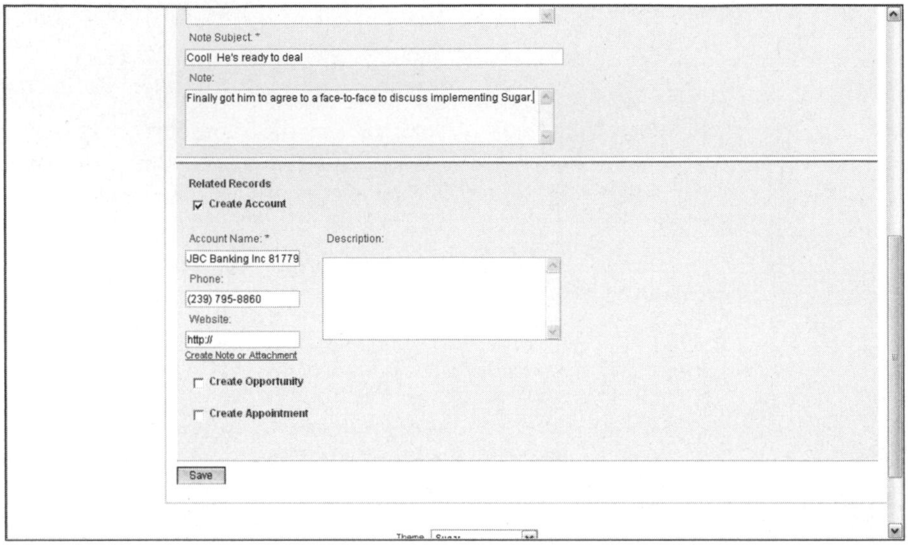

Figure 4-11:
Adding
a note to
the Leads
record
you are
converting.

4. **(Optional) Scroll down further to the Related Records area of the window, select the Create Account, Create Opportunity, and/or the Create Appointment check boxes and fill in the appropriate information.**

   Here's your chance to add an Account, Opportunity, or Appointment — and have it automatically link to the record that you're promoting. If you're adding a new account, the one you previously added for the Leads record will automatically appear. The account phone number will also appear based on the Leads record's *office* phone number.

5. **Click Save to complete the transformation from Lead to Contact.**

There's a Whole Lot of Updating Going On

Good software helps you manage the more mundane aspects of your life. SugarCRM is a great piece of software because it helps make mincemeat of your work.

If you scroll to the bottom of the List view, you'll see the Mass Update portion of the screen. Here's where you can update all the selected records in a click of a button:

1. **Select the records in the List view that you want to update.**

2. **Fill in the field information that you want to change.**

   Figure 4-12 shows you the fields that you can update for your Accounts records. Updating Leads or Contacts records information gives you slightly different choices. Regardless of the record type, you can change the Assigned User field. This list draws from the user list of your Sugar database. You can type a user name, or click the Select button and choose the name of a user.

3. **Click the Update button.**

   A prompt appears, asking you if you really want to update the records.

4. **Click OK to update the records.**

   The field information will update on the records that you selected, and the Account List will show only those records.

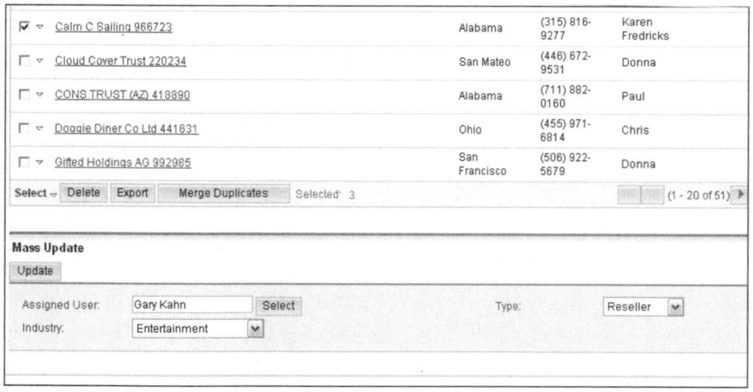

Figure 4-12:
Performing
a Mass
Update
on the
currently
selected
records.

Deleting Records

What do you do if you find that you're no longer doing business with one of your accounts? Or that one of your contacts is MIA — or no longer works for a company? For whatever reason you decide that a record no longer needs to be a part of your database, you can just delete that record.

SugarCRM allows you to delete a single record from the Detail view, or selected records from the List view. In either view, clicking the Delete button brings up the warning shown in Figure 4-13. Click OK and your records will disappear. Forever.

Figure 4-13:
You get an
ominous
warning
when
deleting
records.

Thinking before deleting a record

Although the procedure is rather simple, you might want to rethink deleting records. When you delete a record, you also delete all the associated notes and histories tied to that record. For example, suppose that State College uses SugarCRM to keep track of all the prospective students it has contacted — or has been contacted by. State College admissions personnel receive thousands of inquiries per month and fear that the database will become too large to manage — and subsequently think that deleting all prospects that they haven't had contact with in over a year is the best course of action. However, some of those prospects might be attending different schools that they aren't happy with and might want to enter State College as transfer students. Other prospects might transfer after completing two years at a community college, and still others might consider attending State College as graduate students.

What to do in such a situation? You have a few options. Consider moving the contacts that you no longer need into another archival database. That way, should the need ever arise, you can still find all the original information on a contact without having to start again from scratch. How nice to be able to rekindle a relationship by asking, "So tell me, how did you find the accounting department at Podunk University?" Another option is to change the contact's status to inactive.

Two warnings before deleting a record

Losing contacts in your database is a very scary thought. You undoubtedly rely very heavily on your SugarCRM database; therefore, losing that data can be potentially devastating to your business. Worst of all, when you realize that you just accidentally removed several — or even hundreds — of records from the database, panic can set in!

Avert this panic by following these tips *before* you attempt to delete any of your records:

✔ **Read the warning and make note of the number of contacts that you're about to delete.** Don't be afraid to click Cancel.

✔ **Remember the three rules of computing: back up, back up, back up!** Chapter 16 provides you with instructions on how to create a backup. A good backup provides the easiest method to restore all your information after you accidentally delete it.

Checking for Duplicate Records

It's a good practice to make sure that a record doesn't already exist in your database *before* you set about adding it a second time. However, if you realize that a record exists multiple times in your database, you can easily merge them from either the List or Detail view.

You'll probably run across duplicate records while perusing the List view. Here's how you can fix the problem:

1. **Indicate the duplicated records by selecting the appropriate check boxes.**

   If necessary, you can merge more than two records together, as shown in Figure 4-14.

2. **Click the Merge Duplicates button.**

   The Merge Records With window opens. The left column shows you the data to be kept when the records are merged; the column on the right shows what data — if any — will be lost.

3. **Click the double left arrows next to any data you want to save.**

   In the example in Figure 4-15, you see that the Industry information is different for the two records. If you'd like to retain Communications as the industry, click those arrows and the data will copy over to the first record's information.

4. **Click the Save Merge button when you're finished.**

   A prompt appears, warning you that your record(s) will disappear after the merge.

5. **Click OK to continue.**

   Say sayonara to the old record(s) and howdy to the newly merged record. You might even hear a faint Ta-Dum in the background.

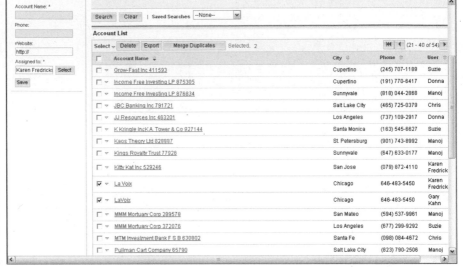

Figure 4-14:
Selecting
the
duplicate
records to
merge.

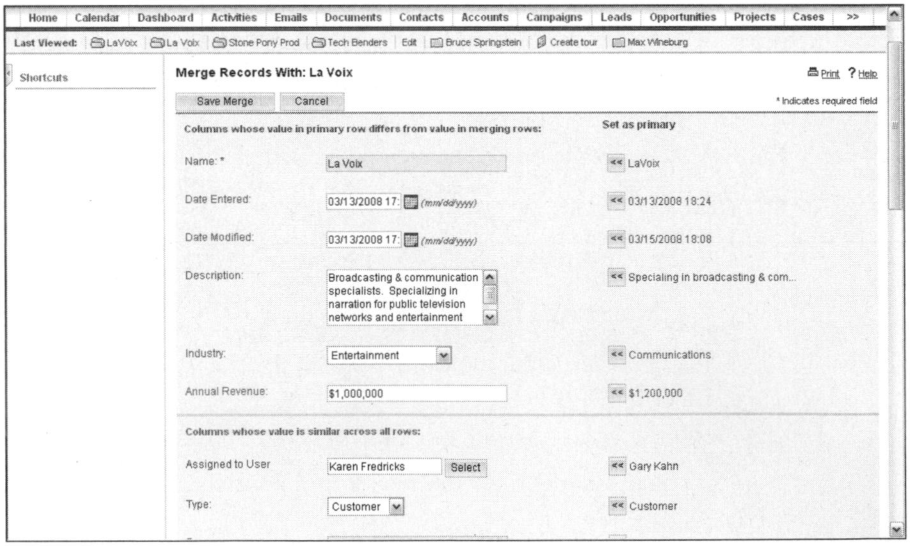

Figure 4-15:
Merging
duplicate
records.

Exporting Your Records

You might want to export a list of your records for a number of reasons. You might need to give a list of your Accounts records to a mailing house in order for them to send out those slick new brochures they've created for you. Or, maybe you want to share a list of the Contacts records belonging to a trade association with a non-Sugar user. Whatever the reason, it's quite simple to export that list by following these steps:

1. **Select the records you wish to export from any List view.**

2. **Click the Export button.**

   The window in Figure 4-16 magically appears, making this a foolproof operation.

Figure 4-16:
Exporting the selected record(s).

3. **Click Save.**

   The Save As window opens.

4. **Navigate to the folder where you want to save the file and give it a name.**

5. **Click Save.**

   Sugar creates a .csv (comma-separated values) file containing all your selected records.

Part II
Cooking with Sugar

The 5th Wave   By Rich Tennant

"I've used several spreadsheet programs, but this is the best one for designing quilt patterns."

In this part . . .

Okay, after you whip Sugar into shape (see Part I of this book), it's time to get your life in order. The CRM in SugarCRM stands for *customer relationship manager,* which (as the name implies) makes it a great place to manage your customers. You can schedule an activity with any one of them, set a reminder, and maybe add some notes for good measure. (Sure beats the heck out of a yellow sticky note!) If you're working on a special project with a customer, you'll want to track it in Sugar. You'll also want to keep track of your sales opportunities so you can add even more customers to the fold. Sugar can even help you keep track of the paperwork associated with your customer. And, after you have everything organized, you'll want to be able to access all that data again from one central location.

Chapter 5

Keeping Track of the Sweet Things in Life

*I*n this chapter, I show you how to schedule activities with your contacts, how to view those activities (and modify them if necessary), and even how to find out whether you completed a scheduled activity. You discover the intricacies of navigating through the various SugarCRM calendars, how to use your Task List to keep you on top of your activities, and the joy of sharing your scheduled activities with others. Finally, you find out how to take notes so you can say "hasta la vista" to the sticky notes and paper scraps decorating your office.

Actively Working with Activities

One of the most useful of Sugar's features is its ability to tie an *activity,* such as a call, meeting, or task, to a specific record. Most basic calendaring programs allow you to view your appointments and tasks on your calendar, but they don't offer a way of cross-referencing an appointment to a record. For example, if you schedule an appointment with me and forget when that appointment is, you have to flip through a traditional calendar until you see my name. Plus, you can't easily see a list of all appointments that you've ever scheduled with me. However, SugarCRM offers these helpful features.

In Sugar, you can associate an activity with just about any record type. You'll probably schedule most activities with Accounts and Contacts records, but you can schedule them with virtually any type of Sugar record including Opportunities, Projects, and even Bugs.

Creating an activity

You can schedule activities from a number of places in Sugar including:

- The Calendar module
- The Activities module
- The Activities subpanel of any record
- The Shortcuts menu on the Home page

Using different methods to schedule different activities is a smart plan of action. For example, I recommend scheduling meetings through the calendars to make sure that you don't have a conflict for a specific time slot. However, when you're scheduling calls and tasks, which are generally "timeless" activities that don't have to be set for a specific time, you might prefer scheduling from the Activities module where you can view your existing Call List.

You might find that many of your individual activities revolve around a single goal or *project*. If this is the case, you'll want to head over to Chapter 6 where you find out how to work with projects.

In an ideal world, you could set up various tasks and have your software complete the tasks for you *automatically* without having to consult your Task List. You might then consider Sugar to be an ideal piece of software because Chapter 16 shows you how you can use the Scheduler to automate various processes, such as following up on leads.

Follow these steps to create an activity:

1. **Open the Calls, Meetings, or Tasks window.**

   The three types of Sugar activities are Calls, Meetings, and Tasks. All three are scheduled in pretty much the same way. There are two ways to get to them:

   - Click Schedule Call, Schedule Meeting, or Create Task from the Shortcuts menu on the Home page, or on the Activities or Calendar modules.

   - Click Create Task, Schedule Meeting, or Schedule Call from the Activities subpanel of any record.

   Not sure which method floats your boat? Consider creating new activities from a record's subpanel. As shown in Figure 5-1, the associated Related To field will already be filled in. Better yet, schedule from a Contacts record and both Contacts and Accounts records' information will automatically associate with the activity!

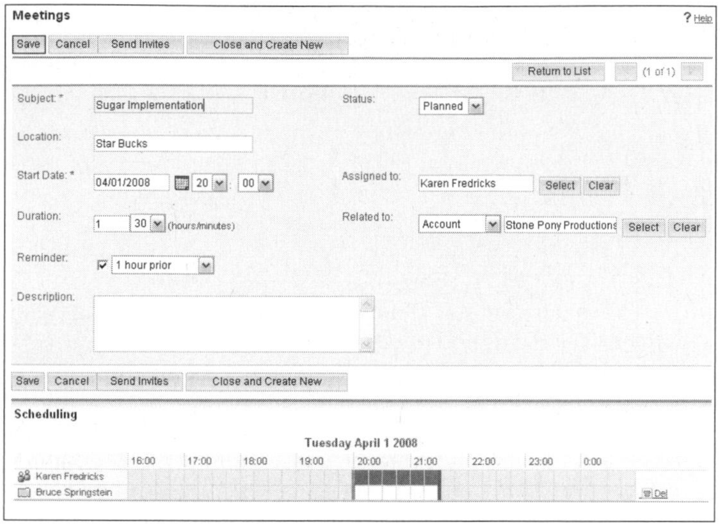

Figure 5-1:
Scheduling
a meeting
from a
Contacts
record.

Two additional methods allow you to create calls and meetings quickly —
albeit in a somewhat abbreviated manner:

- The Calendar tab on the Module Tab bar also includes the Create
Appointment Quick Form (shown in Figure 5-2), which allows you
to schedule a call or meeting by simply adding a Subject, Start
Date, and Time.

Figure 5-2:
Scheduling
a call or
meeting
quickly.

- Clicking a time in the Day calendar view will allow you to schedule
a call or meeting by simply adding a subject.

Hopefully, you live by the "no pain, no gain" philosophy of activity scheduling and used one of the first three methods.

 2. **Fill in the required fields.**

  You'll find the procedures for adding calls, meetings, and tasks to be almost identical because all three activity types use just about the same fields. Here's a run-down of the various activity fields — and where you find them.

  • *Subject:* All activity types require a subject.

  • *Status:* Although all activity types include a Status field, it is only a *required* field for Tasks and Calls.

  • *Location:* It never hurts to let everyone know, including yourself, where the big event will take place. Not surprisingly, only Meetings include a location field.

  • *Inbound/Outbound:* This option is for Calls only and lets you specify whether you'll be placing or receiving the call.

  • *Start Date:* Although all activity types include the Start Date field, it is only *required* when scheduling calls and meetings. Feel free to click the calendar icon to view a mini-calendar if you need help selecting a date.

  • *Assigned To:* Scheduling a task is only half the fun; the other half comes when someone actually completes the task. The Assigned To field shows just who the responsible party is. By default, your name will be that person.

  • *Duration:* I'm not sure of the logic here, but only calls have a required duration; however, feel free to add one for your meetings as well.

  • *Related To:* The beauty of Sugar is that the various components all link together. Here's where you relate the activity to another type of record.

  • *Reminder:* Select this check box if you want the system to send a reminder to everybody on the list prior to the call or meeting.

  • *Description:* Add additional information regarding an activity. For example, you might want to add special instructions about the items that you need to bring to a meeting.

  • *Due Date:* If you're scheduling a task, you can optionally include a Due Date.

  • *Start Time:* Enter a start time for the event. Choose 00 for the Start Time if you're scheduling a call or task that doesn't need to occur at a specific time.

- *Priority:* Although not available when scheduling calls or meetings, this is a required Task field; High, Medium, or Low are your options in the drop-down list.

3. **Click Save.**

   You have a real, live scheduled activity!

Scheduling a sweet rendezvous

A particularly useful feature of Sugar is the ability to invite other users or contacts to participate in a meeting or call. Once invited, Sugar will send out e-mail invitations and keep track of the responses, which you can view directly from the Call or Meeting window.

To add invitees to the party:

1. **Scroll to the Scheduling subpanel of the Schedule Call or Schedule Meeting window.**

   Figure 5-3 shows you what it looks like, just to make sure you don't get lost.

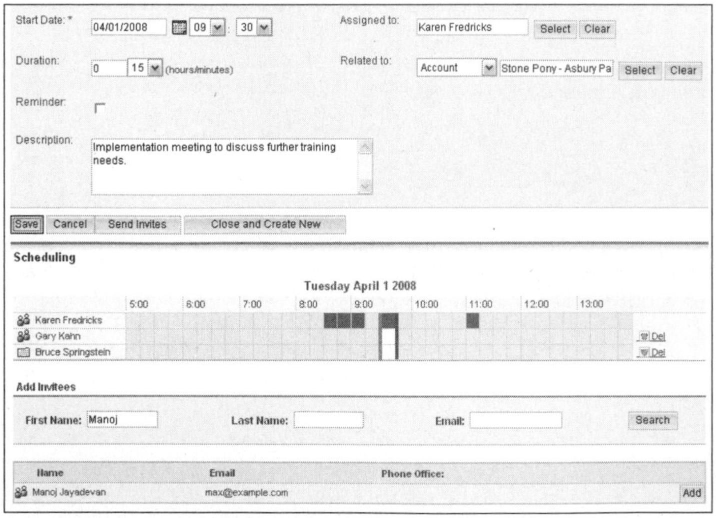

Figure 5-3: Inviting invitees to the party.

2. **Enter the invitee's first name, last name, or e-mail address in the Add Invitees subpanel and then click Search.**

   Sugar will race through your database looking for possible matches.

3. **Click Add to add the name to your list of invitees.**

   If you're into appearances, you'll note that any users you invite to the soiree have a slightly different icon than that of a plain old ordinary contact.

4. **Click the Send Invites button to send out e-mail invitations to all of your invitees.**

5. **Click Save to save your activity.**

   The activity includes two sub-panels: invited Contacts and invited Users. And, as shown in Figure 5-4, you can see whether the invitee has accepted your invitation.

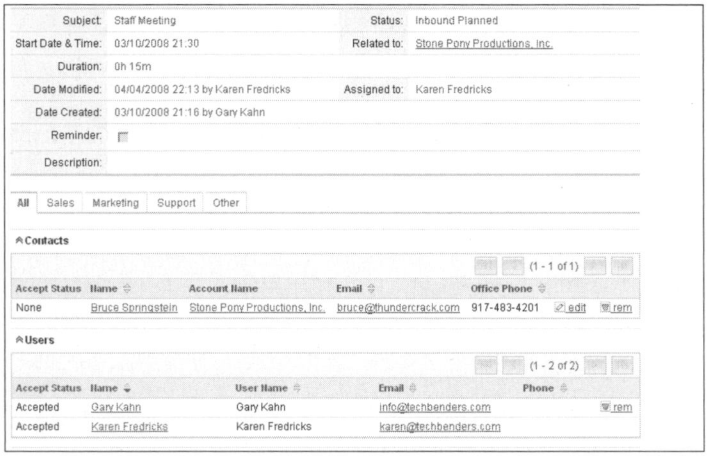

Figure 5-4:
Viewing the responses of invitees of an activity.

Accessing Your Activities

After you create activities, Sugar is a worse nag than your mother! You can see your activities — and Sugar reminds you to complete them — in a number of ways:

- **Per record:** The Activities subpanel for a selected record enables you to see what specific activities you scheduled with that particular record.

- **Per List:** Sugar provides you with a Call List, Meeting List, and a Task List to let you see your calls, meetings, and tasks.

- **Calendar:** The Day, Week, and Month calendars show a listing of the current day's activities. The Year calendar places the date of any day that includes a scheduled activity in bold type.

Viewing the "Honey-Do" lists

Like the "Honey-Do" list hanging from your spouse's workbench, the various Sugar activity lists give you a listing of all the activities.

The lists are readily accessible by clicking the Calendar or Activities modules on the Modules Tab bar and then choosing Calls, Meetings, or Tasks from the Shortcuts menu, which opens the Call, Meeting, or Task List. Figure 5-5 shows you a sample of the Task List.

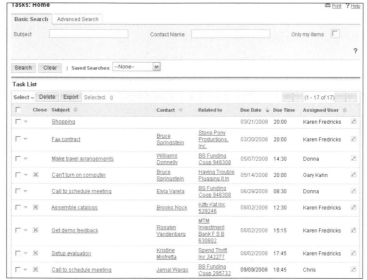

Figure 5-5: Looking at a very full Task List.

Just as your boss will see red if you fail to complete a task, Sugar displays the due date of any overdue tasks in — you guessed it — red.

Quickly printing an Activity List

As great as Sugar is, it can be totally useless if you don't have access to a computer or handheld device. Or maybe you work with a technically challenged co-worker (your boss?) who prefers to have a copy of her Task List printed on a daily basis. No need to fret; Sugar can easily perform this task for you. Although these instructions are for the Task List, they work equally well for the Call List and Meeting List:

Unfortunately, the Shortcuts menu will print right along with your Task List. To avoid its appearance, you'll want to close the Shortcuts menu before proceeding.

1. **Click the Print icon at the top of the Task List page.**

   A new page opens looking pretty much like the page that's *already* open.

2. **Click the Printer icon at the top of your browser window.**

   With luck, your printer will snap to attention.

3. **Race to the printer, collect the hard copy of the Task List, and race it over to your co-worker's desk.**

   I know, you really don't need to race around but it does make for a nice cardio workout!

Viewing the Activities tab

If you scroll to the Activities subpanel at the bottom of any record's Detail view, SugarCRM displays all the activities scheduled with the current record. This is a great way to have a list of all the activities you've scheduled with a contact.

You can see the Activities subpanel for a Contacts record in Figure 5-6.

All	Sales	Marketing	Support	Activities	Collaboration

Activities

Create Task	Schedule Meeting	Schedule Call	Compose Email		(1 -

	Close	Subject ⇕	Status ⇕	Contact ⇕	Due Date ⇕	Assigned User ⇕
	✕	Testing in Sugar	Planned	Bruce Springstein	04/02/2008 18:00	Karen Fredricks
	✕	Training Session	Planned	Bruce Springstein	04/01/2008 09:30	Karen Fredricks
	✕	Fax contract	In Progress	Bruce Springstein	03/31/2008 00:00	Karen Fredricks
	✕	Staff Meeting	Planned	Bruce Springstein	03/10/2008 21:30	Karen Fredricks

History

Create Note or Attachment	Archive Email	View Summary		(1 -

	Subject ⇕	Status ⇕	Contact ⇕	Date Modified ⇕	Assigned User ⇕
	He's a really nice guy	Note	Springstein	03/30/2008	
	chapt 4 graphic	Note	Springstein	03/20/2008	
	company logo	Note	Springstein	03/20/2008	
	Planning next concert	Note	Springstein	03/20/2008	
	Called to confirm appointment	Note	Springstein	03/13/2008	

Figure 5-6: The Activities subpanel.

You can click the column heading of any column to sort your activities.

Editing your activities

Like all the best-laid plans of mice and men, activities change, and you need a way to make note of these changes in Sugar. Changing an activity is all in the click of the mouse. If you can see an activity, you can edit it. That means you can edit your activities from the Activities subpanel, the appropriate list (Task, Call, or Meeting), or from any of the Sugar calendars.

Resist the urge to simply change the date for rescheduled activities. Although this is easy enough to do, you might end up losing some key information. Say, for instance, that a particularly high-maintenance customer stands you up four times — and then complains to your boss about your lack of service. If you simply edit the original activity, you won't be able to document the dates of all four activities. You might like to think of this as CYA (um, *cover your sweet . . .*) technology!

Clearing activities

After you complete a task, clearing the task is very important because then Sugar

- ✔ **Stops reminding you about the activity.**
- ✔ **Removes the X in the Close column of the Task, Call, or Meeting List.**
- ✔ **Changes the activity's status.**

To clear an activity, follow these steps:

1. **Open the Activity List that contains the activity you want to clear.**

   Again, if you can *see* the activity you can *clear* the activity. If you happen to be working in the Task List, you can clear the activity from there. Or, if you happen to be looking at a record that contains an activity — be it an Accounts, Contacts, or Opportunities record — you can clear the activity right from the Activities subpanel.

2. **Click the X to the left of the activity you wish to clear.**

   The Edit page opens. If you look at the Status field, you'll notice that it's changed. For example, if you mark a meeting as closed, the Status field contains *Held*. If you clear a task, the Status field changes to *Completed*.

   It might seem a bit counterintuitive, but Open items have an X next to them; once completed, the X disappears.

3. **Click Save to save your changes.**

Don't hold your breath waiting to hear champagne corks popping in the background. You'll have to be satisfied in knowing that the next time you run across the activity anywhere in Sugar, the item will be missing the X — and you'll have one less thing to worry about!

The miniature Task List

Generally, you schedule meetings — and often times, calls — for a specific time. These items will then appear to a specific time slot on your calendars. On the other hand, tasks have a due date; as long as you complete them by that *date,* the actual completion *time* is insignificant.

Sugar supplies you with a miniature Task List that appears to the right of Sugar's daily calendar. This Task List provides you with a quick way to view your entire day at a glance without having to click elsewhere. The smaller Task List provides all your scheduled tasks for a specific day. Figure 5-7 shows a sample of a Day calendar and its Task List.

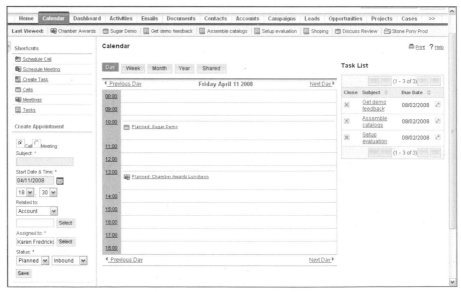

Figure 5-7:
A Day calendar's Task List.

Viewing the various calendars

The various Sugar calendars are great for viewing scheduled tasks. As you might suspect, you can view the calendars by clicking the Calendar tab of the Module Tab bar. Doing so opens your Day calendar.

You can view your calendar (any scheduled activities will appear) four different ways by clicking the appropriate tab at the top of the Calendar module:

✔ **Day calendar:** Shows you the time-specific activities of the selected day as well as a listing of the day's tasks. (Refer to Figure 5-7.) The day is divided into hour intervals.

✔ **Week calendar:** Not surprisingly, the Week calendar shows you the activities of the selected week arranged in a single column, as shown in Figure 5-8.

Figure 5-8:
Wondering about the week's activities.

✔ **Monthly calendar:** As you can see in Figure 5-9, this view shows you the activities of the selected month.

✔ **Year calendar:** Although this view won't show you any scheduled activities, it will show you a calendar of the current year. Click a date to launch the corresponding Day calendar. You'll notice that the dates on the calendar that include scheduled activities will appear bolded.

✔ **Shared calendar:** This is a cool feature. Follow these steps to view another user's calendar:

1. **Click the Shared tab, which launches a slightly different version of the Week calendar.**

2. **(Optional) Click Previous or Next to navigate to the week you want to view.**

3. **Click the Edit link to open a list of Sugar users.**

4. **Select the user whose calendar you want to view.**

   If you'd like to view the calendar of several users, hold down the Ctrl key while selecting the user names.

5. Click Select.

You now can view the weekly calendar of another user, or multiple users, as shown in Figure 5-10.

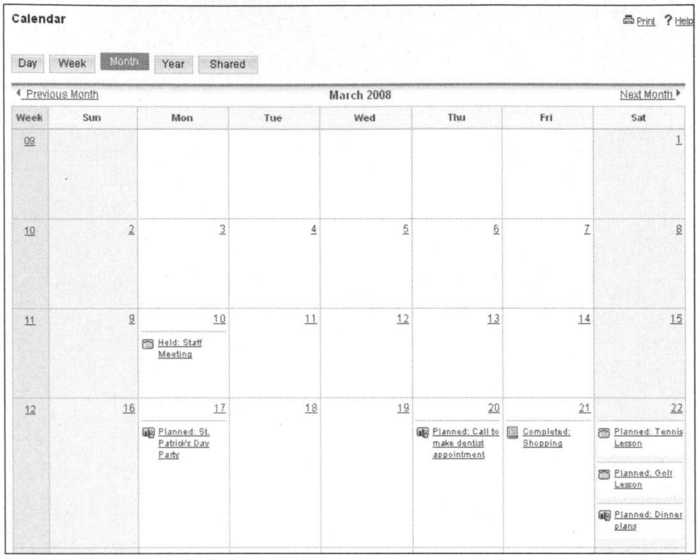

Figure 5-9: The month at a glance.

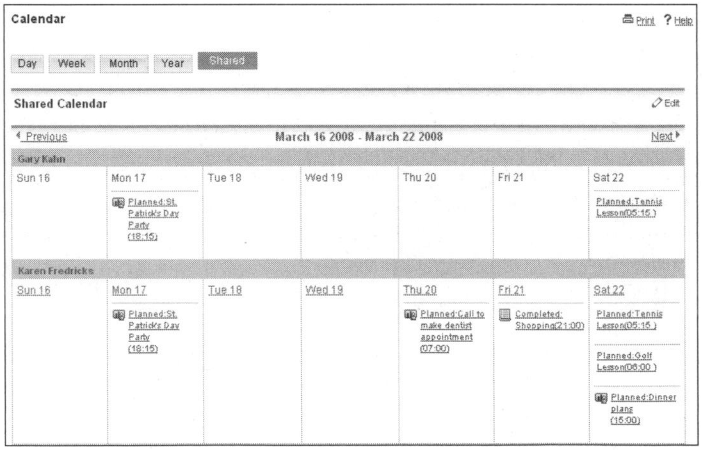

Figure 5-10: Viewing the calendars of others.

No matter which calendar view suits your fancy, they all share some common functionality:

- ✔ **Activity types are represented by specific icons.** For example, scheduled calls are represented by a telephone icon.

- ✔ **Clicking an activity opens the Tasks record in its full glory where you can then edit the activity.**

- ✔ **Hovering your mouse over an activity reveals any additional details you might have included about the activity.** Figure 5-11 shows you an example of those details.

Figure 5-11:
Hovering
your mouse
over an
activity.

- ✔ **Clicking a date in the Week, Month, or Year calendars opens that date in the Day calendar.**

- ✔ **Clicking the Previous and Next links moves you backward or forward in a calendar.** For example, to view next month's calendar, click the Next Month link located at both the top and bottom of the Month calendar.

Creating Sweet Love Notes

Look around your desk. If you have more than one sticky note attached to it, you need to use SugarCRM. Look at your computer monitor; if it's decorated with sticky notes, you need to use SugarCRM. Does a wall of sticky notes obscure your file folders? Do you panic when you can't find your pad of sticky notes? Do you have small sticky notes clinging to larger sticky notes? You need to use SugarCRM!

What if one of your best clients calls requesting a price quote? You quote him a figure from the top of your head — and then promptly forget what you quoted him. Or imagine that one of your more high-maintenance customers calls you on March 1 in immediate need of an imported Italian widget. You check with your distributors and guarantee him one by March 15. On March 10, he calls you, totally irate that he hasn't yet received his widget.

Sound familiar? Creating notes is one of the easiest features to master but one that too many users overlook. A simple note in Sugar provides you with several benefits:

✔ **Your entire office can operate on the same page by having access to the same client data.**

✔ **You have a record, down to the date and time, of all communications that you have with each of your contacts.**

✔ **You won't forget what you said to your customer — or what your customer said to you.**

✔ **You have pertinent information at your fingertips without having to strip-search your office looking for a lost sticky note.**

Adding a note

Considering the importance of notes to the overall scheme of your business, they are amazingly easy to add. Most importantly, notes can be attached to a contact in your database. In addition, a note can be attached to most Sugar records, including Accounts, Contacts, and Opportunities records.

Here's all you have to do to add a note to Sugar:

1. **Open the Detail view of the record you want to attach a note to.**

   For example, if you want to add a note about John Smith, you'd open his Contacts record.

   An alternative way of adding a note is to click the Activities tab on the Module Tab bar, choose Notes from the Shortcuts menu, and then fill in the Note Quick Form. Resist the temptation to use this method! As you can see in Figure 5-12, the Quick Form does not allow you to associate the note with a record type — thus depriving you of the true power of a note.

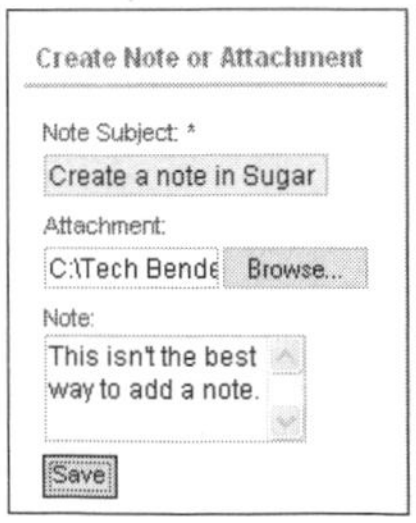

Figure 5-12:
Warning – don't be too quick in creating a note.

Create Note or Attachment

Note Subject: *
Create a note in Sugar

Attachment:
C:\Tech Bende Browse...

Note:
This isn't the best way to add a note.

Save

2. Scroll down to the History subsection of the detail screen and click the Create Note or Attachment button.

The History tab expands, revealing the Note input screen shown in Figure 5-13.

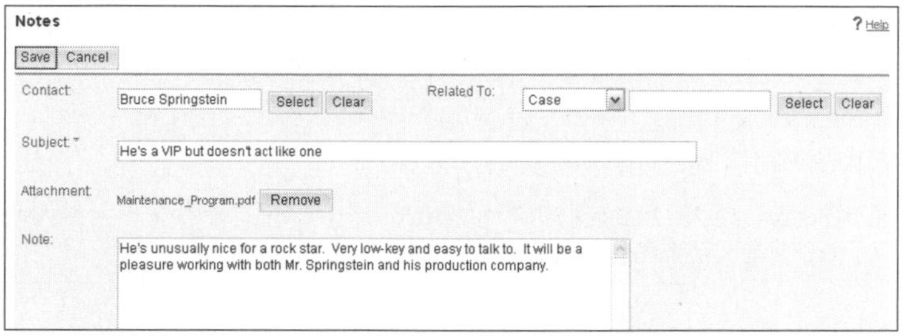

Figure 5-13:
Adding a Sugary note.

Notes					? Help

Save   Cancel

Contact: Bruce Springstein   Select Clear   Related To: Case ▾   Select Clear

Subject: * He's a VIP but doesn't act like one

Attachment: Maintenance_Program.pdf Remove

Note: He's unusually nice for a rock star. Very low-key and easy to talk to. It will be a pleasure working with both Mr. Springstein and his production company.

3. Fill in the appropriate information (only the note's Subject field is required).

Although Subject is the only field that's required, you'll want to add as much information as possible. Some of the information may already be filled in, depending on the type of record you started with and the amount of information the record contains. For example, if you start with a Contacts record that you've already associated with an Accounts record, both items fill in automatically in the Note input screen.

Sugar makes entering the Contact and Related To fields as easy as pie; type the first few letters and Sugar will supply you with a list of choices that match. Alternatively, you can always select the appropriate record from the drop-down list.

4. Click Save to record your note.

Your note will appear on the History subpanel along with any other notes you added to the record.

As strange as it may seem, Notes is the only module that does not automatically fill in the user's name who created the note — nor can you add it after the fact. Don't look for a name in the Assigned User column of the History subpanel because you won't find one.

Working with notes

After you create a note, it appears on the record's History subpanel. Being the astute reader that you are, you might notice that the note's creation date displays as well.

After you create a note, you can work with it in a number of ways:

- ✔ **Click the Edit link to the right of the note to edit a note.**
- ✔ **Click the Rem link to remove a note.**
- ✔ **Click the View Summary button to view or print a list of your notes, including the body of the note.**

Working with the Note List

You'll probably access most notes through the record's Detail view. After all, it's nice to be able to view all the information relating to a record from one location. However, should you want to view all of your notes at one time, you can do so from the Note List. Here's all you need to do:

1. **Click the Activities tab on the Module Tab bar.**

2. **Select Notes from the Shortcuts menu.**

   The Note List, similar to the one in Figure 5-14, opens.

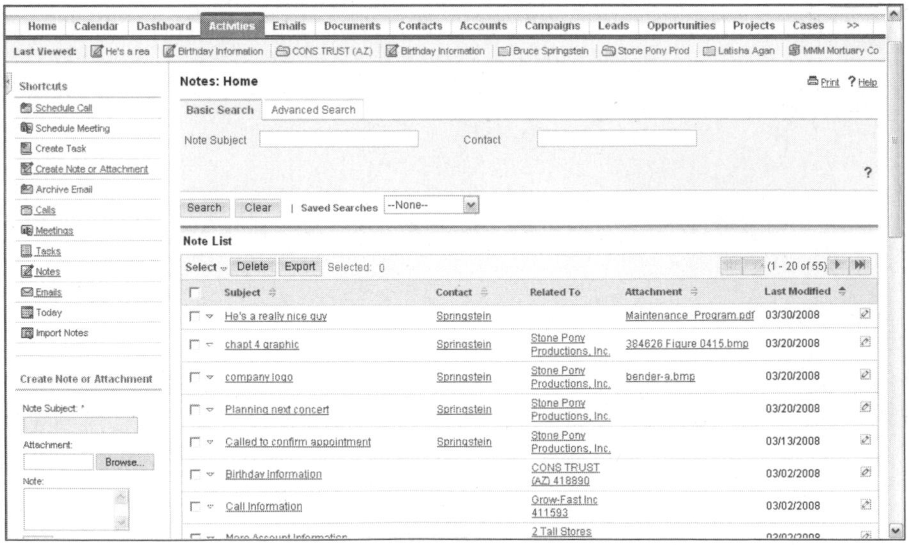

Figure 5-14: The Note List.

You can perform several tasks while in the Note List:

- **Delete a note:** To delete a note, you must first select it by selecting the check box to the left of the note and then clicking the Delete button. You can select as many notes as you'd like. Sugar presents you with a warning before you remove the note(s) permanently.

  Now that you know how easy deleting a note is, you might want to prevent other users of your database from deleting them. If you're the database administrator, check out Chapter 16 to find out how.

- **Export notes:** You might want to share your Note List with other, non-Sugar users — if those people actually exist! Again, select the note(s) you want to export and then click the Export button. You're prompted to give the file a name and location; click the Save button and you'll be the proud owner of a `.csv` file containing your Note List.

- **Duplicate a note:** You might want a note from one contact record attached to another record. Or maybe you're so pleased with the contents of a note that you want to clone it for future use. Luckily, Sugar gives you the ability to copy notes:

  a. *Click the subject of the note you want to duplicate. The Notes Detail window opens, as shown in Figure 5-15.*

  b. *Click the Duplicate button. The Notes input screen appears; notice that the fields are already filled in.*

  c. *Change the Contact and/or the Related To record type information and then click the Save button.*

Figure 5-15: Duplicating a note.

Chapter 6

Creating a Project Isn't a Major Project

*T*he Projects module is designed to create and manage projects for your organization. Working with the Projects module in SugarCRM is a three-step process and that's exactly how I organize this chapter. First, you create a Projects record, then you create the individual tasks necessary to complete the project, and finally, you track the progress of the project. In addition, this chapter looks at the additional tools for the Projects module that come with the Professional Edition of SugarCRM.

Adding a Bit of Management to Your Projects

You've probably been involved in projects of some sort ever since you had to create your first science project back in the third grade. By the time you advanced to high school, you had probably moved on to group projects in which the various members of your group were responsible for different aspects of the project.

By definition, a *project* is a large or major undertaking that usually requires many steps. In the business world, most projects resemble your high school group projects because several players are needed to reach your goal. But, unlike high school group projects, business projects often involve considerable money, personnel, and equipment. Additionally, rather than receiving a report card, business projects are often graded by how much money the project makes — or loses. Ultimately, a poorly managed project may result in hearing those words made famous by Donald Trump: "You're fired!"

Although Sugar can't guarantee that you'll get an A on your report card, it can make sure that you stay on top of your projects — and that nothing falls through the cracks.

Creating a Projects record

Creating a Projects record is your first step when working with the Projects module. You create a Projects record in just about the same way you create any other Sugar records, so you might have a vague feeling of déjà vu as you follow along the steps:

1. **Click Projects on the Module Tab bar.**

   Expectedly, doing so opens the Projects Home page shown in Figure 6-1.

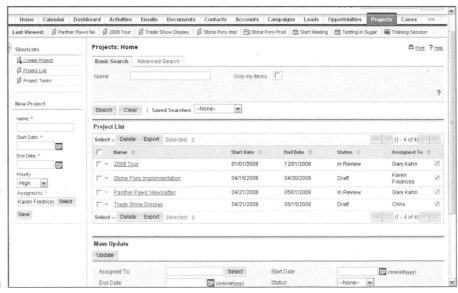

Figure 6-1: The Projects Home page.

2. **Choose Create Project from the Shortcuts menu on the left.**

   The new Projects record page opens; you can see it for yourself in Figure 6-2.

   Alternatively, you can use the Quick Form to create the Projects record quickly by supplying only the project name and its start and end date.

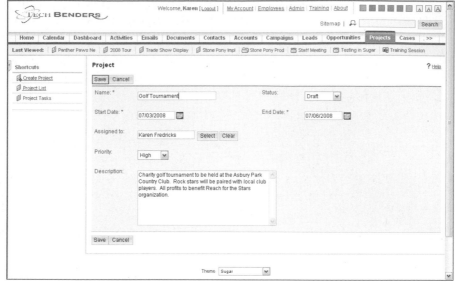

Figure 6-2:
The new
Projects
record
page.

3. Fill in the Projects record's fields.

Although you can probably do this in your sleep, I want to give you the 411 on the Projects record's fields and tell you which ones are required.

- **Name (required):** Enter a name for the project, hopefully one that will help identify the project to both you and your co-workers.

- **Status:** From the drop-down list, choose the project status of Draft, In Review, or Published.

You might scratch your head wondering about the choices in the Status drop-down menu; feel free to skip over to Chapter 15 to find out how to change those wacky choices.

- **Start Date (required):** Click the calendar icon and select the project start date.

- **End Date (required):** Click the calendar icon and select the project end date.

Having an end date *prior* to the start date doesn't make much sense to anyone, including Sugar. If you try to forge ahead in this direction, Sugar will display an error message — and not allow you to save the Projects record.

- **Assigned To (required):** Every Projects record is assigned to a user. The assigned user is the project manager. Enter the name of the user who has ownership of the project. By default, this is the user who created the Projects record. The assigned user can assign the Projects record to another user if he'd like to pass the buck.

Although Assigned To doesn't have the asterisk normally associated with a required field, it is required.

- **Priority:** From the drop-down list, choose the importance of the project (Low, Medium, or High).

- **Description:** Enter a brief description of the project if it needs a bit more explanation.

4. **Click Save to create the Projects record.**

   You'll now see the Projects record's detail page.

5. **(Optional) Associate the Projects record with other subpanel records.**

   You can associate a project with multiple Activities, Contacts, Accounts, Opportunities, Bugs, and Cases records by following these steps:

   a. *Scroll down to the appropriate subpanel.*

   b. *Click Select.*

      The Record search page opens.

   c. *Fill in the parameters you are searching for.*

      For example, if you are attaching a Contacts record to the Projects record, you might search on last name.

   d. *Click Search.*

      If there are matches in your database, they appear at the bottom of the search page.

   e. *Click the hyperlink of the record you'd like to add to the Projects record.*

      The search page closes, and the record is added to the appropriate Projects record's subpanel.

Unfortunately, you can't associate a Projects record with *multiple* users; there's only one project manager, so everyone knows whom to blame should things not work as planned. However, you can associate multiple tasks to a Projects record — and those tasks can be the responsibility of various users, as you'll see in the next section.

Creating Project Tasks

Projects include lots of minute details that someone — usually you — has to take care of. So, after you've defined your Projects record, you'll probably be itching to jump into it a bit further to start taking care of business.

You can define multiple Project Tasks for each project. A *Project Task* differs from a plain vanilla *Task* in that you must associate a Project Task with a Projects record.

To create a Project Task:

1. **Click Projects on the Module Tab bar and then choose Project List from the Shortcuts menu.**

2. **Click the name of the Projects record to which you want to add a Project Task.**

   The Project Details view opens. Figure 6-3 shows you what it looks like.

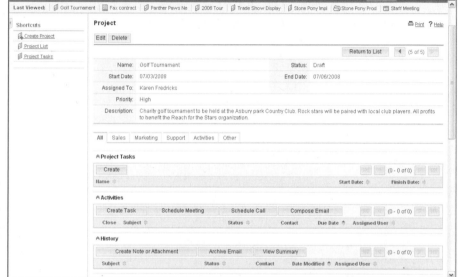

Figure 6-3:
The
Project
Details
view.

3. **Click Create in the Project Tasks subpanel.**

   The new Project Tasks page opens, as shown in Figure 6-4.

4. **Enter information on the Project Tasks page for the following fields:**

   • *Name (required):* Enter a name for the task. Try something catchy like "get this done or else."

   • *Task ID (required):* I'm not sure why, but you need to include a number for the task. Guess you can refer to a task by its number instead of its name, as in "did you finish your twenty."

   • *Start Date:* Click the calendar icon and select a start date for the task.

   • *Finish Date:* Click the calendar icon and select the due date for task completion.

   • *Percent Complete (%):* Enter the percentage of the task that has been completed. You'll want to continue to edit this percentage while your task reaches its completion.

- *Priority:* Choose a priority level, such as High, Medium, or Low from the drop-down list.

- *Milestone:* Select this check box if the completion of this task is considered a milestone for project completion.

- *Project Name (Required):* Fill in the name of the project. Alternatively, you can click Select and search for the project name.

    Although Project Name is missing the asterisk used to denote a required field, it is, indeed, required.

- *Description:* If you feel that that name of the project isn't enough, enter a brief description of the task.

5. **Click Save to create the task.**

    You return to the Project Detail view where you can add additional tasks if necessary.

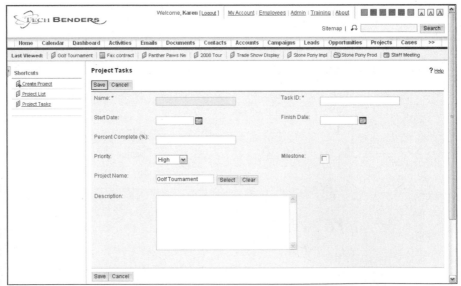

Figure 6-4: Creating a new Project Task.

Managing a Project

After you define your Projects record — and create a handful of Project Tasks to help move you along to your final goal — it's time to kick back and relax, right? Wrong! Creating the Projects record is only half the fun — now you have to put your nose to the grindstone and start on that project. Fortunately for you, Sugar will be with you every step of the way.

You can edit or delete projects, or even export a list of your current projects to a non-Sugar user (if such an animal actual exists) on the Projects Home page.

Here's how you access the Projects Home page:

1. **Click Projects on the Module Tab bar.**

   The Projects Home page opens. Refer to Figure 6-1 if you want to follow along at home.

   Click any column title to change the sort order of the Projects Home page.

2. **(Optional) Pick the Projects record you want to work with by selecting the corresponding Select check box.**

   This will allow you to perform one of the following operations:

   • *Delete*

   • *Export*

   • *Mass Update*

3. **Click on a project name to edit it.**

   The Project Detail view opens.

4. **Click Edit.**

   You are now free to roam around the cabin — or make whatever editing tweaks you feel are appropriate.

5. **Click Save to save the Projects record changes.**

Adding a Professional Touch to Your Projects

As I mention in Chapter 1, the three flavors of Sugar are Community, Professional, and Enterprise. You might be very content with the functionality of the Sugar Community Edition. However, if your company is involved in lots of large projects, you'll want to move up to Sugar Professional where you have access to several additional project management tools.

Passing the project buck

One of the big differences between the SugarCRM Community and Professional editions — besides the price — is that the Professional version gears itself toward larger organizations. This doesn't necessarily mean that your company is part of the Fortune 500, but it generally means that your company has many users that interact with each other.

By definition, a *project* is a compilation of many tasks. If you're the head cook and bottle washer of your company — or need to have your head examined — then the sole responsibility for most projects rests smack dab on top of your head. However, if you've learned to delegate — or pass the proverbial buck — then you'll find a couple of the features found only in the Professional version to be quite appealing.

Relying on your resources

In Sugar-speak, a *resource* is a user of the Sugar database; one who can be added to a Projects record and in turn be responsible for Project Tasks.

Follow these steps to add resources to a Projects record:

1. **Click the project's name on the Projects Home page.**

   The Projects Detail view opens.

2. **Scroll to the Resources subpanel and then click Select User to add one of your users to the project.**

   The User panel (shown in Figure 6-5) opens.

   Two kinds of resources can be added to a project: *Users* (people who are part of your organization) and *Contacts* (folks who are not part of your organization).

   You can only manage resources for projects that are assigned to you.

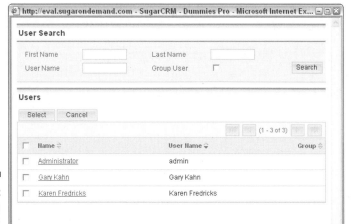

Figure 6-5: Adding users to a project.

3. **Select the names of the users you want to add to the project (by selecting the corresponding check boxes) and then click Select.**

   The assigned users are now listed in the Resources subpanel.

4. **(Optional) Click Select Contact in the Projects Detail view.**

   You can select the names of contacts using the exact same method that you do for users.

Taking the team approach

If you're working with a great big project, you just might need a great big team of folks to help you complete it. The Professional version allows you to create teams of users who work and play together happily for a unified goal. Chapter 14 shows you how to create a team. The Team field appears in the Projects Detail view when you create a new project.

Going, going, Gantt!

A company that deals with project management generally will purchase special software to help organize the mountains of tasks associated with a large project. Most project management software includes the ability to create a Gantt chart. A *Gantt chart* is a chart that graphically depicts the progress of tasks and schedules as they relate to a project. If you're using SugarCRM Professional, you can save your pennies because you're able to create Gantt charts directly in Sugar.

If you — or someone else on your team — has already invested in Microsoft Project you can save a Sugar project in MS Project format. Once saved, you can open the MPX file in MS Project. Simply click Export to MS Project in the Projects Detail view. When the message appears, opt to save the MPX file.

You create *Projects records* exactly the same way in both Sugar Community Edition and Sugar Professional. However, when you start creating *Project Tasks,* you use Gantt charts — and you have many more ways to track and view the progress of those tasks.

Follow these steps to create a Project Task in SugarCRM Professional:

1. **Click Project on the Module Tab bar.**

   The Projects Home page appears.

2. **Click the project's name in the Project List area of the Projects Home page.**

   The Projects Detail view opens.

3. Click the View Gantt butto in the Project Tasks subpanel.

You can view your Project Tasks in any one of the following ways:

- *Grid view:* The Grid view displays such details as the task name, completion percentage, project start and end dates, estimated and actual duration time, dependencies, and assigned resources. You can view specific information (such as completed tasks or milestones) by choosing an option from the View drop-down list. Project managers can edit any task and add additional tasks as needed. Users can specify the completion percentage and actual duration for their assigned tasks. You can export the project tasks to a PDF file by clicking the Export to PDF button.

- *Gantt view:* The Gantt view displays the total time needed for each task from start to finish. Figure 6-6 shows you a sample Gantt view.

Figure 6-6:
Sugar's
Gantt view.

- *Grid/Gantt view:* As you might guess, the Grid/Gantt view is a combination of both the Grid and Gantt views.

You can view a project in Grid/Gantt, Grid, or Gantt view, but you can only *create* and *edit* Project Tasks in Grid/Gantt or Grid view.

4. Click the Grid view button.

Although you can create your Project Tasks in the Grid/Gantt view, you might find the Grid view to be a bit less confusing. The various icons on the Grid view are labeled in Figure 6-7 to help you with the following instructions.

You can also right-click anywhere within the body of the grid to view the contextual menu shown in Figure 6-8.

Paste

Cut | Delete

Copy | Expand All

Outdent Row | Collapse All

Indent Row | Save | 2 weeks

Insert Row | Week | Month

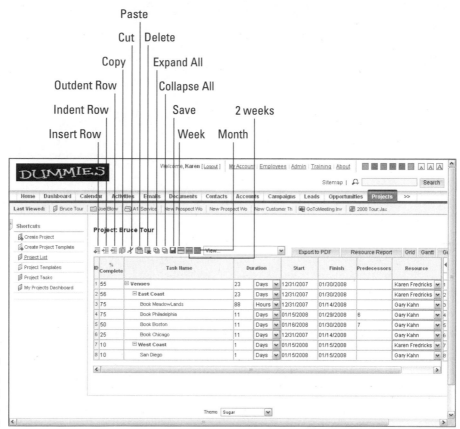

Figure 6-7:
The Project
Grid view.

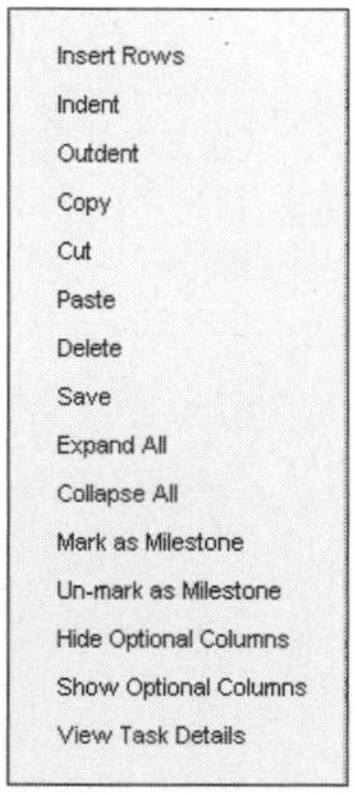

Insert Rows

Indent

Outdent

Copy

Cut

Paste

Delete

Save

Expand All

Collapse All

Mark as Milestone

Un-mark as Milestone

Hide Optional Columns

Show Optional Columns

View Task Details

Figure 6-8:
Using
the Grid
contextual
menu.

5. **Click the Insert Row icon to create a new Project Task.**

   A new row is added at the end of the grid. Tasks are listed in numerical order in the ID column.

   To add a new row above an existing row, click the task ID number to select that row and then click the Insert Row icon.

6. **(Optional) Select a row and then click the Indent icon on the toolbar.**

   Your project might be so large and complex that you need subtasks to help you manage it. By clicking the Indent icon, you can make the selected line item a subtask of the preceding task. You can then use the Expand All and Collapse All icons to view all or some of your tasks.

7. **Double-click the Task Name cell and give the Project Task a name.**

8. **Add a Start and Finish Date.**

   A little calendar appears if you click either of the date fields so that you can click the date you want. Alternatively, you can type a date and ignore the calendar. In any event, Sugar automatically calculates the duration of the task.

9. **(Optional) Specify any Predecessors.**

   When managing a project you might find that you can't complete one task prior to finishing another task. When you create Project Tasks, you can specify Predecessors. For example, if you need to receive inventory (Task 1) *before* barcoding (Task 2), you can specify Task 1 as the predecessor of Task 2.

10. **(Optional) Choose a Resource from the drop-down list in the Resource column.**

    I know the naming convention seems a bit strange, but Resources are actually the users assigned to a project.

11. **(Optional) Tweak your Project Tasks if necessary.**

    If you want to delete a task, select the task and then click the Delete icon. Or, if you're adding many similar tasks, you might want to select the task, click the Copy icon and then paste the task to another location

12. **Click the Save icon to save your tasks.**

    You might be wondering about the last column in the Task Projects grid — Actual Duration. That column fills when you actually complete a task.

Creating Project Templates

Many companies experience a sense of déjà vu when creating projects. For example, swimming pool contractors might find that all their projects require pretty much the same steps in the same order. If you are very lazy — or extremely smart — you might turn to SugarCRM Professional, which includes the ability to create Project Templates.

You can create a Project Template for projects with similar tasks. When you create a Project Template, you can include the Project Tasks. You can also assign resources to a Project Template if the same loyal group of folks works on similar projects repeatedly. You can then use the saved Project Template to create new Projects records. And, once created, the Projects records you create based on a template can be edited exactly like any other project.

The two methods for creating Project Templates are

- ✔ Create one from scratch.
- ✔ Save an existing project as a template.

Cloning existing projects

You might prefer to create a Projects record first just to get comfortable with the process. You can then save it as a template after you have the opportunity to fine-tune the project. This procedure is extremely easy:

1. **Click Projects on the Module Tab bar.**

   The Projects Home page opens.

2. **Select the name of the Projects record you want to copy from the Project List subsection.**

   The Project Detail view displays.

3. **Click the Save as Template button.**

   A new page opens, prompting you for a Template name.

4. **Give the Template a name and then click the Save as New Template button.**

Creating a new Project Template

As easy as it is to transform an existing Projects record into a template, sometimes you need to create a Project Template from scratch. Perhaps your company has already created project guidelines which you now need to capture in Sugar.

Creating a new Project Template from scratch isn't a whole lot harder than cloning an existing Projects record if you follow these steps:

1. **Click Projects on the Module Tab bar.**

   The Projects Home page opens.

2. **On the Projects Home page, choose Create Project Template from the Shortcuts menu.**

The Project Template page opens as seen on stage, screen, and Figure 6-9.

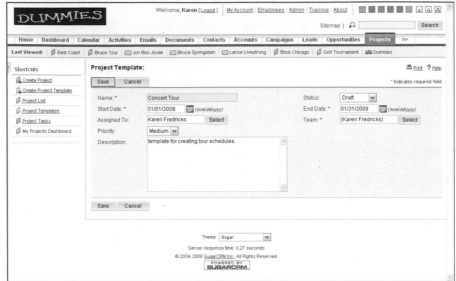

© 2004-2008 SugarCRM Inc. All Rights Reserved.

Figure 6-9:
Creating
a Project
Template.

3. **Fill in the Project Template information.**

You need to fill only a few fields. If you fail to add information to one of the required fields, SugarCRM has a hissy fit — or at least highlights the missing fields in bright red and stops you from continuing until you add information to the required fields:

- *Name (required):* Enter a name for the template.

- *Status:* Specify the template's status (Draft, In Review, or Published) from the drop-down list.

- *Start Date (required):* Enter a start date for the project.

- *End Date (required):* Enter an end date for the project.

- *Assigned To:* Click Select to select an individual from the Users list. By default, it is assigned to you.

- *Team (required):* Click Select to select a team from the Team List.

- *Priority:* From the drop-down list, specify the project's priority, such as High, Medium, or Low.

- *Description:* Feel free to write a book — or at least add a few words — to describe the Project Template.

4. **Click Save to save the template.**

Using Project Templates

After you save a template, it is added to the Project Template List. You can now edit the template by adding Project Tasks or use it to create a new Projects record.

1. **Click Projects on the Module Tab bar to open the Projects Home page.**

2. **Choose Project Templates from the Shortcuts menu to open the Project Templates Home page.**

3. **Click the name of the Project Template from the Project Templates Home page to open the Project Template Detail view.**

   • Click the View Gantt button to add Project Tasks to the Project Template in the same way that you add Project Tasks to a Projects record.

   • Click Save as Project to create a new Projects record from the Project Template. A new window opens. Give the Projects record a new name, click Save as New Project, and you have a new project waiting for you.

Taking a holiday from your project

All work and no play makes most of us pretty cranky. Additionally, having two projects to complete at the same time might result in serious damage to any small inanimate objects that aren't firmly attached to your desk.

When you create a Projects record, you may need to take *holidays* into consideration. The project manager can create a Projects Holiday to account for someone's absence. Any holidays that you schedule appear in the Projects Holiday subpanel so panic doesn't set in when one of your teammates is MIA.

You can schedule a holiday for one of the following reasons:

✔ A project team member takes a vacation.

✔ A project team member takes time off from one project while working on other projects.

Although you aren't guaranteed an all-expense paid trip to the Caribbean, you will have a reprieve from your existing project(s) if the project manager follows these steps:

1. **Click Projects on the Module Tab bar.**

   The Projects Home page opens.

2. Click a project name to view its details.

The Project Detail view opens.

3. Scroll to the Project Holidays subpanel and then click Create.

To avoid scrolling past a whole lot of subpanels, you might consider clicking the project's Other tab, which cuts to the chase and just displays the project's Resources, Project Tasks, and Project Holidays subpanels.

A Holidays form opens, which looks very much like the one shown in Figure 6-10.

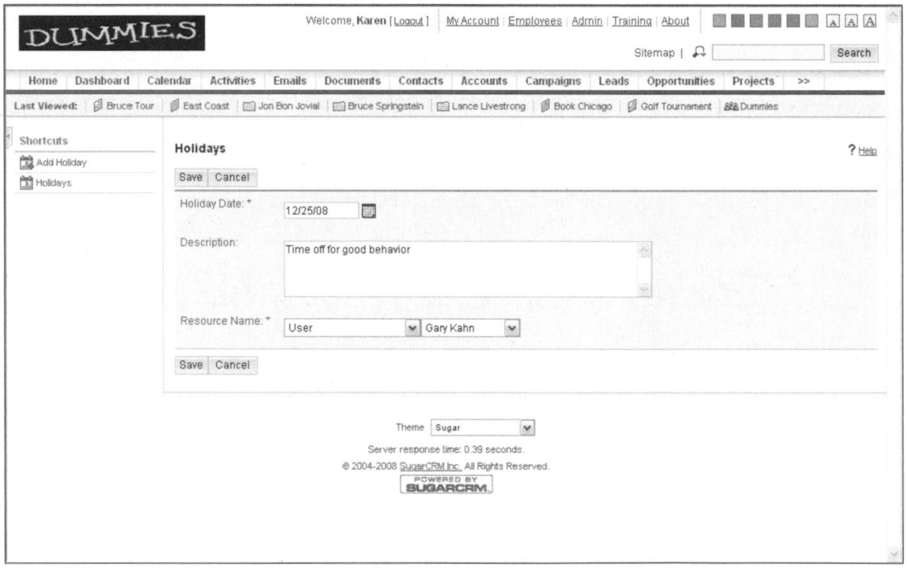

Figure 6-10:
Taking a
holiday from
a project.

4. Enter information for the following fields:

- *Holiday Date:* Enter the holiday or vacation date.

- *Description:* Enter a description or reason for the holiday.

- *Resource Name:* From the Resource Name drop-down list, choose the resource type (User or Contact) who is taking the holiday and then select the appropriate name in the second drop-down list.

5. Click Save to save the holiday.

The saved holiday is listed in the project's Holidays subpanel in the Projects Detail view.

Taking a look at the big picture

SugarCRM Professional edition is the flavor of choice among small to mid-sized businesses. Larger companies thrive on cubicles, trips to the water cooler, and reports.

Project reporting is one of the areas in which Sugar shines. Chapter 14 shows you how to create custom reports — and you can create a custom project report if you wish. This section, however, shows you a couple of cool "out of the box" ways to help keep your grubby finger on the pulse of your projects.

Creating Project Resource Reports

One of a project manager's main tasks is making sure that all the players are on task and completing their tasks according to schedule. You can run a Resource Report from either the Grid view or the Gantt view. The Resource Report displays all the Project Tasks along with other pertinent tidbits of information, including the project name, the workload percentage per project, duration of each project, and any scheduled holidays. The Resource Report not only breaks down a user's workload across projects but also lists the percentage of busy time for each day. This enables managers to better evaluate the status of ongoing projects.

Resources are either the *users* or *contacts* that you have associated with a project.

Here's how to create a Project Resource Report:

1. **Click Project on the Module Tab bar.**

   The Projects Home page opens.

2. **Click the name of the Projects record you'd like to report on in the Project List subpanel.**

   The Project Detail view opens.

3. **Click the View Gantt button in the Project Tasks subpanel.**

   The Grid/Gantt view opens. If you prefer to work in the Grid or Gantt view, feel free to click the appropriate tab.

4. **Click the Resource Report button.**

   The Resource Report form opens.

5. **Choose the user from the Resource drop-down list.**

6. **Click the Tasks That Start or Finish After field and select the start date of the report.**

You might find that the field name is a bit confusing — I know I did! The purpose of the Resource Report is to view the tasks scheduled to occur within a specific time frame.

7. **Click the And Before field and select the end date of the report.**

8. **Click the Report button to run the report.**

The report opens in a new window and displays the daily status, assigned Project Tasks, and any scheduled Holidays that occur during the specified period. As shown in Figure 6-11 the % Busy column indicates if the user has one (100%), two (200%), or even four (400%) tasks scheduled for a specific day.

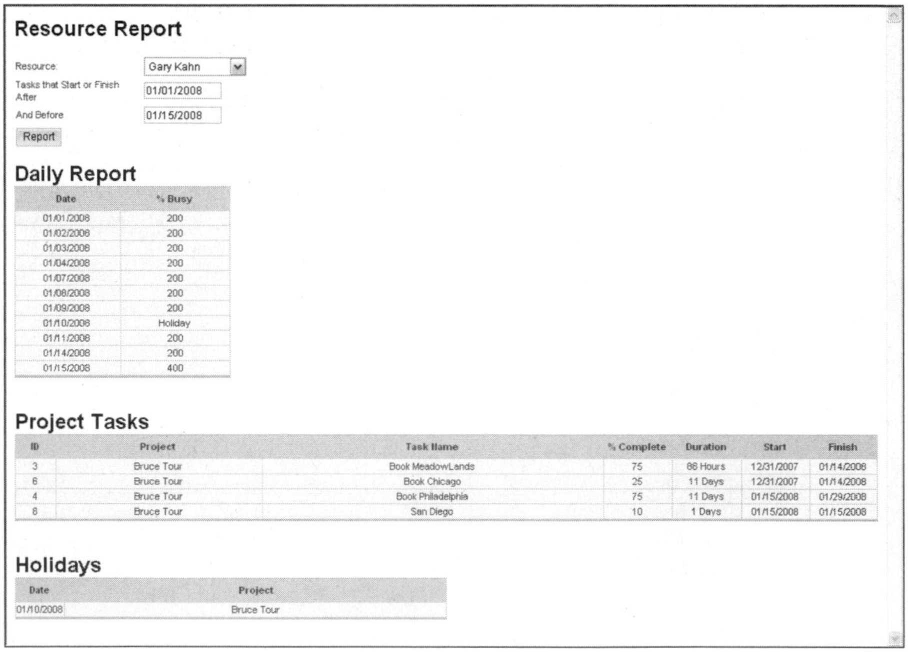

Figure 6-11:
Viewing the
Resource
Report.

Resource Report

Resource: Gary Kahn
Tasks that Start or Finish After: 01/01/2008
And Before: 01/15/2008

Report

Daily Report

Date	% Busy
01/01/2008	200
01/02/2008	200
01/03/2008	200
01/04/2008	200
01/07/2008	200
01/08/2008	200
01/09/2008	200
01/10/2008	Holiday
01/11/2008	200
01/14/2008	200
01/15/2008	400

Project Tasks

ID	Project	Task Name	% Complete	Duration	Start	Finish
3	Bruce Tour	Book MeadowLands	75	88 Hours	12/31/2007	01/14/2008
8	Bruce Tour	Book Chicago	25	11 Days	12/31/2007	01/14/2008
4	Bruce Tour	Book Philadelphia	75	11 Days	01/15/2008	01/29/2008
8	Bruce Tour	San Diego	10	1 Days	01/15/2008	01/15/2008

Holidays

Date	Project
01/10/2008	Bruce Tour

Chapter 7

Working with Opportunities

*I*n this chapter, I lead you through the entire sales process with SugarCRM. I show you how to create an initial opportunity, make changes to it while a sale makes its way through the sales pipeline, and view your opportunities in a variety of ways. And, if you're using SugarCRM Professional, I show you some of the advanced Opportunities functionality.

Creating Opportunities

In SugarCRM, an *opportunity* is a potential sale to an Accounts record. Each opportunity must be associated with an Accounts record. All sales information for an Accounts record appears on the Opportunities subpanel of the Accounts record. When you create an opportunity, you associate it with a sales stage and forecasted close date so that you can see how close you are to closing the sale.

You can associate an opportunity with additional record types, typically Contacts and Leads records. You can associate an opportunity with only one account, but you can associate it with multiple leads and contacts. Opportunities records are often linked to Campaigns records so you can measure the success — or failure — of a campaign.

After creating an Opportunities record, you can go to the Opportunity List where you can see all your opportunities listed together. Additionally, you can view the opportunity from any record you've associated with the opportunity. If that weren't enough, there are a slew of sales dashlets ranging from a basic pipeline to a Campaign ROI (return on investment). Whew!

By automating the sales process with Sugar, you have a better chance of closing more sales. First, if you follow up on your activities, as I show you in Chapter 5, you have significantly fewer contacts falling through the cracks of your database. Secondly, you can adjust your predictions while the opportunity moves through the sales stages. Most importantly, you can filter the Opportunity List (Chapter 9), allowing you to focus on the deals that you think you have the best chance of closing.

Initiating the opportunity

Sugar gives you several methods of creating an opportunity, depending on which module you happen to be working in at the time. Opportunities records can be created with

- **The Create Opportunity link from the Shortcuts menu on the Home module or on the Opportunities module's Home page.**
- **The Create Opportunity Quick Form on the Opportunities module's Home page.**
- **The Create button in Opportunity subpanels within Accounts and Contacts records.**
- **The Convert Lead button in the Leads Detail view; when you convert a lead, you also find an option to create an opportunity.**
- **The Create Opportunity from Quote button in the Quotes Detail view (Professional version only).**

For the purposes of this book, I use the first method, but feel free to experiment with the other methods to find the one that works best for you. Who knows? You might even find that you eventually generate opportunities using *all* the methods.

So why are you sitting around reading a book? It's time for you to go out there and make some money. Here's how you'll make your first million:

1. **Click the Opportunities tab on the Module Tab bar.**

   The Opportunities module's Home page opens.

2. **Create a new opportunity by choosing Create Opportunity from the Shortcuts menu.**

   The Opportunities record opens, as shown in Figure 7-1.

If you've been following along from chapter to chapter, you might already be a few steps ahead of me. You are correct in assuming that you can simply use the Quick Form to create an Opportunities record quickly (albeit slightly abbreviated). And yes, you can scroll to the Opportunities subpanel of just about any record and click Create to create the new Opportunities record.

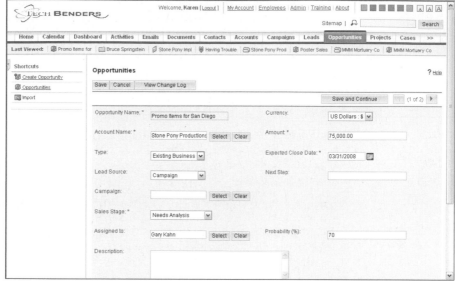

Figure 7-1:
Creating
a new
Oppor-
tunities
record.

3. Fill in the pertinent information for the Opportunities record.

Knowledge is power, so the more information you enter about an opportunity the more power you will have to (hopefully) make the sale. You can supply a lot of information here. Although much of this information is optional, you'll find that the little bit of extra effort you spend now to enter data will result in huge benefits down the road.

Here's a rundown of the Opportunities record fields:

- **Opportunity Name (required):** After you create the opportunity, you can track it down by searching for its name, so consider assigning a name that starts with the company name that you're doing business with or the Purchase Order number.

- **Account Name (required):** Type the first several letters of the account related to the opportunity and Sugar will supply you with a list of possibilities. Alternatively, click the Select button, and click the account name.

- **Type:** From the drop-down list, specify whether the opportunity is from an existing customer or a new customer.

- **Lead Source:** Select the lead source, such as Trade Show or Cold Call, from the drop-down list.

- **Campaign:** Enter the campaign name or click **Select** to choose one from the Campaigns list if the opportunity was the direct result of one of your marketing campaigns.

- **Assigned To:** Enter the name of the user who is responsible for the opportunity, or click **Select** and choose the person from the User List. By default, a new opportunity is assigned to you.

- **Amount (required):** Enter the estimated amount of the sale.

- **Expected Close Date (required):** Indicate when you estimate the opportunity will close.

- **Next Step:** Enter your next step in closing a sale.

Not happy with some of the choices in the drop-down lists, or not sure what information to add to a field? Chapter 15 shows you how to change the drop-down items in the various drop-down lists, or add a drop-down list to an existing field.

- **Sales Stage (required):** If you're hearing a nagging voice in the back of your head, it's because I'm nagging you. An important concept in computing is *Garbage In, Garbage Out (GIGO)*. You want to set the sales stage to know where this opportunity lies in your sales pipeline so the opportunity doesn't fall by the wayside.

- **Probability (%):** In this field, you can assign a probability to each sales stage when you set up the sales process. Feel free to overwrite the probability percentage based on your hunch for each opportunity.

- **Description:** Generally, a database consists of many fields with each containing a single piece of information. But sometimes, storing all your important information into a bunch of teeny-tiny fields isn't possible. That said, you can use the description to write The Great American Novel — or at least a few important tidbits of additional info — about your opportunity.

4. **Click Save to save the Opportunity.**

At this point, you're essentially done with creating the Opportunities record. Sit back and relax a moment while Sugar records the Opportunities record on the subpanel of any associated records.

Editing Opportunities records

The Opportunities subpanel provides you with the sales information on any given record. You can use the information contained on the Opportunities subpanel to create a 360-degree view of a record. For example, you might be trying to sell some white widgets to ABC Company. By taking a peek at the Opportunities subpanel, you can see when they placed their last order and even the dollar amount of their order. Figure 7-2 shows you an example of an Opportunities subpanel.

Figure 7-2:
The Oppor-
tunities
subpanel.

Opportunities						
Create Select					(1 - 2 of 2)	
Name	Sales Stage	Close	Amount	Assigned User		
Promo Items for San Diego	Needs Analysis	03/31/2008	$75,000.00	Gary Kahn		edit
Poster Sales	Proposal/Price Quote	03/31/2008	$10,000.00	Gary Kahn		edit

The Opportunities subpanel serves another important purpose. As your opportunity progresses, you'll find it's often necessary to modify the sales stage.

Sales information appears in the various dashlets, so updating your Opportunities records is vitally important.

The process of updating your sales information is quick and painless:

1. **Go to the record of the account for whom you want to track the opportunities.**

   Because you must associate every Opportunities record with an account, you might start by going to the Accounts Detail view of the account in question. However, because it's possible to associate multiple Leads, Contacts, Campaigns, and Projects records, you'll find the Opportunities subpanel on those records as well.

2. **Click the Edit link to the right of the opportunity you want to view.**

   The Opportunities record opens (refer to Figure 7-1).

3. **Change the information as necessary.**

   The purpose of Sugar's Opportunities records is to allow you to track a potential sale from its inception to its outcome. You'll want to edit the Sales Stage field while the opportunity progresses through the sales pipeline. This allows you to view any of your opportunities to assess exactly where you stand.

   Naturally, you'll also want to record that you *won* an opportunity; unfortunately, you might also find it necessary to record an opportunity as *lost.* And — win, lose, or draw — it's a good idea to change the Expected Close Date to the actual date that you closed the opportunity so that the information displays correctly on any date-driven sales dashlets.

4. **Click Save when you finish editing the opportunity.**

   As usual, Sugar scurries around trying to make life easier for you. The dashlets will update automatically and the Opportunity List and subpanel will reflect the updated information.

   Additionally, you can add contacts to the Contact subpanel that are associated with the opportunity. The more accurately you cross-link information like this, the more effective Sugar becomes.

Keeping an Eye on the Prize

You poor reader, you! You work so hard in filling out the numerous Opportunities record fields. Knowing that you need a little break, SugarCRM rewards you with an abundance of ways to view your opportunity information.

Viewing the Opportunity List

The Opportunity List provides you with a way to view all your opportunities for all your contacts. Chapter 9 shows you how to filter the Opportunity List to display only those opportunities that match your specifications. You can then print the Opportunity List by clicking the Print button at the top of the Opportunities Home page.

Getting to the Opportunity List is almost too easy: Just click the Opportunities module tab to open the Opportunities Home page. Scroll to the Opportunity List to see your opportunities (see Figure 7-3). Notice that the Opportunity List comes equipped with its very own toolbar containing buttons that allow you to Delete, Export, and Merge Duplicates.

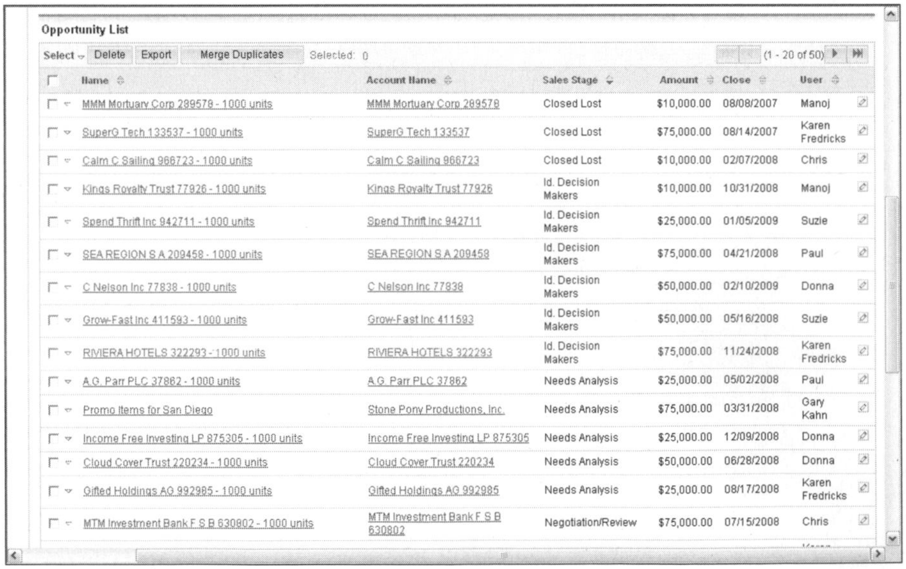
Opportunity List
Select Delete Export Merge Duplicates Selected: 0
(1 - 20 of 50)
Name
Account Name
Sales Stage
Amount
Close
User
MMM Mortuary Corp 289578 - 1000 units | MMM Mortuary Corp 289578 | Closed Lost | $10,000.00 | 08/08/2007 | Manoj
SuperG Tech 133537 - 1000 units | SuperG Tech 133537 | Closed Lost | $75,000.00 | 08/14/2007 | Karen Fredricks
Calm C Sailing 966723 - 1000 units | Calm C Sailing 966723 | Closed Lost | $10,000.00 | 02/07/2008 | Chris
Kings Royalty Trust 77926 - 1000 units | Kings Royalty Trust 77926 | Id. Decision Makers | $10,000.00 | 10/31/2008 | Manoj
Spend Thrift Inc 942711 - 1000 units | Spend Thrift Inc 942711 | Id. Decision Makers | $25,000.00 | 01/05/2009 | Suzie
SEA REGION S A 209458 - 1000 units | SEA REGION S A 209458 | Id. Decision Makers | $75,000.00 | 04/21/2008 | Paul
C Nelson Inc 77838 - 1000 units | C Nelson Inc 77838 | Id. Decision Makers | $50,000.00 | 02/10/2009 | Donna
Grow-Fast Inc 411593 - 1000 units | Grow-Fast Inc 411593 | Id. Decision Makers | $50,000.00 | 05/16/2008 | Suzie
RIVIERA HOTELS 322293 - 1000 units | RIVIERA HOTELS 322293 | Id. Decision Makers | $75,000.00 | 11/24/2008 | Karen Fredricks
A.G. Parr PLC 37862 - 1000 units | A.G. Parr PLC 37862 | Needs Analysis | $25,000.00 | 05/02/2008 | Paul
Promo Items for San Diego | Stone Pony Productions, Inc. | Needs Analysis | $75,000.00 | 03/31/2008 | Gary Kahn
Income Free Investing LP 875305 - 1000 units | Income Free Investing LP 875305 | Needs Analysis | $25,000.00 | 12/09/2008 | Donna
Cloud Cover Trust 220234 - 1000 units | Cloud Cover Trust 220234 | Needs Analysis | $50,000.00 | 06/28/2008 | Donna
Gifted Holdings AG 992985 - 1000 units | Gifted Holdings AG 992985 | Needs Analysis | $25,000.00 | 08/17/2008 | Karen Fredricks
MTM Investment Bank F S B 630802 - 1000 units | MTM Investment Bank F S B 630802 | Negotiation/Review | $75,000.00 | 07/15/2008 | Chris

Figure 7-3: The SugarCRM Opportunity List.

Graphically viewing your Opportunities

In Sugar-speak, a *dashlet* is one of the charts and graphs located on the Dashboard Home page. You can monitor the opportunities that you have at each stage of the sales development cycle and display this information graphically by making use of Sugar's pre-defined sales dashlets. Whether you want to compare the progress of your sales people or measure the success of your lead sources, Sugar has a way of giving you the information, as you can see in Figure 7-4.

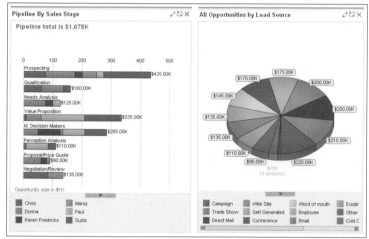

Figure 7-4: Viewing your Opportunities graphically.

All you need to do to see all your opportunities translated through the wonder of modern technology into a graph is to click Dashboard on the Module Tab bar.

For added excitement, try performing one of these neat party tricks:

- ✔ Hover your mouse over any section of a dashlet and a mouse over appears that gives you the details of the particular dashlet.

- ✔ Click on any section of a dashlet and Sugar drills down to the underlying data.

Chapter 9 gives you more information on working with the Dashboard.

Seeing what's changed in the Change Log

All record types include a Change Log and Opportunities records are no exception. And, because Opportunities records tend to be one of the most volatile of all record types, they're a great way of tracking an individual opportunity.

By now, you're an old hand at opening an Opportunities record using one of the following methods:

- ✔ Click the opportunity from the Opportunity List that's located on the Opportunities Home page.
- ✔ Click the opportunity from the Opportunities subpanel of any record Detail view associated with the opportunity.

Click the View Change Log button located at the top of the Opportunities Detail view and the Change Log will open in a new window, like the one shown in Figure 7-5.

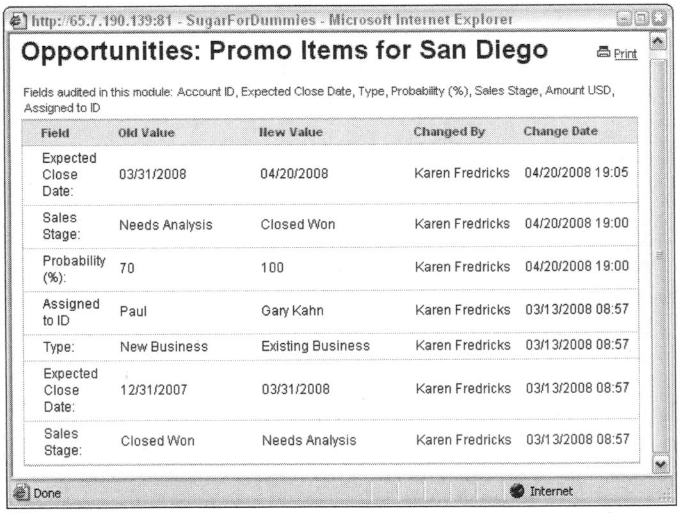

Figure 7-5:
The Opportunities Change Log.

The Change Log shows you the important milestones for the opportunity, such as when it moved from one sales stage to another. It will also detail any changes that were made to key fields — such as Expected Close Date and Amount — and give you the name of the user who made the change. You can click the Print link to create a hardcopy of the Change Log.

SugarCRM Professional Opportunities

So far, this chapter has focused on the Opportunities functionality found in the Community Edition of SugarCRM. The remainder of this chapter shows you some of the advanced Opportunities features that are a part of SugarCRM Professional. Specifically, you'll see how to add Products to Sugar, associate those products with an Opportunities record, and even create a quote using those products. If that isn't enough to get your juices flowing, the Professional Edition allows you to e-mail your quote as a PDF file and even pull up some nifty Opportunities reports to help you keep track of the entire operation.

Producing sugary products

If you're like most people, you'll find this part to be fun. Here's where you get to count the cash, bill for the beans, dream of the dollars . . . In any event, the Products module is where you get to add all of the products and/or services that you sell. Once added, you can add the product line items to a quote for your opportunity and sit back while Sugar crunches the numbers for you.

The Products module helps you to create and manage products for your company. You can either select an item from the product catalog, or create a new product that is not in the product catalog.

Sounds like a job for the Administrator!

If you happen to find yourself wearing the Database Administrator hat, you'll need to read this section — and possibly asks for a raise and/or a corner office. If you aren't a database administrator, feel free to skip this section unless you're wondering what the administrator does to deserve a raise or a corner office.

The database administrator is responsible for several very important product areas. You'll want to make sure that he's doing the job before you set your users loose on the Products module in SugarCRM Professional.

The administrator defines all the products, product types, categories, and manufacturer information within Sugar. If your organization doesn't maintain a product catalog or if users need to create a product that isn't in the catalog, you can create a freestanding product. However, freestanding products aren't added to the product catalog.

You can have more than one administrator for a Sugar database. If you have lots of users and only one administrator, you might consider letting another user share the fun — and responsibilities — of being an administrator.

You can enter into the land of Administrative Products by using either of the following methods:

✔ Click the Admin system link at the top of any Sugar page and then click Create Product from the Shortcuts menu shown in Figure 7-6.

Figure 7-6:
The Admini-
strative
Products
Shortcuts
menu.

✔ Click the Admin system link at the top of any Sugar page and scroll to the Products and Quotes subpanel (see Figure 7-7).

Figure 7-7:
The
Products
and Quotes
subpanel.

Product and Quotes			
Manage the product catalog, along with the related information on manufacturers and shipping providers.			
Product Catalog	Enter items in the product catalog	Manufacturers	Set up the list of manufacturers
Product Categories	Update the list of product categories	Shipping Providers	Set up the list of available shipment methods
Product Types	Configure the list of product types	Tax Rates	Configure the list of available tax rates

Manufacturing Manufacturers

For centuries, man has contemplated his navel and the age-old question of which comes first — the product, the catalog, or the manufacturer. Okay, maybe that discussion was about eggs and chickens, but I'm going to veer slightly from the order of the Shortcuts menu and start by adding some of the simpler Products elements:

1. **Click Create from the Manufacturers Home page.**

   The Manufacturers Home page expands to show you the new Manufacturers record. Figure 7-8 gives you a good idea of what all this looks like.

2. **Enter the manufacturer information.**

   When I say I like to start simple, I mean just that. You have only three fields to fill in here:

   • *Manufacturer:* Enter the manufacturer's name.

   • *Status:* Select Active to add the name to the manufacturer's drop-down list.

- *Order:* Enter a number to specify the order in which the manufacturer will display in the manufacturer's drop-down list.

3. **To create the manufacturer, click Save; to create another manufacturer, click Save & Create New.**

Figure 7-8:
Adding
a Manu-
facturers
record.

Typecasting your products

When you first start creating a product list in Sugar, it seems fairly simple: create a product or two and you're off and running. However, as you add more and more products, your list can become more and more disorganized. Adding product types is an easy way to control the chaos.

Here's all you need to do to add a product type:

1. **Click the Create button in the Product Type List subpanel.**

   The Product Types Home page opens, as shown in Figure 7-9.

   Not sure how to get there? The easiest way is to click Product Types in the Products and Quotes subpanel of the Administration Home page.

2. **Enter information into the following fields:**

   - *Product Type:* Enter a name for the new product type. You might want to divide your products into Retail and Wholesale, or include various types of services.

   - *Description:* Enter an optional description for the product type.

- *Order:* Enter a number to specify the order in which the product type will appear in the Product Type drop-down list.

3. **Click Save to save the Product Type, or** click **Save & Create New** to create another product type.

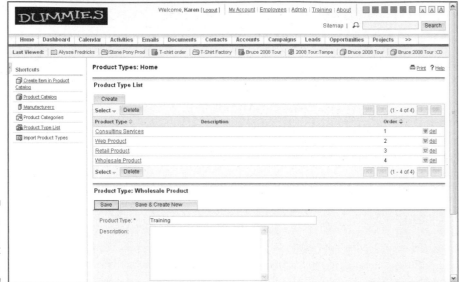

Figure 7-9:
Creating
Product
Types.

Categorizing your products

It's good to walk before you run, look before you leap — and enter in the various product parameters before you delve too deeply into the exciting world of product management.

After you have the feel for adding product types and manufacturers, you're ready to start thinking about how your products will be categorized.

1. **Click the Product Categories option in the Product and Quotes subpanel on the Administration Home page.**

   Just try saying that instruction five times fast! While you tie your tongue in circles, the Product Categories Home page opens (see Figure 7-10).

2. **Click the Create button on the Product Categories Home page.**

   The Product Category subpanel displays fields to let you create a new product category.

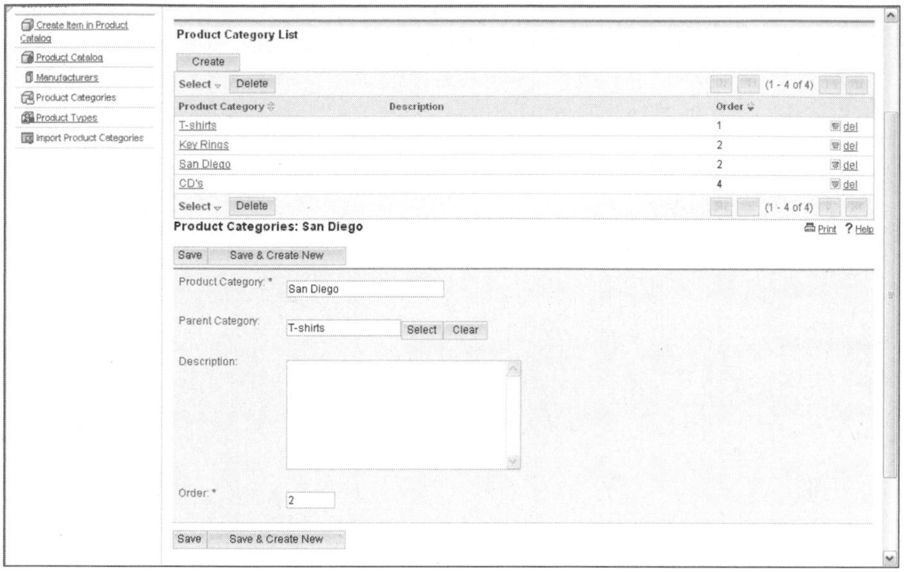

Figure 7-10:
The Product
Categories
Home page.

3. **Enter information for the following fields:**

   • **Product Category:** Enter a name for the category. You can have *parent* categories and subcategories. And, if you really want, you can have subcategories of your subcategories. For example, you might sell red, white, and blue widgets. You could set up Widgets as the first category before setting up the additional categories of Red, White, and Blue.

   • **Parent Category:** Here's where you can sculpt your product hierarchy. In the widget example above, you could indicate Widgets as the Parent category when setting up the Red, White, and Blue products by clicking Select to choose the parent from the Product categories. Figure 7-11 shows you a sample of the hierarchy that appears when you click Select.

   • **Description:** Enter a brief description of the category.

   • **Order:** Enter a number to specify the order in which this category will appear in the Product Category List. I'm not sure how why, but this is a required field — and conceivably all your product types can have the same order number.

4. **Click Save to create the category or click Save & Create New to create another category.**

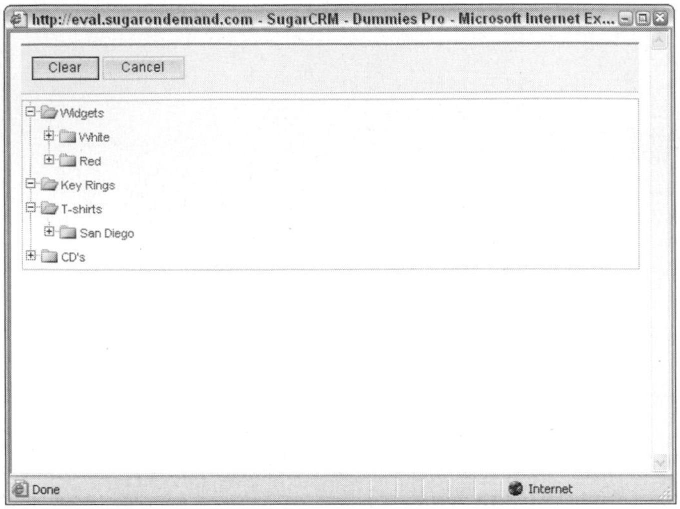

Figure 7-11:
Categorizing
your
products.

Giving the taxman what he's owed

The only certainties in life are death and taxes — or so I'm told — and I'm fairly certain that if you sell products you're going to have to pay taxes on them somewhere down the line. Sugar takes the bitter edge off taxes by providing you with a handy dandy way of configuring the various tax jurisdictions you deal with.

1. **Click Admin on the Home page, scroll down the Administration Home page to the Products and Quotes subpanel, and then click Tax Rates.**

   The Tax Rate Home page opens, as shown in Figure 7-12.

2. **Click Create.**

3. **Fill in the required fields.**

   Actually, *all* the fields are required but don't worry — there's only four of them. Kind of ironic that something as complicated as taxes (at least according to the bill I receive every year from my accountant) is so easy to set up.

   • *Tax Rate Name:* Give the Tax Rate a catchy name; you might find that the name of the appropriate state works rather well.

   • *Percentage:* Add in the tax percentage.

   • *Status:* Choose Active from the drop-down list to display the rate in the appropriate areas of Sugar.

   • *Order:* Enter a number to specify the order in which the tax rate will display in the Tax Rate drop-down list.

4. **Click Save to save the tax rate.**

For additional fun and excitement, you might prefer to click Save & Create New if you want to save this tax rate and create a new one.

Figure 7-12:
The Tax
Rate Home
page.

Sending your products via carrier pigeon

Sometimes it seems as though Sugar has thought of everything. Granted, it hasn't thought of a way to help me win an argument with my significant other, but it sure makes life easy when running a business.

Unless people are coming to you to pick up all their purchases in person, you'll probably need to have a method of delivering your products directly to their fat, little fists. Here's how you can set up the shipping methods:

1. **Click Admin on the Home page to open the Administration Home page.**

2. **On the Administration Home page, scroll to the Product and Quotes subpanel and click Shipping Providers.**

   The Shipping Provider Home page opens.

3. **Click Create.**

   The Shipping Provider Home page expands to include the Shipping Provider page, as shown in Figure 7-13.

4. **Fill in the Shipping Provider fields, all of which are required.**

   • *Shipping Provider:* Enter the name of the shipping provider.

   • *Status:* Choose Active from the drop-down list so that you can actually use the shipping method.

- *Order:* Enter a number to specify the order in which the name will display in the Shipping Provider drop-down list.

5. Click Save to save your new shipping method for posterity.

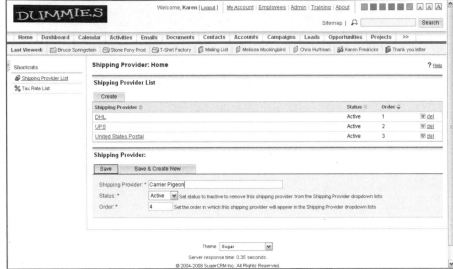

Figure 7-13:
The
Shipping
Provider
Home page.

Producing a Catalog

In Sugar, you don't actually *create* a catalog. Rather, any products that the administrator adds are automatically placed into the Catalog and grouped by product types. The Catalog List allows the administrator to keep track of how much inventory she has on hand as well as other important tidbits of information, including the cost and price of each item.

After you've done all the initial setup, you're ready to start entering your widgets, gadgets, and other products into the product catalog:

1. Click Admin on the Home page to open the Administration Home page.

2. Choose Create Product from the Shortcuts menu.

The Product Catalog page opens. If you prefer, you can also scroll down the Administration Home page to the Products and Quote subpanel, click Product Catalog, and then choose Create Product for Catalog from the Shortcuts menu, but I was always taught that the shortest distance between two points is a single click.

3. Enter the product information into the various fields.

You might start to see the method to my madness. Many of the areas that you had set up previously, such as Manufacturer and Category, will now be available to you. The thing to remember here is that you are actually creating a *catalog* of your products. By that, I mean that in addition to adding information about your product, you're adding information that will help you with reporting and tracking later.

There are lots of fields to enter here, but I want to share a few of the more important ones with you:

- *Product Name (required):* Enter the name of the product.

- *Category:* Click Select to choose the category to which the new item belongs.

- *Date Available:* If this is a new product, you might want to indicate exactly when it's going to be available to your adoring fans.

- *Quantity in Stock:* I don't know about you, but I'm pretty disappointed when I order something — only to learn that it's out of stock.

- *Tax Class:* Choose the appropriate option from the drop-down list to specify whether the item is taxable.

- *Manufacturer:* Choose the manufacturer of the item from the drop-down list.

- *Cost (required):* Enter the cost price of the item. This price will not appear in quotes.

- *List Price (required):* Enter the list price of the item.

- *Discount Price (required):* Show the discounted price; if you don't offer discounts, just enter the List Price.

4. **Click Save to save your product to the product catalog.**

Creating a product using the Products module

Products set up using the Products module are not part of the product catalog. For that reason, it's probably a better idea to let the administrator deal with *setting up* products and let the users *sell* the products.

The Products Home page typically lists products that you create but not those from the product catalog. However, when you create a quote from the product catalog, the products in the quote are automatically added to your Products List.

One reason you may want to set up products from the Products module is that you can also associate a product with an Accounts record. This enables you to view and edit the product from the Accounts' Detail view. This functionality is helpful if you manufacture specific items for specific accounts.

Follow the bouncing ball to create a product from the Products module:

1. **Click the Products module tab on the Home page.**

   The Products Home page opens.

2. **Click Create Product on the Products Home page.**

   The Products page opens.

3. **Enter information for the fields on the Products page.**

   If you've been following along at home, you might think that this form is slightly different from the form you see when you create a product from the product catalog. Smart reader! Although the fields are fairly similar, they are arranged a wee bit differently. And, if you really want to be lazy, only one field — Product Name — is required. Either you can feel sorry for the administrator who was required to add more fields, or you can roll up your sleeves and start entering information.

   One of the problems with being lazy is that you might inadvertently enter default information into some of the non-required fields. For example, the Manufacturer and Product Type fields auto-populate with the first item that appears on their drop-down lists.

   You might see Product fields that you just plain don't need. For example, the Support fields show when support starts and expires. You can opt to leave those fields blank — or flip over to Chapter 15 where you find out how to edit and/or delete those fields.

4. **Click Save to create the product.**

Adding a touch of product management

If you've hung in there during the entire Product section, you deserve a gold star on your forehead — and to make lots of money in the future. At last, your hard work is over and you can sit back and relax. First, however, you might want to tear yourself away from the golf course for a minute and review some of the neat things you can do with your products — besides sell them, of course!

As you might have guessed, you're able to see a list of your products from the Product List that you access by clicking Products on the Module Tab bar.

Not seeing all of your products? Items that the administrator added to the product catalog will not appear in the Product List *until* you use them in a quote.

You can manage your opportunities directly from the Product List in a number of ways:

- ✔ **Sort:** Click any column title to sort the List view.

- ✔ **Delete:** Select a product and then click Delete to delete it.

- ✔ **Edit:** Click a product name in the list to view the details of the product. Once there, you can click Edit to edit the product details.

✔ **Duplicate:** Click Duplicate in the Product Detail view. This is a great timesaver if you have a lot of similar products, such as pink, magenta, and chartreuse widgets; click Duplicate, stick in a new product name, and you're good to go.

✔ **Export:** Select the products you want to export and then click Export to export a list of your products to Excel.

You can quote me on that

Wouldn't it be lovely if all your customers simply picked up the phone, placed an order, and ka-ching — the money was in the bank. Dream on! Many — if not all — of your customers are going to require, request, and/or demand that you send them a quote before they send you the money. If that's the case with your business, you'll want to use the Quotes module that comes with SugarCRM Professional.

Quickly creating quotes

The Quotes module lets you create, view, and manage quotes for your organization. When you create a quote, you can select a product from the product catalog, or you can manually enter information on products that aren't in the catalog. *Quotes* specify the quantity and the price per unit for the products and services that you sell to a customer. When you select from the catalog, the system automatically fills in information, such as the manufacturer's number and tax class.

1. **Choose Create Quote from the Home page's Shortcuts menu.**

   The Quotes page opens. The top half of a Quotes page is shown in Figure 7-14.

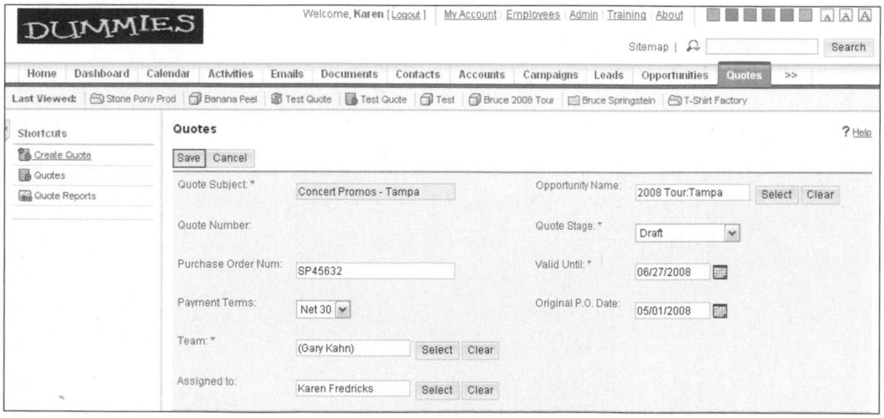

Figure 7-14: The Quotes page.

Alternatively, you can click Quotes on the Module Tab bar and use the Create Quote Quick Form displayed below Shortcuts. This form contains only the required fields. However, you can add information after you save the form.

2. **Enter information into the fields on the Quotes page.**

   - **Quote Subject (required):** Give the quote a name that will make it easy to identify.

   - **Quote Number:** You can be lazy here because Sugar will assign a number automatically.

   - **Purchase Order Num:** Enter the P.O. number if you have one.

   - **Payment Terms:** Choose the customer's payment terms from the drop-down list.

   - **Team (required):** Enter the name of the team that is allowed to view the Opportunities record.

   - **Assigned To:** Add the name of the individual who is working on the Opportunities record.

   - **Opportunity Name:** Here's where you can associate an existing Opportunities record with a quote.

   - **Quote Stage (required):** Choose the current stage from the drop-down list.

   - **Valid Until (required):** Click the calendar icon and select an expiration date.

   - **Original P.O. Date:** Click the calendar icon and select the Purchase Order date.

3. **Add information to the Bill to and Address Information subpanels, as shown in Figure 7-15.**

   You must associate every quote with a Billing Account. Happily, any address information you have on record for the account will automatically fill in to the billing address information. Select the Copy Address From Left check box if the shipping address is the same as the billing address.

4. **(Optional) Add the basic Line Items information.**

   You can cram a lot of information into the Line Items subpanel; follow along so you won't get lost. You start by filling in a few non-required fields:

   - *Currency:* Choose the currency used in the quote from the drop-down list.

   - *Tax Rate:* Choose the tax rate for the account from the drop-down list.

- *Shipping Provider:* Choose a shipping provider from the drop-down list.

The administrator defines the currency, tax rate, and shipping provider information that display in the drop-down lists.

- *Grand Total:* Check this box if you want Sugar to get out its abacus and add up all the products you include in the quote.

- *Line Numbers:* Check this box if you want to number your products when you save the quote in PDF format.

5. Click the Add Group button.

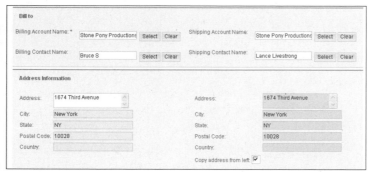

Figure 7-15: The Bill To and Address Information subpanels of the Quote form.

The Line Items subpanel expands, as shown in Figure 7-16.

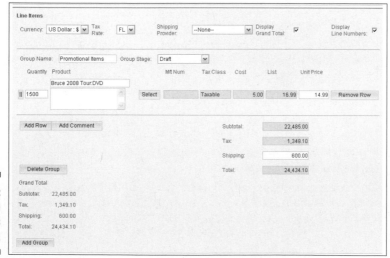

Figure 7-16: The Quote Line Items subpanel.

- *Enter a name for the product group in the Group Name field.* All products must be in a group in the quote.

- *Choose the status of the group from the Group Stage drop-down list.* For example, you might have a group of products that are backordered; you would place them all in the Backordered status.

6. Click the Add Row button.

This allows you to enter your first product within the group. Now the fun begins and some of your long hours of setup start to pay off — you add your products to the Quote. For each row, add the following product information:

- *Quantity:* Enter the quantity that you're quoting.

- *Product:* Enter the product name or click Select to select it from the product catalog.

- *Description:* Add a description of the product if desired.

    Sugar will automatically enter information for the remaining fields — Mft Num, Tax Class, Cost, List, and Unit Price — if you select an item from the catalog that contains this information. If not, feel free to add it manually.

The cost price doesn't display in the quote you e-mail customers.

You can't modify the pricing information of products you added directly from the product catalog. However, you can modify the pricing for items that you manually enter into Sugar.

7. Add additional Groups and/or rows.

Typically, you continue to add products to the group you create in Step 5. However, you might want to have more than one group on the quote to help distinguish between different types of products or services. For example, if you offer both products and services, you might have a Products group showing the products you're selling, and a Services group showing the services you'll render.

8. Click Save to create the new quote.

After you save the quote, the system displays the Quotes Detail view. You can also find the quote listed on the Quotes List.

Creating a PDF of a quote

Sugar treats a quote exactly like any other record. You can edit, duplicate, and delete a quote directly from the Quotes Detail view. You can also create Activities, History, Projects, and Contracts from the Quotes Detail view that are then associated to the Quote. If you're not sure how to perform these wondrous tasks, flip back to Chapter 4, which focuses on creating Contacts, Accounts, and Leads records.

One cool thing you can do with a quote that you can't do with other records is to convert it to a PDF. You can then print the PDF or e-mail it directly to the customer. And of course, Sugar lets you do all this PDF (pretty darned fast!).

1. **Click the Quotes module tab on Sugar's Home page.**

   As expected, the Quotes Home page opens.

2. **Click the quote name to open it.**

   The Quotes Detail view springs open.

3. **Click the Print as PDF button and then click Open in the dialog window that appears.**

   A PDF version of your quote opens in Adobe Reader (see Figure 7-17). Try to avoid jumping up and down in delight because your cubicle mates might look at you strangely. From here, you can save the PDF and attach it to an e-mail, or you can print it, squeeze it into an envelope, and send it on its way via US Snail Mail.

Figure 7-17:
A sweet quote in PDF format.

The only modification that you can make to the quote template is to add your logo to it. Chapter 16 shows you how.

4. **Close Adobe Reader.**

    You'll end up right back where you started — in the Quotes Detail view.

5. **Click the E-mail as PDF button.**

    The E-mail page opens with an e-mail message already addressed to the contact that is linked to the quote. And even better, the subject and body of the e-mail are filled in as well (which of course you can edit if necessary).

6. **(Optional) Click the Options button on the e-mail icon bar and select a different e-mail template.**

    If you've read Chapter 12, you might have set up some e-mail templates. Feel free to choose one of them from the Templates drop-down list.

7. **Click Send and your e-mail — with the attached quote in PDF form — will hurtle through cyberspace on its way to Mr. or Ms. Customer.**

Chapter 8

Working with Documents

*T*he Documents module is the module you turn to when you want to share documents with the rest of your company. You can use the Documents module to store, share, and supervise the versions of your documents. And, just like with a traditional library, you can decide who is allowed to check out documents — and monitor what kind of shape the documents are in when they return.

Creating Your Documents with the Documents Module

If you've ever tried to e-mail a large attachment to a colleague, you know that a seemingly easy task can run into a whole bunch of snags. The file might be too big to get past your ISP or, if you can send it out, it might be too big for your *recipient's* ISP. If the file is large, it might take a long time to transmit — during which you're unable to receive any other e-mail. Your recipient might have a spam blocker, or his company might have e-mail policies that prohibit receiving file attachments.

By using the Document List, you can create a library of documents and graphics that can be shared by all members of your staff. For example, you might be collaborating with a colleague who works from home on a brochure. Or perhaps you're building a custom-ordered widget for your best customer and want to share the specs and some sketches of the final product with your boss who's vacationing in Botswana. By placing documents and graphics in the Document List, you — and anyone else you authorize — can view files *whenever* and *wherever* needed.

You can find the Documents module — and add a few documents to the Documents List — by following these steps:

1. Click Documents on the Module Tab bar.

As you'd expect, the Documents Home page opens. Don't just take my word for it — view it for yourself in Figure 8-1.

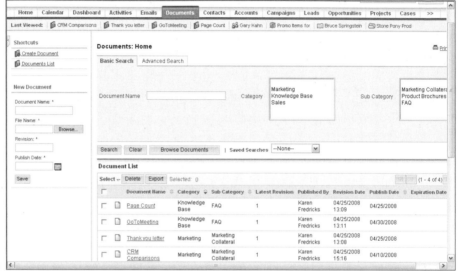

Figure 8-1:
The
Documents
Home page.

2. Choose Create Document from the Shortcuts menu.

The Documents form opens. You might be surprised at the number of fields you see here. The only required fields are the document name, the publish date, the revision number, and the file itself.

No pain no gain! The more information you enter *now,* the more organized you'll be in the *future*.

3. On the Documents form, enter information for the following fields:

- *Document Name:* Enter a name for the document. It doesn't have to be the same as the actual filename.

- *File Name:* Click Browse to navigate to the location of the document file and then click Open to add it to the Document form. The form will not reflect the path and filename.

If you leave the Document Name field blank, it will automatically fill with the filename.

- *Revision:* Enter the revision number; if you're adding a document for the first time, type in **1**.

- *Template:* Select this box if you are creating a template to be used in merges.

- *Document Type:* Choose a pre-defined document type from the drop-down list. Just like a library makes use of a filing system, this is a great way to help keep those documents organized if you're planning on housing a lot of them. At the very least, you might want to differentiate your templates from your pictures from your sound bites.

  If you're less than thrilled with the options in the drop-down list, you'll want to go Chapter 15 where you discover how to change those options.

- *Category:* Choose a category from the drop-down list. If you're groaning at all these fields, just remember that the Dewey Decimal System contains more than one number. Here's where you might group documents, such as Marketing Materials and FAQ's (Frequently Asked Questions).

- *Sub Category:* If you selected a category, select the category subset if possible. If you add a category and subcategory for the document, you create a document tree, which helps you to organize files and find documents.

- *Status:* Choose the status from the drop-down list to indicate the current state of the document. Consider using choices such as Draft, Under Review, and We've Got a Winner.

- *Publish Date:* Click the calendar icon to memorialize the date of the download.

- *Expiration Date:* Like milk sitting too long in your refrigerator, it's good to have an expiration date. For example, a brochure for an April sale loses its potential on May 1.

- *Related Document:* Click Select to associate a related document. The window you see in Figure 8-2 opens, revealing the documents you've already downloaded to Sugar. Click the appropriate document name to associate it with the current document.

- *Related Document Revision:* Choose the revision number of the associated document from the drop-down list; if only one revision of the document exists, you'll only have the choice of one number.

- *Description:* Enter a description of the document just in case the document name and filename don't do the trick.

4. **Click Save to add the document to your Sugar database.**

   Sugar actually clones the document and adds it to Sugar. You can delete the original document if you want without worry because the *cloned* copy remains safely in Sugar.

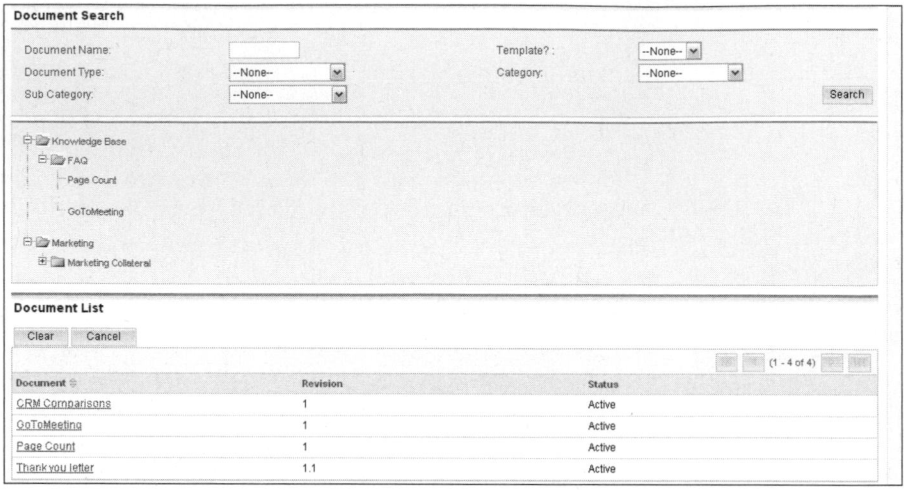

Document Search

Document Name:	Template? : --None--
Document Type: --None--	Category: --None--
Sub Category: --None--	Search

⊟ 📁 Knowledge Base
   ⊟ 📁 FAQ
      └─ Page Count
      └─ GoToMeeting
⊟ 📁 Marketing
   ⊞ 📁 Marketing Collateral

Document List

Clear   Cancel

(1 - 4 of 4)

Document ⇕	Revision	Status
CRM Comparisons	1	Active
GoToMeeting	1	Active
Page Count	1	Active
Thank you letter	1.1	Active

Figure 8-2:
Adding
a related
document
to a new
document.

Dealing with Your Documents

After you add documents and graphics to the Documents module, you'll probably find it even more useful than the local library. You can view your files, save a copy to your desktop, create updated versions, and even send them to your adoring masses.

Any file that you attach when you create a document displays on the Document List subpanel of the Documents Home page for your viewing pleasure.

Accessing your documents

For your first trick, you'll want to learn how to access files. If you're thinking that you'll have to paperclip this page for future reference you're wrong — unless you just want to keep reminding yourself how easy it is to work with the Sugar Documents module.

1. **Click Documents on the Module Tab bar.**

2. **Choose Documents List from the Shortcuts menu.**

   The Documents Home page opens, complete with the Document List subpanel. This list works exactly like all the other lists sprinkled throughout Sugar, so you can sort the List view or even delete selected documents.

3. Click the name of the saved file.

For your convenience, the document names appear as hyperlinks, so you know something cool will happen when you click one of them. In this case, the Documents page opens, as shown in Figure 8-3.

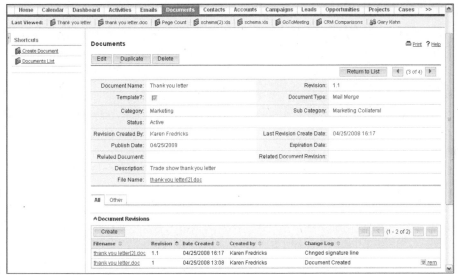

Figure 8-3: The Documents page.

Notice our good friend the Duplicate button on the top of the page. Duplication is particularly popular among the smart and lazy of the crowd. After you create a prize-winning document — or at least one that you're happy with — you can duplicate the document, make a few minor changes, save the document again with a *different* name, and *voilà!* — new document.

4. Click the file that you want to see.

You find out how to make document revisions in the next section, but I want to give you a preview of how this is going to play out. You'll notice a file name; that represents the most *current* version of the file. However, you'll also notice the Document Revisions subpanel, which shows you *all* versions of the document. And, Sugar very sweetly marks them with a date and time stamp so you can view *any* of the versions. Usually, you'll just click the filename, but if you need to see the original document or one of its earlier updates, you can click those as well. In all cases, the File Download window will open.

5. Click Open to view the document immediately, or Save to save the document.

If you open the document, it will open immediately. At this juncture, you can edit the document exactly how you would any other document. And, you can save your changes.

If you're going to be loading your changes back into Sugar, you'll want to save the document as a different name. Sugar, helpful as always, suggests a name change for you; if the original document was called `myfile.doc`, Sugar will automatically suggest `myfile(2).doc` as the new name.

Sugar gives you tons of software functionality but it can't give you licenses for software that you don't own. If one of your users uploads an Excel spreadsheet — and you don't own a copy of Excel — you won't be able to view that document. You need to have a copy of the software originally used to create a document loaded on to your computer before you can view the document.

Verifying your versions

Sharing documents is a great timesaver, particularly for those of you who often work from remote locations. Very often, just being able to download and review a document is enough to make you a very happy — and productive — camper.

However, hosting shared documents opens a whole other can of worms. For example, two employees are collaborating on new sales materials from separate, remote locations. They both download copies of the same document and make changes to it. The first employee uploads the document to the library when she is finished. An hour later, the second leader uploads his copy of the document to the library — which overwrites the first employee's document. Yikes!

The folks at Sugar must have run into the exact same problem because they came up with a great solution. *Versioning* enables you to track and manage multiple revisions of the same document and to view and recover earlier editions if necessary.

Here's how you can add a revised copy of a document back into Sugar:

1. **Click Documents on the Module Tab bar.**

2. **Choose Documents List from the Shortcuts menu and then click the name of the document you want to revise in the Document List subpanel.**

    The Documents Detail view opens. I hate to make assumptions, but I'm going to make an assumption here: I'm assuming that you've already read the previous section, opened a document, made a few changes, and saved it.

3. **Click Create in the Document Revisions subpanel of the Documents Detail view.**

The Document Revision page, shown in Figure 8-4, displays the current document name and revision number.

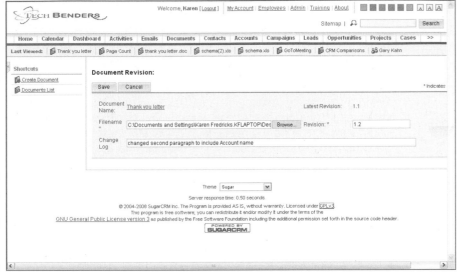

Figure 8-4:
The
Document
Revision
page.

4. Enter information into all the fields.

I know all the fields aren't *required*, but in this case, all the fields are really *important* ones.

If you leave one of the fields blank or input incorrect information, you can't go back and edit it after the fact. Proceed with caution!

- *File Name:* Click Browse to navigate to the file location, and then click Open to add it to Sugar. You cannot change the filename of the attached file; Sugar supplies it automatically.

- *Revision:* Specify a revision number for the revised document. If you're making fairly minor changes you might use a decimal, such as 1.1 or 1.76. If you're making fairly radical changes you might want to increase the ordinal to the next integer.

- *Change Log:* Enter a brief description of the changes. You'll find this field to be really helpful if you have to track multiple document versions.

5. Click Save to save your changes.

The revised file now appears at the top of the Documents Revisions subpanel, which displays the revision number, the date and time of the last revision, and the Change Log comment.

If you look closely, you'll notice the Remove icon next to all the older documents. That's because you can remove any of the older documents if you want. However, the most recent version can't be deleted.

I'll Take a Bit of Sugar with My Word

A particularly useful Sugar feature enables you to create customized document *templates*. Templates are forms in which your selected data fields are filled by Sugar. You can send these forms to a thousand people as easily as you can send them to just one person. You can send routine documents one at a time on a continual basis, or you can send a document one time to all or part of your database.

A good way to understand the concept of mail merge is to visualize this simple equation:

template + data field(s) = personalized document

Note the *(s)* at the end of *data field,* which suggests that you can use either one name or many names. Some of you might think that you'll never perform a mail merge because you have no desire to send a mass mailing. Others of you might have already perfected the art of mass mailing but never realized that a mail merge can be directed to one person or to thousands of people. I hate to be the one to break your bubble, but if you have any kind of routine documents that you're generating repetitively, you should be using Sugar to do so.

The three things necessary to create a mail merge are

- ✔ **A name or a list of names:** If you've followed this book to this point, you're the happy owner of a database chock full of Account and Contact information.

- ✔ **A document template:** A *document template* is a letter or form that substitutes field names in place of names and addresses or whatever other information comes directly from your database.

- ✔ **A program that can combine the names into the template:** After you have a list of names and a document template, you need something to combine them. You could try to use your food processor, but I prefer to use the mail merge feature.

Sugar has a nifty plug-in that allows you to create mail merge templates in Microsoft Word. The plug-in comes as part of the SugarCRM Professional, or can be purchased separately if you're using Sugar's Community Edition.

You create the templates in Word and upload them to the Sugar Document module. Once uploaded, you can initiate a mail merge in either Sugar or Word.

Installing the plug-in for Microsoft Word

Because the ability to link Word to Sugar requires a plug-in, you have to install the plug-in if you're running Sugar's Community Edition (the plug-in is included in SugarCRM Professional). Fear not; this isn't a particularly difficult thing to do:

1. **Close Microsoft Word.**

   You're going to be able to access a special Sugar toolbar from within Word, but in order for the fun to begin, make sure Word is closed.

2. **Download the Sugar plug-in for Word.**

   a. Go to www.sugarexchange.com.

   b. Select Integration on the left side of the screen under Browse By Category.

   c. From the alphabetical listing, scroll down and select Sugar Plug-in for Microsoft Word.

   The plug-in will come in the form of a .zip file. It doesn't matter *where* you save the download file as long as you *remember* where you saved the file.

Unfortunately, it's not very easy to find the Office plug-ins so you might need a road map. You'll find them by going to the Sugar exchange (www.sugar exchange.com/). For the Word plug-in you'll want to click on the Integration category and then scroll down through the list of product until you find the Sugar Plug-in for Microsoft Word. For the Outlook plug-in you'll select the e-mail category and then scroll down to Sugar Plug-In for Microsoft Outlook.

3. **Double-click and follow the prompts to extract the file.**

   You're now the proud owner of your very own Sugar Word plug-in file.

4. **Double-click the .exe installation file and follow the prompts to install the Word plug-in.**

   No need to get fancy here — simply clicking Next and Next will get you where you're going.

5. **Start Word after the installation completes.**

   Try to curb your enthusiasm! The SugarCRM drop-down menu displays below the Word menu exactly like the one shown in Figure 8-5.

   This menu gives you all the options you need to make Sugar and Word play nicely together.

The Sugar drop-down menu in Word.

Figure 8-5:
Accessing
Sugar in
Microsoft
Word.

6. In Word, choose SugarCRM⇨Settings and fill in your SugarCRM credentials.

Figure 8-6 shows you what the SugarCRM Settings window looks like. You just need to add your user name and password, and the URL you use to access Sugar.

Figure 8-6:
Connecting
Word to
Sugar.

7. In Word, choose SugarCRM⇨Login.

You are now safe to roam around the cabin — and start creating mail merge templates.

Creating a mail merge template

Before you can win friends and influence prospects with your dazzling display of personalized documents, you need two basic elements: the data and the document template.

You're creating a template, not a document, to perform your mail merge. A *document* is a plain old file that you create and use in Word. You use it once, save it, and store it away for posterity or delete it as soon as you're done with it. Comparatively, a *template* is a form that merges with your database information. The convenience of templates is that you use them over and over again.

With your data tucked away nicely in your database, all you have left to do is to create the document template, which involves creating a form document. Your document template contains placeholders that are then filled with information from your database after you perform a merge. Create a document template by following these steps:

1. **If you haven't done so already, open Word and choose SugarCRM⇨Log in.**

2. **Choose SugarCRM⇨Define Template.**

   The Select Master Module dialog box displays, as shown in Figure 8-7.

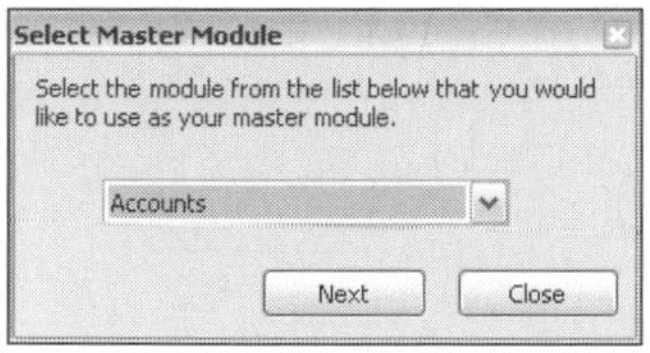

Figure 8-7: Creating a document template.

3. **Select the module that you want to create a template for and then click Next.**

   You can add most any field to your template. Typically, you'll want to use Accounts, Contacts, Leads, and Prospects fields because that's where you'll find basic contact information, such as name and address. However, you can add Cases and Opportunities fields as well.

   Depending on the module you choose, a list of record field names displays, as shown in Figure 8-8.

Figure 8-8: Adding fields to the document template.

4. **Start typing your document.**

   You are, after all, in Word and can use all of its features. Write your thank you letter or create a few slick marketing pieces.

5. **Click the spot in your document where you want contact information to appear, select the appropriate field name, and then click Add to Document.**

   Here's where the fun begins. Every time you get to a part that could be populated with Sugar information, scroll down the list of fields, select one to insert into your template, and then click Add to Document.

   The record type and field name appears in your document set off by lovely double-angle brackets. Treat these field names exactly as you do any other words in your template. For example, if you want to see them set in bold, bold the field name. You also want to place the appropriate punctuation next to an inserted field if necessary; for example, if you place the «Contacts_salutation» field in the greeting line, you'll want to follow it with a colon.

   You can also double-click a field name to insert it into your document.

6. **Click Next to continue.**

   Here's where you can add other record type fields into your document. For example, you might want to use Accounts fields for the address information, but Contacts fields for the first and last name information.

   When you select Campaign Prospects in the Master Module dialog box, Sugar won't give you the option to include other record types.

7. **Click Finish.**

   The Add Fields window closes. Fear not, you can get it back again if necessary by clicking SugarCRM⇨Define Template.

8. **Check your document for accuracy and edit as necessary.**

9. **Choose File⇨Save As.**

   Figure 8-9 shows Accounts billing address fields along with Contacts name fields.

10. **Choose SugarCRM⇨Upload.**

    The Upload Document to SugarCRM dialog box opens, which looks remarkably like the one shown in Figure 8-10. Creating a document template is only half the fun. The other half comes from getting your template into Sugar.

11. **Enter a document name and revision number for the document and then click OK.**

    Notice that the Is Mail Merge Template check box is selected to ensure that the document is correctly identified as a template in the Documents module.

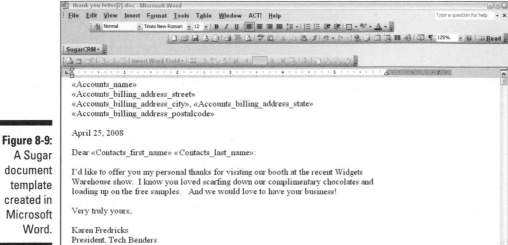

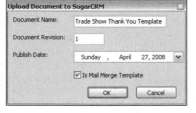

Figure 8-9:
A Sugar
document
template
created in
Microsoft
Word.

Figure 8-10:
Uploading a
template to
Sugar.

We're off to see the Mail Merge Wizard

Now that you've created a document template, you're ready to fill your template with record information. Don't assume that creating a mail merge implies sending a single message to thousands of people at one time. A mail merge can also be used to automate the most mundane and routine of tasks. You can use Sugar's document templates to write a thank you letter every time you land a new client or to write an inquiry letter each time you receive a new lead. After you discover this timesaver, I guarantee that you'll never go back to your old way of creating documents again!

If a document is a Mail Merge template, the document type will automatically show as Mail Merge on the Documents Detail view.

Here's how you create a mail merge in Sugar:

1. Navigate to the appropriate module's Home page.

For example, if you want to send a letter to a contact, go to the Contacts module.

You can also initiate a mail merge by choosing Mail Merge from the Shortcuts menu on the Documents Home page. However, by starting at a record's Home page, you can select the appropriate record(s) prior to the mail merge.

2. **Select the record of whom you want to send a letter.**

If you're just sending the template to one record, then you only need to select that record. However, if you'd like to send the template to multiple records, you'll want to search for those records and then choose Select All Records.

Chapter 4 shows you how to select records, and Chapter 9 shows you how to query among your records.

3. **Click Mail Merge.**

The Mail Merge button is conveniently located next to the Export button above the record list. Clicking it starts the Mail Merge Wizard.

The Mail Merge option must be enabled on both the Administration page and the My Accounts page to display the Mail Merge option. If you're a database administrator, go to the Administration Home page and check the System Settings to make sure that the Enable Mail Merge option is selected. If you're an end-user, go to the My Account page and make sure there's a check next to Mail Merge. If Mail Merge is not enabled, you will not see a Mail Merge button.

4. **Choose a template from the Select Template drop-down list on the Select Module and Template page.**

Take a look at Figure 8-11 just to make sure you're on the right track.

Figure 8-11:
The Select
Module and
Template
page.

Although you can also choose a different module from the Selected Module drop-down list, you'll probably find it easier to select the record(s) you plan on merging prior to starting the mail merge. You might also notice that only mail merge templates appear in the Select Template drop-down list.

5. **Click Next to continue.**

   The Merge page that displays depends on the module that you selected. Any records that you select appear in the Selected section on the right. If you did not select any records, you can do so here. Use the left and right arrows to add or remove records.

6. **Click Next to continue.**

   The third step of the Wizard — the Review and Complete page — gives you a recap of your choices.

7. **Click Begin Merge.**

   You might hear a bit of clanging as the Wizard starts combining the data with the template. A dialog box opens that requests you specify whether to open the merged document in Word, or save it to a disk.

8. **Make your selection and click OK.**

   If you choose to open the document in Word, the merged document displays on the screen. If you choose to save the document to a disk, you can now specify the location to which you'd like to save the document.

Performing a mail merge in Word

You'll probably find it much easier to run your mail merges in Sugar rather than in Word. Sugar allows you to make use of its queries, which makes targeting your mailings much easier. However, some of the folks in your organization might find Word to be more familiar territory and want to use Word for their mail merges. Not a problem if you follow these steps:

1. **In Word, open the template you want to use for the merge.**

   You'll want to close any other Word documents that you might already have open.

2. **Click SugarCRM⇨Perform Mail Merge.**

   Similar to the dialog box shown in Figure 8-12, a list of records for the module that you selected in the template appears.

   You must be logged in to the Word plug-in for this to occur.

3. **Use the right arrow to move the records that you want from the Available records list to the Selected Recipients list.**

   You can use some of your old Windows tricks to help you here, such as holding down the CTRL key while selecting records to select several at one time.

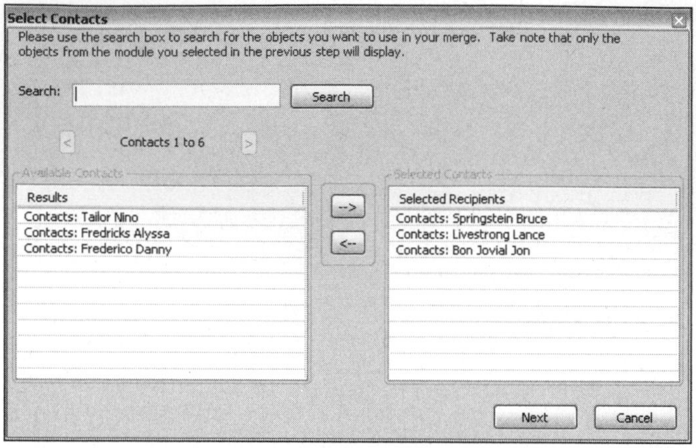

Figure 8-12:
Selecting
records
for a mail
merge.

4. **(Optional) Click Next to continue.**

   You might be asked to select more records depending on the module(s) that you choose when you set up the document template. For example, if the template included both contacts and opportunities, you'll be asked to select your opportunities.

   The Complete Mail Merge dialog box displays the selected records.

5. **Click Complete Merge.**

   The merged document displays in all its glory. At this juncture, you are free to print the document — or save it to Sugar for future reference.

Chapter 9

Watching Your Sugar Content

After you enter information into Sugar, you need a way to find it again. Sometimes, you'll want a 360-degree view of all your information. You can accomplish this easily by making use of the Home page and dashboards. Other times, you'll want to hone in on a single record. Or, you might want immediate access to a group of records based on very specific criteria. Knowing how to search in Sugar will provide you with the power you need to find the information you need. And, once you find the data, you might even want to print it for posterity.

There's No Place Like Home

The Home module is the first thing you see when you log in to Sugar. The Home page consists of *dashlets* — individual components that summarize your various activities. A dashlet displays a list of item records that is similar to the List view displayed on a module's Home page. You can remove the dashlets that you don't use and add other dashlets that are better suited to your needs.

By default, the Home page displays the following dashlets:

  ✔ **My Calls:** Lists all the phone calls you're scheduled to make, regardless of time period.

  ✔ **My Meetings:** Lists all your meetings.

  ✔ **My Leads:** Shows your recently added Leads records.

- ✔ **My Top Open Opportunities:** Lists your top open Opportunities records.

- ✔ **My Accounts:** Displays the Accounts records that are assigned to you.

- ✔ **My Open Cases:** Here's where you can view a list of customer issues that you — or some other nice person — has assigned to you to resolve.

- ✔ **Jot Pad:** This is your virtual sticky note; feel free to jot down anything you need to.

- ✔ **My Pipeline:** Displays a chart of your sales opportunities based on their current sales stage.

Figure 9-1 shows a sample of the My Top Open Opportunities dashlet.

Figure 9-1:
The My
Top Open
Oppor-
tunities
dashlet.

Opportunity Name	Amount	Expected Close Date
JJ Resources Inc 463201 - 1000 units	$25,000.00	03/29/2008
Kaos Theory Ltd 628887 - 1000 units	$10,000.00	05/15/2008
Gifted Holdings AG 992985 - 1000 units	$25,000.00	08/17/2008
RIVIERA HOTELS 322293 - 1000 units	$75,000.00	11/24/2008
Kitty Kat Inc 529246 - 1000 units	$10,000.00	12/27/2008

My Top Open Opportunities (1 - 5 of 6)

Honing in on the Home page

After you decide on the dashlets you want to display on your Home page, the real fun begins. All dashlets have several common elements:

- ✔ **To rearrange your dashlets, place your mouse on the dashlet title and then drag-and-drop it to a new position.**

- ✔ **To remove a dashlet, click the Delete (X) icon.**

- ✔ **To refresh a dashlet, click the Refresh (double-arrow) icon.** By refreshing the dashlet, you're able to see any changes that have been made in Sugar.

- ✔ **To zoom in for more information, click the record name or subject.**

- ✔ **To sort your information, click a column header.**

Changing the Home page dashlets info

You'll probably find the Home page to be one of your best resources because it allows you to see the various aspects of your business on one page. However, you might not be satisfied with the information displayed on a dashlet. For example, the My Top Open Opportunities dashlet only displays your top *five* opportunities; with a little tweaking you can make it display *ten — or as many as you want.*

You can configure each dashlet to display various rows and columns. Additionally, you can change the filters to display the exact information you need. Best of all, it's really easy to tweak the dashlets if you follow these steps:

1. Click the Edit (pencil) icon of the dashlet you'd like to modify.

The Options dialog box displays in a separate window similar to the one shown in Figure 9-2.

Figure 9-2:
Editing a
Home page
dashlet.

2. Change the dashlet title.

For example, you might rename the My Top Open Opportunities dashlet to simply My Top 10 Ops.

3. **Select the columns to display by selecting a column title from the Hide Columns area and then clicking the left-pointing arrow.**

   Your column choices are dependent on the type of dashlet that you're editing. You can also remove columns from the Display Columns area. And, feel free to use the up and down arrows to rearrange things a bit.

4. **Change the Filters.**

   You can opt to show only your items or to filter items according to date range or some other criteria.

5. **Click Save when you finish editing the dashlet.**

   You might want to take a moment to appreciate your artistry. Or, if you're not satisfied with your changes, you can always try, try again!

Adding new dashlets to the Home page

You can add and remove dashlets as needed. Simply click the Add Dashlets button at the top-right side of the Home page and the dialog window shown in Figure 9-3 opens.

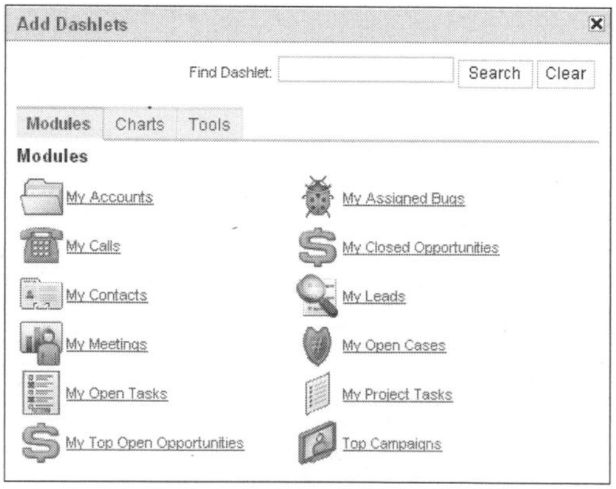

Figure 9-3:
Adding
dashlets to
the Home
page.

Notice that many of the dashlets already appear on your Home page. However, you might want to add multiple dashlets of the same kind and give them different names and filters. For example, you might add a dashlet for your top five opportunities, and another similar dashlet with the top ten opportunities company-wide. After you added a dashlet, you can move it using the technique described in the previous section.

By default, you can only add ten dashlets to your Home page. However, if you feel an overwhelming desire to increase that number, consider wandering over to the administrator with a subtle bribe because she can change this setting. And, if you find you can't modify the Home page at all, you might consider finding an even larger bribe because the administrator has control of that setting as well.

Got the "I've done a bit too much Home page customization" blues? There's a sure-fire cure. Click My Account from the Home page and then click the Homepage button in the Reset to Default area at the top of the Users page. *Voilà!* — you're back to the original Home page layout.

You Can't Drive Your Business without a Dashboard

The Dashboard is quite similar to the Home page. However, most of the Home page dashlets are in list format whereas the Dashboard dashlets take the form of neat graphical charts and graphs like the ones shown in Figure 9-4.

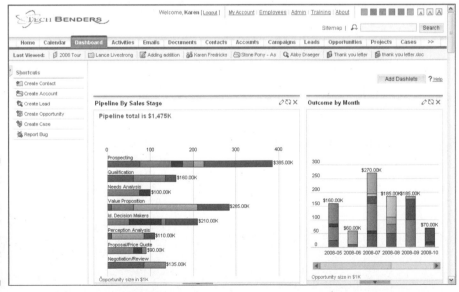

Figure 9-4: The SugarCRM Community Edition Dashboard Home page.

You access the dashboards by clicking Dashboard on the Module Tab bar. If you've mastered the dashlets on the Home page, then you've mastered the Dashboard dashlets because you add, remove, edit, and move the dashlets in both modules exactly the same way.

Basic dashboarding 101

The Dashboard module contains six dashlets, all of which focus on information it gathers from the Opportunities module:

- **All Opportunities by Lead Source by Outcome:** A bar chart displaying opportunities segmented by each lead source.

- **All Opportunities by Lead Source:** A pie chart that shows the proportion of total opportunities for each lead source.

- **Campaign ROI:** If you're using the Campaign module (see Chapter 14), this displays a campaign's return on investment.

- **My Pipeline by Sales Stage:** This one is a funnel chart that shows the total dollar amount for your opportunities grouped by sales stage.

- **Outcome by Month:** A bar chart displaying the total sales pipeline for each month.

- **Pipeline by Sales Stage:** A funnel chart that displays the total dollar amounts for all your opportunities grouped by sales stage.

Click the Add Dashlets button to add an additional dashlet to the Dashboard page. Remember, you can add the same dashlet multiple times and then edit it to change the names and filtering criteria.

Not satisfied with the available dashlets? Chapter 20 talks about the SugarForge and SugarExchange where you find lots of additional dashlets.

Professional dashboarding

SugarCRM Professional Edition comes complete with mag wheels and enhanced dashboard functionality. It also comes with two additional dashlets:

- **My Closed Opportunities:** Shows a gauge chart of your opportunities that you've closed.

- **My Forecasting:** Compares your sales quota against the actual amount of your opportunities. You read about the Forecasting module in Chapter 16.

You can also perform an additional party trick using SugarCRM Professional: the ability to group your dashlets into pages.

If you look closely at Figure 9-5, you'll notice two tiny — albeit important — differences from what you see in Figure 9-4:

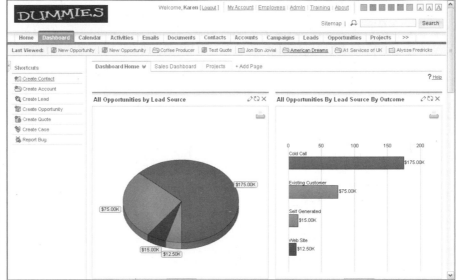

Figure 9-5:
The SugarCRM Professional Edition Dashboard Home page.

✔ **The Add Dashlets button disappeared.**

✔ **The Dashboard features additional page tabs.**

In Professional Edition, you modify the Dashboard by clicking on a page of your dashboard and then clicking the double down arrows. This opens the dialog window shown in Figure 9-6.

Figure 9-6:
Modifying the Dashboard Home page in Sugar Professional.

From here you can

- ✔ **Rename:** Rename the dashboard page by replacing the existing page name with a new one.

- ✔ **Add Dashlets:** Add additional dashlets to the page using the same technique as you do for Community Edition dashboards. In addition to the dashlets mentioned above, you can also add any customized charts that you've created.

    If you're not sure how to add your customized charts, you might want to take a gander at Chapter 16.

- ✔ **Change Layout:** Change the dashboard layout to have a one, two, or three column layout.

- ✔ **Delete Page:** Delete a dashboard page. However, you can't delete the Dashboard's Home page.

Seek and Ye Shall Find

If all roads lead to Rome, surely all processes in SugarCRM lead to the Search window. A *search* is a way of looking at only a portion of the records in your database, depending on your specifications. A good practice in Sugar is to perform a search and then perform an action. For example, you might perform a search and then follow up on your key opportunities. Or, you might do a search and then perform a mail merge.

The theory behind the search is that you don't always need to work with all your contacts at one time. Not only is working with only a portion of your database easier, at times, doing so is absolutely necessary. If you're changing your mailing address, you probably want to send a notification to everyone in your database. Comparatively, if you're running a special sales promotion, you probably notify only your leads and accounts. And if you're sending overpriced holiday gift baskets, you probably want the names of only your very best customers.

In Sugar, you can search for information across several modules or restrict your search to one specific module. You can also perform a quick search based on a single field.

The three types of Sugar searches are

- ✔ **Global Search**
- ✔ **Basic Search**
- ✔ **Advanced Search**

Doing the Global Search

A *Global Search* can be an extremely useful way to find data about your records no matter where that information might be lurking. In fact, you might nickname this search the "Super" search. As your database increases, you might want to see all the records that revolve around a single Contacts or Accounts record. Sugar's Global Search enables you to dig for that information in the Accounts, Bug Tracker, Cases, Contacts, Leads, Opportunities, Projects, and Quotes modules of Sugar.

For example, suppose that you're looking for all the information about a key Accounts record. You perform a Global Search by filling in your search criteria in the search box located at the top-right corner of any Sugar screen and then clicking the Search button.

The percent sign (%) is the universal wildcard in a MySQL database. Sugar automatically adds the % wildcard to the end of a search. For example, searching for "The Big%" matches such records as The Big Kahuna or The Big Bopper. Searching for "%Big" returns Mr. Big.

Depending on the type of database you're using, a Global Search may or may not be case-sensitive. Sugar databases that use the MySQL database are not case-sensitive whereas those using Oracle are case-sensitive.

A Gobal Search searches throughout your database — checking all records — and returns all records relating to your criteria in a page that looks similar to Figure 9-7.

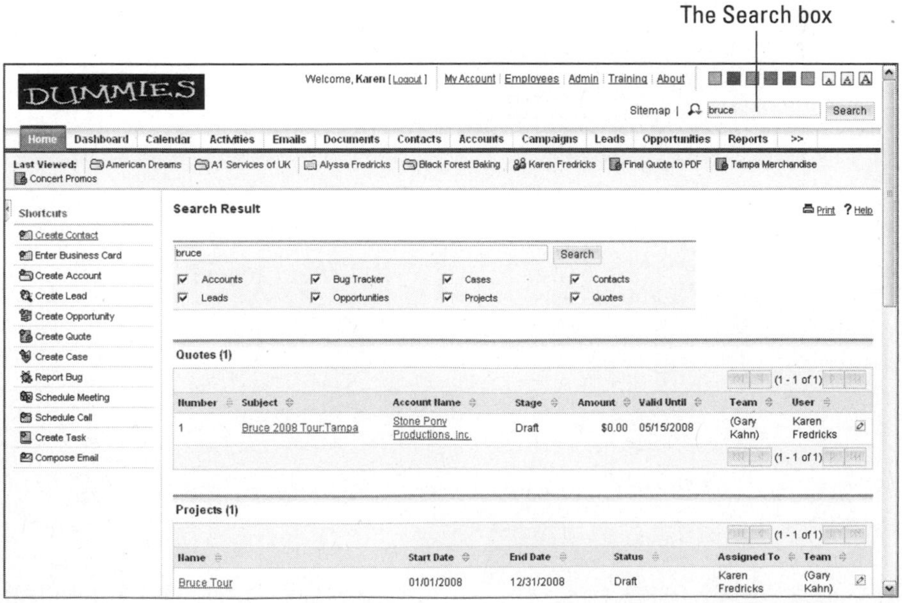

The Search box

Figure 9-7:
The results
of a Global
Search.

The modules with the most records display at the top of the Search Result page. When the search has completed, you can further refine your search by selecting only the modules you wish to query and then clicking the **Search button**.

Getting back to basics

You can perform a Basic Search from the Search subpanel, which is conveniently located at the top of most module Home pages. The Basic Search limits your search options to a few crucial fields.

Performing a Basic Search is easy if you follow these steps:

1. **Select the tab of the module that you'd like to search.**

   Unlike a Global Search, the Basic Search is limited to a single module.

2. **Fill in the criteria on which you'd like to search.**

   For example, Figure 9-8 shows you the Basic Search tab of the Contacts Home page, which includes the First Name, Last Name, and Account Name fields. You can search by any — or all — of the fields.

   The search fields are context-sensitive; when you type a character in a field, the system performs a search and presents a list of values starting with that character.

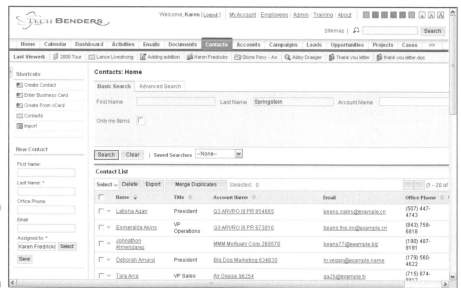

Figure 9-8: Performing a Basic Search.

3. **(Optional) Select the Only My Items check box to find only those records that are related to your tasks and activities.**

4. **Click the Search button.**

   Quick as a wink, your List view modifies to show only those records that match your search criteria. If you enter information into more than one field, then a record must match all those fields to be included.

   At this point, you can continue on your merry way. Feel free to perform a mass update, delete the selected records, and perform any function that you can normally perform in the List view.

5. **Click the Clear button when you finish working with the selected records.**

   You might feel a momentary feeling of panic right after performing a search, wondering what happened to the rest of your records. Sugar believes in the "Mother May I" school of computing. After you perform a search, those records — and only those records — will display in the List view even if you log out of Sugar and log back in again. Make sure you hit the Clear button to bring the rest of the records out of hiding.

Advancing your way through the searches

After you use your database for a while and it slowly but surely fills up with more and more records, you might feel the need to add a little more power to your searches. You also might find yourself constantly creating the same search and wishing you could save that search. In fact, you might even start using the term *query,* which is computer-speak for *search.*

If you need to base your search on multiple criterions, you can perform a query to create the search. In Sugar, a *query* searches all the records in your database based on the criteria that you specify and then creates a list of the records that match that criteria. Additionally, you can rearrange the list to show the fields you deem to be most important.

Many of you might associate *advanced* with *difficult,* but that's certainly not the case here. In Sugar, the Advanced Search is powerful, but not difficult, if you follow these steps:

1. **Click the Advanced Search tab of the module's Home page.**

   As you probably know by now, most every module includes the Search subpanel on its Home page. The Advanced Search page displays various fields depending on the selected module. The fields are blank; your mission — should you choose to accept it — is to specify the fields and values that define the query.

2. Fill in any criteria on which you want to search.

The Advanced Search allows you to create an exact profile for the contacts you're hoping to find. For example, you might want to have a look at all of your Accounts records from the state of Arizona who are manufacturers.

Fill in as much criteria as you need. The whole purpose of doing an Advanced Search is to look for records that fit more than one criterion. If you're looking for all customers who are located in Arizona, select Customer from the Type list and type AZ in the State field, as I do in Figure 9-9.

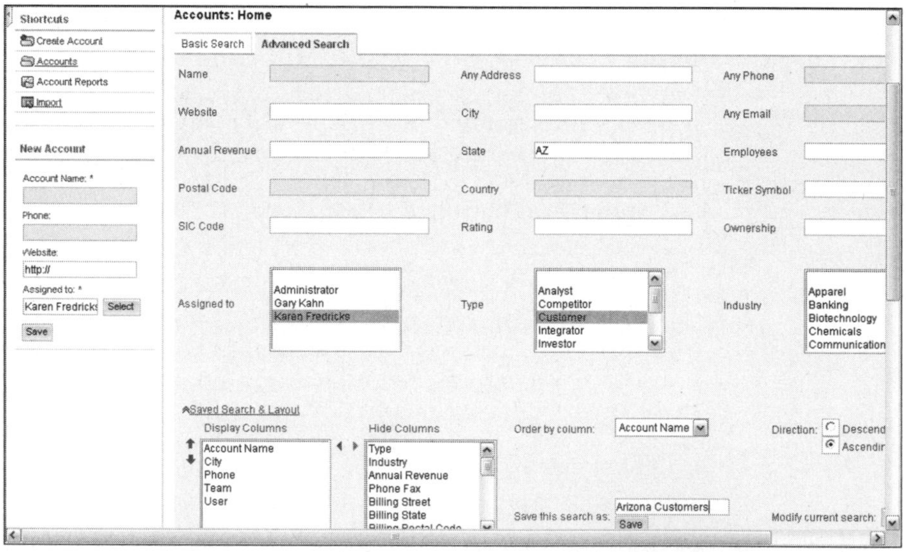

Figure 9-9:
The
Advanced
Search
page.

3. Click the Search button.

Sugar happily displays a list of all the Contacts records that match your search criteria in the List view.

4. Click the double down arrows next to Saved Search & Layout.

The Saved Search & Layout subpanel expands. The Saved Search & Layout option lets you save the search criteria as well as how you want that information to display.

5. Select a field from the Hide Columns list and click the left arrow to add a column to the List view.

The object of the game is to decide which fields you want to display — and the order in which they'll be displayed.

To change the order of the displayed fields, select a field from the Display Columns list and then use the up or down arrow to move it. To remove a column from the List view, select it from the Display Columns list and use the right arrow to move it to the Hide Columns list.

6. **Choose the column you wish to sort by from the Order By Column drop-down list.**

   Only those fields you select in the Display Columns list will show in the Order By Column drop-down list.

7. **Select the appropriate Direction radio button.**

   Most folks like to see things in Ascending or A–Z, low-to-high order. However, you might choose descending order if you're searching for opportunities and want to see the big-ticket items first.

8. **Enter a name for the search results in the Save This Search As field and then click Save.**

   Creating an Advanced Search is only half the fun; the other half comes from being able to use it again — and again and again!

9. **Choose None from the Saved Searches drop-down list to clear the current search, and then select your saved search from the Saved Searches list to view the saved search.**

10. **(Optional) Make any necessary changes to the search criteria and/or the layout and then click Update.**

    Mistakes happen. The world evolves. And you may need to tweak your saved search. Feel free to do so.

11. **(Optional) Click Delete to delete the saved search.**

    Over time, your list of saved searches might get very l-o-n-g; you'll want to prune it a bit.

Saved searches can be a bit confusing. You might find yourself using a saved search, changing the filters and actually creating a new search — even though the Saved Searches drop-down displays the original search name. It's a good practice to choose None from the drop-down and then click Clear to rid yourself of any evidence of the prior search.

Part III

A Spoonful of Sugar Keeps Your Customers Happy

The 5th Wave   By Rich Tennant

"Ms. Lamont, how long have you been sending out bills listing charges for 'Freight,' 'Handling,' and 'Sales Tax,' as 'This,' 'That,' and 'The Other Thing?'"

In this part . . .

*E*ven the best-laid plans of any business can result in unexpected outcomes. Hard as it may be to believe, your customers will find things to complain about — and you'll want to be responsive to their concerns. Using Sugar, you can set up and manage cases for those problematic customers as well as report on any bugs that you uncover in your product line. And, as your company grows, you might consider creating custom portals for each of your customers as a way of handling their problems immediately — before they have a chance to escalate.

Chapter 10

Adding a Bit of Case Management

*C*ase management is the collaborative process of assessing a problem, planning its solution, and ultimately providing a favorable outcome. In this chapter, I show you how to use Sugar's Cases module to identify and fix the problems that are bothering your customers before they snowball into major headaches. And, after you solve the problem and/or resolve the issues, you can document your findings in the company Knowledge Base.

I'm on the Case

Fortunately, some of you may never have to use Sugar's Cases module. Maybe you sell a product that never breaks — or one that you don't have to worry about fixing. Perhaps the services that you offer are so stellar that you never receive a complaint. Lucky you! If that's the case, feel free to skip this chapter.

For the rest of the crowd, the Sugar Cases module will seem heaven-sent. Many other CRM products require you to purchase expensive add-on software if you need to manage a help desk or incident tracking. By having one integrated product, however, your support personnel can attach the issues to existing records without having to retype address and other contact details in the database.

With Sugar, you can use the Cases module to deal with a variety of complaints and questions that all too often land on your desk. Maybe you sell products or equipment that can break from time to time. Maybe you run a call center that fields questions about various products. Or maybe your company has a customer service department that needs a place to log the complaints they have to deal with. Whatever the situation, Sugar is there to handle all the negative aspects with a sweet smile.

Generally, the bigger the company the greater the possibility that things will go wrong. The Cases module is fairly generic, so you can use it company-wide to help resolve the issues facing various departments. This is very important in a small or medium-sized company where typically a single solution is used for multiple purposes:

- ✔ **Customer service department:** A customer service department can use Sugar to keep track of all the issues and problems your customers report about your product or services. Issues no longer slip through the cracks. Sugar tracks the life of support issues from the day they're reported to the day they're resolved so that you keep your customers happy — and don't lose them to your competition!

- ✔ **Sales department:** Because the entire database is integrated with the customer support issues, your sales folks can see how your customers are being taken care of and what issues they face.

- ✔ **Marketing department:** Marketing can refer to the Cases module to analyze the nature of the problems your customers are reporting and use the insight to improve your product or services.

- ✔ **Internal IT department:** Your overworked and underpaid IT folks can use Sugar to keep track of internal, employee-related tasks so they can prioritize their time.

Although the Cases module is fairly basic at first glance, a trip to Chapter 15 shows you how to customize and make Cases as robust as you need.

Let's Make a Federal Case Out of It

Creating Cases records and resolving them with Sugar is a very easy process. In essence, the customer notifies the help desk or customer service department of his issue and the support personnel assigns a ticket that details the problem. If the first person is able to solve the issue, he closes the case. However, if he is unable to resolve the problem he can assign a follow-up to someone else in the company who might have better luck in helping Mr. Customer — and ultimately closing the case. Anyone in the company can view the details of the case from the Cases subpanel of the associated Accounts record.

Creating a Cases record is much easier than waiting for a small problem to develop into a mountain of trouble:

1. **Choose Create Case from the Shortcuts menu.**

   The Cases page opens. Check out Figure 10-1 to see what it looks like.

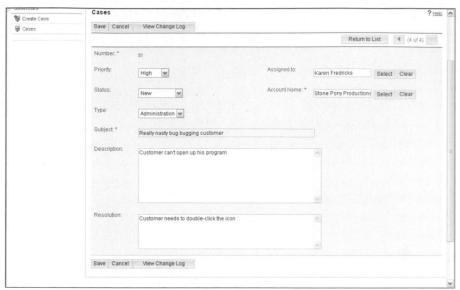

Figure 10-1:
Creating a
Case.

2. **Enter information into the fields on the Cases page.**

   - **Number (required):** You may wonder how exactly you fill in information for this required field. Gotcha! You don't; Sugar automatically assigns the next sequential number to a new case.

   - **Priority:** Specify the urgency of the problem (High, Medium, or Low) from the drop-down list.

   - **Assigned To:** Specify the lucky person who is in charge of the Cases record.

   If the administrator has enabled e-mail notification, then the case owner will receive an e-mail whenever a Cases record is assigned to her. Chapter 16 shows you this and a few more tricks available to the database administrator.

   - **Status:** Specify the status of the problem from the drop-down list; typical choices include items like New, Closed, and I'm really stumped.

   - **Account Name (required):** You must associate a Cases record with an existing Accounts record. You can type in the first few letters of the account name and Sugar will magically suggest possible matches, or you can click the Select button to manually search for an Accounts record.

   - **Type: The type of case you're creating. The choices are Product, User and Administration.**

- **Subject (required):** Enter a brief summary of the Cases record to help identify it among the rest of the Cases records.

- **Description: For some record types, a description offers little or no value. However, in the case of case management this is where you'll want to write a litany that** clearly describes the problem.

- **Resolution:** Enter the results of the investigation into the problem.

3. **Click Save to save the Cases record.**

   The Cases Detail view displays, as shown in Figure 10-2.

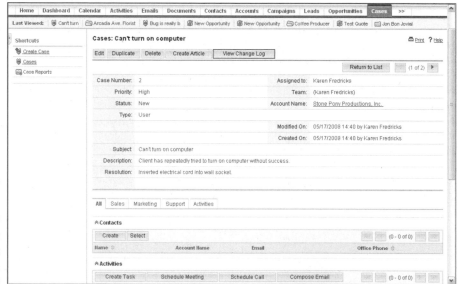

Figure 10-2:
The Cases
Detail view.

I Rest My Case

Some cases have easy resolutions and you're able to open and close the case at the same time. However, many cases are more complex and involve a bit more intervention before they can be closed.

Here's how you can monitor a Cases record from start to finish:

1. **Click the Cases module tab from the Sugar Home page.**

   You can access your entire case load by clicking the Cases module tab from your Home page. The Cases Home page allows you to search for Cases by Number, Subject, or Account Name. In addition, Figure 10-3 shows how you can opt to view only those Cases records assigned to you.

By now, you're pretty much a Sugar List expert. You can sort, delete, export to Excel, or merge Cases records using exactly the same method you use for any other List in Sugar.

2. **Click the case record's name to view the details of a Cases record.**

   Clicking the name of a Cases record from the Case List opens the Case page. This page is extremely important in the life cycle of a Cases record.

3. **Click Edit to change the case record's details and then click Save to record your changes.**

   Because Cases records are fairly volatile, you need to edit them frequently. In particular, you'll want to change the Status field — especially when you close the Cases record.

4. **(Optional) Click the View Change Log button to view any recent changes to the Cases record.**

5. **Scroll to the Contacts subpanel and click Select to associate additional Contacts records with the Cases record.**

   You can associate as many Contacts records as you like to a Cases record. By associating the Cases record to various Contacts records, you give the rest of your organization a bit of a heads-up that there's a problem before they step into a possible minefield.

   Figure 10-4 shows you the various Case page subpanels.

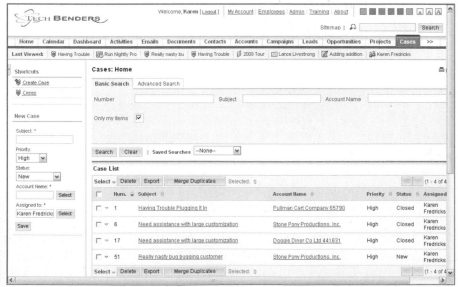

Figure 10-3:
The Sugar Cases Home page.

6. Scroll to the Activities subpanel.

You can perform a variety of case-related tricks from the Activities subpanel.

- *Task:* Here's where you can hand the next step of the case to one of your unsuspecting colleagues.

- *Meeting:* If the case requires some major fine-tuning on the part of the customer, you might want to schedule a face-to-face meeting with him to discuss it.

- *Call:* Schedule a follow-up phone call for either yourself or one of your co-workers.

- *E-mail:* This really sweet option automatically opens an e-mail pre-filled with the case record's number and subject in the subject line so that you can keep Ms. Customer informed via e-mail.

7. Scroll to the History subpanel.

Need to fill in a few more tidbits of info? Here's the place!

8. Scroll to the Bugs subpanel.

Chapter 11 tells you about the crawly critters and insects that infect software; here's where you can associate a bug with your Cases record.

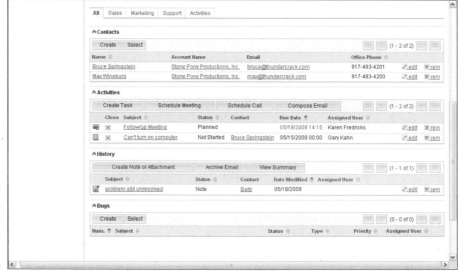

Figure 10-4:
The sub-panels of a Case page.

It's a Case of Reporting

You have a couple of nice ways to really stay on top of your case load. My favorite is to make sure you include the My Open Cases dashlet on your Home page — and place it in a prominent position so that you see it each time you fire up Sugar. Chapter 9 walks you through that task.

Another way to keep track of your cases is by using a report to view your cases. SugarCRM Professional Edition comes with both a price tag and a bunch of case reports.

You can access the Case Reports by clicking the Cases module tab on the Sugar Home page and then choosing Case Reports from the Shortcut menu. As you see in Figure 10-5, the four "out of the box" reports are

- ✔ **Open Cases By User By Status**
- ✔ **Open Cases By Month By User**
- ✔ **Open Cases By Priority By User**
- ✔ **New Cases By Month**

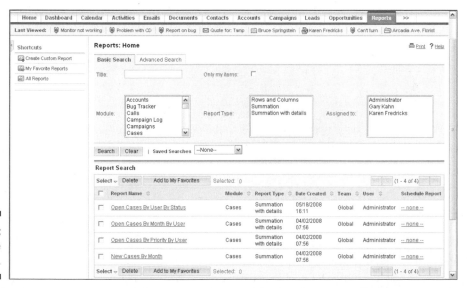

Figure 10-5:
The Case
Reports.

The default reports all display in graphical format. Once displayed, you can change the filters or opt to have a report display as text rather than as a graphic; Chapter 14 explains how to change the report options. You can also drill down on any portion of the report to see more detail. Figure 10-6 shows you a sample of the Open Cases By Priority By User report.

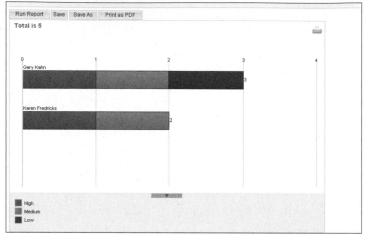

Figure 10-6:
The Open Cases By Priority By User report.

Building Your Base of Knowledge

The beginning of this chapter deals with the issues that your customers face — and the process you go through to provide a solution. You might think that after the customer goes away — hopefully with a smile on his face — your problems are over. However, chances are pretty good that other customers will come to you with the very same issues somewhere down the line. You might start the process all over again — or you might try to learn from your experiences.

SugarCRM Professional Edition includes a Knowledge Base module. A *knowledge base* is a collection of articles that pertains to a specific topic. Generally, knowledge base or *KB* articles include a problem and its solution. Typically, a knowledge base includes the ability to search the articles to find the answers to your specific questions.

Using the Knowledge Base module, you can create articles on any subject to develop your own searchable library of answers to common questions as well as create FAQs (Frequently Asked Questions). You can attach a file to the article, create an article from an existing case, and even e-mail the article directly to one of your customers.

Creating a KB

The steps for creating a new Knowledge Base article are easy. Here's all you have to do:

1. **Open a new Knowledge Base article.**

   You can create a Knowledge Base article using any one of the following three methods:

   - *From scratch:* Click Knowledge Base on the Module Tab bar from the Home page and then choose Create Article from the Shortcuts menu.

   - *From an existing Cases record:* If you have an existing case — preferably one you've already resolved — open the case and then click Create Article on the Cases record's Detail view. This method saves you from having to enter a Title, Subject, Description, or Resolution because that information automatically fills in from the corresponding fields in the Cases record.

   - *From an existing e-mail message:* Hard as it may be to believe, a problem might stump the stars of your company only to be solved by the customer himself. In cases like these, the customer e-mails you with a solution, which you can use to generate a new article without having to start from scratch.

   Whatever method you use, the Knowledge Base article page opens, as shown in Figure 10-7.

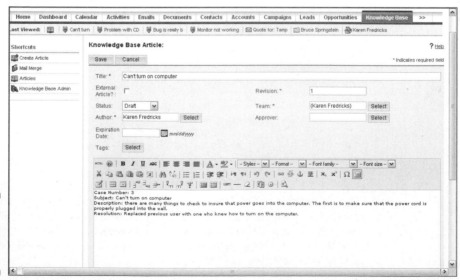

Figure 10-7:
Creating a
Knowledge
Base article.

2. Enter information into the Knowledge Base Article fields.

Although not all the fields are required, they're all important so take the time to fill them all in.

- **Title (required):** This is the main way you identify an article so give it a good title.

- **External Article:** Select this check box to make the article available to both your *internal* Sugar users and your *external* SugarPortal users.

- **Revision (required):** Enter the article's revision number. Typically, the revision number of a new article is 1, followed by 2, 3, 4, and so on.

- **Status:** Choose the status of the article from the drop-down list to indicate whether it's ready for prime time viewing.

To make the article available for viewing, the status must be set to Published.

- **Team (required):** Enter the name of the team that's allowed to access the article. If an article is an external one, Team will default to Global so that everyone can access it.

- **Author (required):** By default, the article creator is the assigned author. However, you can click **Select** and choose a different user.

Make sure that the author is a member of the assigned team so that she will be able to access — and subsequently edit — the article.

- **Approver:** Click **Select to select** the name of the lucky user who's responsible for the final rendition of the article.

- **Expiration Date:** Old news is, well, old news, so you might want to include an expiration date to ensure that your article will not display when it is no longer relevant.

When an article reaches its expiration date, it no longer appears in any internal search results or in the SugarPortal.

3. Click the Tags Select button to link the article with a new or existing tag.

The next section, "Playing tag with your KB articles" talks about *tags,* which is the method Sugar uses to organize your articles.

4. Enter the text of the article in the Body field.

This is the main purpose — and most important part — of the article. The body includes a nice HTML editor so you can format your text using familiar tools, such as bold, italics, underline, colors, and font size. You'll even find buttons that allow you to create a hyperlink within the article and preview the final product.

Typically, KB articles include a description of the problem and its resolution.

5. **(Optional) Click Browse to navigate to the location of a file and select it to attach the file to the article.**

   For example, if you are a software company, you might have created a *hot fix* to fix a problem and want to attach it to the article.

6. **(Optional) Click Browse to navigate to the location of a graphic and select it to embed an image into the article.**

   A picture is worth a thousand words so you might want to include one in the body of your document to illustrate your point.

7. **Click Save to save the article.**

   The article's Detail view displays.

Playing tag with your KB articles

Tags are similar to folders. They allow you to group articles so that it's easy to find the ones you want. When you *tag* an article, the system creates a link between the tag and the article.

Sugar comes with two tags: FAQs and Untagged Articles. You also have the capability to create custom tags. If you're a software company, for example, you might create additional tags such as Hardware Errors, Software Errors, and Nut Behind the Keyboard Errors. An article can be linked to more than one tag, and a tag can be linked with multiple articles.

As your Knowledge Base grows, you can organize your tags into *root* tags and *subtags*. Root tags are the main categories, and subtags are the subcategories.

When you create an article, you can create a new tag for it or select an existing one. It's probably a bit easier to create tags prior to creating the articles so that you give some thought to the organization you want the Knowledge Base to follow.

Here's how to start creating tags:

1. **Click Knowledge Base on the Module Tab bar on the Sugar Home page and then choose Knowledge Base Admin from the Shortcuts menu.**

   The Knowledge Base Admin page opens. A list of existing root tags displays under the Tags heading.

2. **Choose an action from the admin options drop down list and then click the folder to which you'd like to create a new tag.**

   Don't be fooled by the check boxes — you need to click the actual filename here. Click the Tags folder if you'd like to create a root tag; click one of existing root tags if you'd like to create a subtag.

3. **Fill in the name of the new folder and then click Save.**

Figure 10-8 gives you an idea of what adding a new tag looks like.

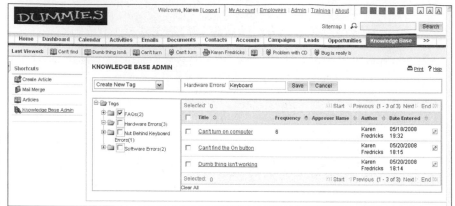

Figure 10-8:
Creating a
new tag.

Being the KB Editor and Chief

After your Knowledge Base grows, you'll probably need to reorganize it a bit by renaming or deleting tags, or maybe changing which articles correspond to a given tag. The Knowledge Base Admin page is just the place to make these changes.

Notice in Figure 10-8 that you can select both Tags and the corresponding articles associated with a tag. By selecting Tags and/or articles and making use of the admin options drop-down list, you have a whole bunch of editing options available to you:

- **Delete Tag:** Choose Delete Tag from the admin options drop-down list, select a tag, and then click the Delete Tag button.

    Only administrators can delete tags because they can view all the articles associated with a tag, whereas some of your users might not have the necessary permission to view all articles.

    Only empty tags can be deleted.

- **Rename Tag:** Choose Rename Tag from the admin options drop-down list, click a Tag name, and type in the new tag name.

- **Move article(s):** Choose Move Selected Articles from the admin options drop-down list, select the article(s), click the Select Tag button, and then click the name of the desired tag.

✔ **Apply new tags to an article:** Choose Apply Tags to Articles from the admin options drop-down list, select the article(s), click the Select Tag button, and then click the name of the tag you want to associate with the article.

Seek and ye shall find the article

Ah. The hard work is over. You've solved the problem, saved the world — and created a Knowledge Base article so that everyone else can benefit from your brilliance. But, like most of life, there's a slight catch — how are people going to find your article?

If your Knowledge Base contains only a handful of articles, it's easy to browse for the article in question. However, as your Knowledge Base grows, you'll want to search for articles.

Browsing the base

It's very easy — albeit a bit time-consuming — to browse for an article. Here's how you do it:

1. **Click Knowledge Base on the Module Tab bar on the Sugar Home page and then choose Articles from the Shortcuts menu.**

   The Browse tab of the Knowledge Base Home page appears in all its glory, as shown in Figure 10-9, and displays a list of existing tags.

2. **Click a tag name to view its contents.**

   All the articles within a selected tag display in the right panel.

3. **(Optional) Click the plus (+) sign to view the sub tags and the articles contained within.**

4. **Click an article name to view the contents of that article.**

   From here, it's a question of clicking a tag to reveal the articles it contains. You even have an Untagged Articles tag that you can use to search for any articles that might not have been tagged.

Figure 10-9: The Knowledge Base Home page's Browse tab.

All tags are visible to all users. However, you can see only those articles you have permission to see.

Quickly querying the Knowledge Base

Browsing works well for tiny knowledge bases — or if you have lots of time on your hands. However, as your Knowledge Base grows, you'll want to search for articles by keywords, tags, and/or titles to find the articles that you want.

The Knowledge Base Home page has three tabs: Search, Browse, and Advanced. Your first trip to the Knowledge Base lands you in the Browse tab, which I discussed in the previous section. In this section, I discuss the two other tabs, which you use to find just the article you're looking for.

Simply searching for an article

1. **Click Knowledge Base on the Module Tab bar on the Sugar Home page and then choose Articles from the Shortcuts menu.**

   The Knowledge Base Home page opens.

2. **Click the Search tab.**

   The Knowledge Base Search tab opens, as shown in Figure 10-10.

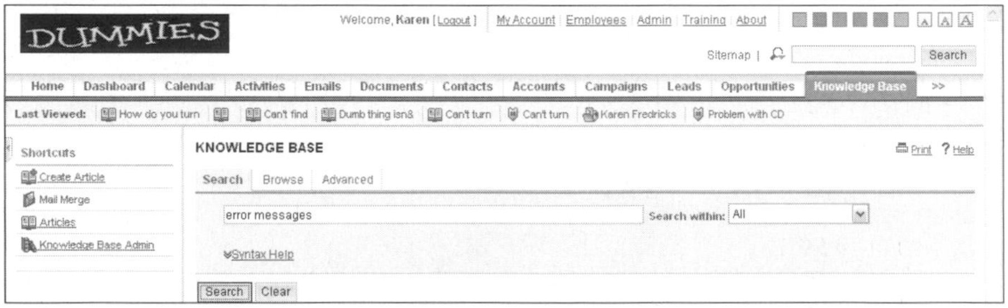

Figure 10-10:
The Knowledge Base Home page's Search tab.

3. **Enter one or more words in the search field to find related articles.**

   You can search by supplying a part of a title or the information found within the article.

4. **(Optional) To restrict the search, choose a criterion from the Search Within drop-down list.**

   The Search Within list allows you to restrict your search a bit more by allowing you to choose such options as Pending Approval or Added Last 30 Days.

5. **Click the Search button.**

   Any articles that match your request will appear in a list at the bottom of the search page.

Building a better query

On the simplest level, Sugar tracks down any articles that include a specified word or phrase in either the title or the body of an article. However, if you're using a MySQL database with Sugar, you can make use of SQL's advanced querying language to build more sophisticated queries.

Here are a few query rules to keep in mind:

- **Words and phrases are not case sensitive.**

- **Use spaces to specify multiple words.** A space works like the word *or.* For example, if you search for *error message,* the search results will return articles that contain either the words error or message.

- **Specific phrases must be enclosed in quotes.** If you are looking for articles that contain the specific phrase *software error messages,* then you must type **"software error message"** in the search field. Without the quotes, you'll end up with a bunch of articles that contain either the words

software, error, and/or *message* anywhere within the article.

- **Use the plus (+) sign to find articles that contain multiple words.** For example, *software +error* will find articles that only contain both words. Additionally, you can combine a word with a phrase; for example, to find articles on keyboard error messages, you can search for *"error messages" +keyboard.*

- **Use the minus (–) sign to exclude words or phrases.** For example, *error messages – keyboard* will find only those articles about error messages that don't include a reference to the keyboard.

- **SQL uses the percent sign (%) as a wildcard.** For example, searching for *%dem* will retrieve demo, democracy, and epidemic.

- **MySQL ignores words with three letters or less unless they are part of a phrase.** Therefore, the search results will not display articles containing *the, or,* and *of.*

Performing an Advanced search

As your Knowledge Base grows, so too will your need to perform bigger, more powerful searches. And, like the reliable software program that it is, Sugar is ready to grow with you.

The Advanced tab of the Knowledge Base allows you to plug in lots of additional criteria to your search. And, although it's advanced and powerful, the Advanced search is every bit as easy to perform as the basic search.

1. **Click Knowledge Base on the Module Tab bar on the Sugar Home page and then choose Articles from the Shortcuts menu.**

   The Knowledge Base Home page opens.

2. **Click the Advanced tab and then click the More Options link.**

   By clicking the More Options link, you can view all the fields shown in Figure 10-11 that are available to you.

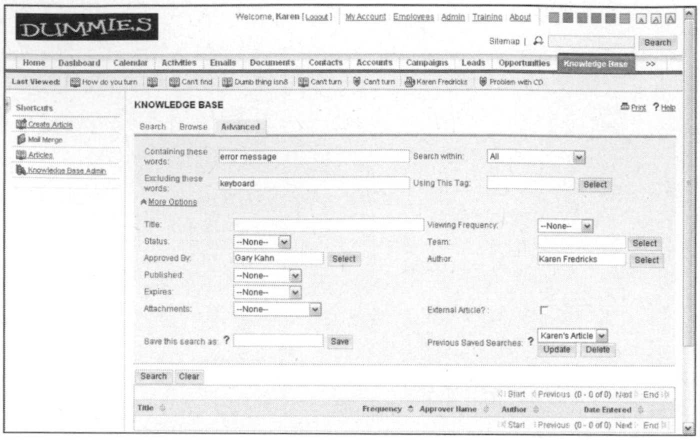

Figure 10-11:
Using
Advanced
Search
to find a
Knowledge
Base article.

3. **Specify any of the search criteria.**

You can make your searches as simple — or as complex — as you like.

- *Containing These Words:* Type the words or phrases you're looking for.

- *Search Within:* Choose additional criterion from the drop-down list, such as a time period or a tag.

- *Excluding These Words:* Enter a word or phrase to exclude from the search.

- *Using This Tag:* Select a tag from the list of existing tags.

- *Title:* Enter the name of the article you're looking for.

- *Viewing Frequency:* Choose the most popular (Top 10) or least popular (Bottom 10) from the drop-down list.

- *Status:* Choose the article's status, such as Draft or Published, from the drop-down list

- *Team:* Click **Select** to choose the team assigned to the article you're looking for.

- *Approved By:* Click **Select** to choose a user from the Users list to search for articles assigned to a specific approver.

- *Author:* Click **Select** to choose the name of the person who wrote the article.

- *Published:* Click the calendar icon to select a specific date for the article.

- *Expires After:* Click the calendar icon to search for articles that expire after a specific date.

- *Attachments:* You can search for all articles with attachments, or specify the name of the specific attachment you're looking for.

- *External Article:* Here's where you can look for only those articles that are accessible by people outside your circle of Sugar users.

- *Save This Search As:* If you'd like to use this search again, enter a name for the search and then click Save.

- *Previous Saved Searches:* Choose the name of the saved search from the drop-down list to reuse a search.

4. **Click Search to start the search.**

   A list of articles that match your criteria will appear.

Chapter 11

Keeping Bugs Out of the Sugar Bowl

*I*n this chapter, I show you how to use SugarCRM to keep track of — and hopefully find solutions for — software bugs. I also show you how to create a forum so that the members of your team can collaborate to solve the problems of the world — or at least fix what's bugging your software.

Nobody likes to think that bugs are roaming around in either their picnic basket or in their software! If your company develops software, this chapter will be particularly useful to you. Even if you don't develop software the Bugs module is a great place for your users to report issues on the Sugar installation itself.

Learning to Fix What's Bugging You

In computer-speak, a *bug* is an error or defect in software or hardware that causes a program to not work correctly. Typically, bugs appear in one of the following situations:

▶ **Software conflicts:** It's almost impossible to test to see how your software program is going to react with every other piece of software that's on the market today. You might find that the software mysteriously stops working when you upgrade your operating system or install a new piece of accounting software.

▶ **Hardware conflicts:** Just as with software, many types of hardware are out there. Again, your software might function perfectly well until you purchase a new computer. Sometimes, even peripherals (such as printers) can cause a problem.

> ✔ **Defect:** If you're a software manufacturer, this is probably the most annoying — and easiest to fix — of all the bugs. A *defect* is a problem with the software that prevents it from working correctly.

Bug Tracking is fairly similar to Case Management. In both instances, something is not working correctly and it's up to you to get it corrected. Sugar's Case Management module is fairly generic and can be used with a wide variety of goods and services. Comparatively, you'll probably want to use the Bug Tracking module specifically for software-related problems because bugs are generally tied to a specific release version of your software. In fact, if you're a software developer, you'll probably find that the folks in your Q&A department will love the Bug Tracker because it will allow them to easily identify software defects — and hopefully get the bugs corrected in the next release of the software.

Waiter! There's a bug in my software!

Sugar's Bug Tracker module allows you to report, track, and manage product bugs. After you create a bug, you can associate it with a related Cases record. Alternatively, you can create a bug directly from a Cases record.

The first step in fixing bugs is to *report* them. When you report a bug, you are in essence identifying it for all to see. Here's how it's done:

1. **Click Bug Tracker on the Module Tab bar on Sugar's Home page.**

   The Bugs Tracker Home page opens.

2. **Choose Report Bug from the Shortcuts menu.**

   The Bugs page opens, as shown in Figure 11-1.

3. **Enter information for the bug fields:**

   Subject is the only mandatory field. However, the more information you add, the more helpful it will be toward resolving a problem.

   - *Number:* No worries, here. Sugar fills in the number automatically.
   - *Priority:* Specify the urgency of the problem from the drop-down list.
   - *Type:* Choose the type of problem you're dealing with from the drop-down list.

     The administrator can make changes to the drop-down lists to give you choices that better fit your needs. Not sure how to get that done? Hand him a nice bribe — and direct him to Chapter 15.

   - *Source:* Bugs reporting can come from a variety of places — internally from your own staff or externally from your customers.

Figure 11-1:
Helping to
stamp out
bugs.

- *Category:* Select the portion of your product associated with the bug. For example, the bug might deal with e-mailing, printing, or saving.

- *Found in Release:* Bugs are often fixed in later releases so it's important to know what version a user is using when they report a bug.

  Along with a corner office and large salary, the administrator is the person responsible for making sure that all your software versions are listed here.

- *Subject:* Enter a brief statement of the problem.

- *Assigned To:* Click the Select button to select the name of the lucky individual who's responsible for fixing the bug. By default, that lucky person is you.

- *Status:* Indicate whether the bug is New, Fixed, or Mind-Boggling from the drop-down list.

- *Resolution:* Select the resolution to the bug, such as Fixed in Later Version, or Not Able to Replicate.

- *Fixed in Release:* Indicate the product version in which the bug was fixed.

- *Description:* Here's where you can expand on the subject if you need to describe the bug with a bit more detail.

- *Work Log:* Use this field to record the steps you've taken to try to stamp out the bug.

4. Click Save to report the bug.

The Bug Detail view displays on the screen.

It's a case of too many bugs

While Sugar can't help you to fix the bugs in your software, it can help you keep them organized so that eventually you'll have enough information to stamp them out. The Bug Tracker Home page is a great place to keep track of your bugs. On this page, you can create a new bug, view the details of a bug by clicking its subject, or edit an existing bug by clicking the Edit (pencil) icon.

The Bug Detail view, shown in Figure 11-2, is the hub of the Bug Tracker.

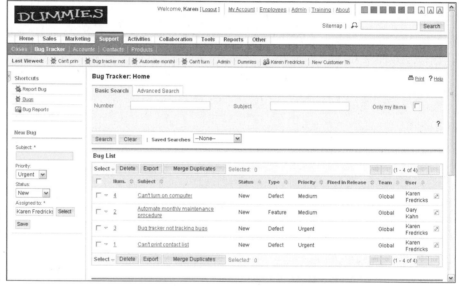

Figure 11-2:
The Bug Detail view.

As is the case with all the other record types, the Bug Detail view contains many subpanels. You can use the Activities subpanel to schedule a task, meeting, or call, or to compose an e-mail. The Contacts and Accounts subpanels give you the opportunity to associate the bug with one of your Contacts or Accounts records.

The Cases subpanel is the one that you'll probably find to be the most helpful. By associating existing Cases records to a bug, you can get a feel for how prevalent the bug is — or in what situations it's likely to appear.

So far, you've read how to report a bug. If you have the Professional version of Sugar, you can also create and run a bug report. Chapter 14 shows you how to create reports; any reports that are based on the Bug Tracker module will automatically appear when you click the Bug Reports shortcut on the Bug Tracker Home page.

Focusing on Forums

A *forum* is an online discussion group. Sometimes called *newsgroups,* forums allow participants with common interests to exchange ideas. Forums are typically based on a topic that is of interest to most members of the group. The group members then post *threads* or messages to the forum. Sugar's Forum module is a great way to allow your users to collaborate on a variety of topics, such as bugs, sales, and marketing — and find out what the members of your staff are thinking.

The Forums module is not a core Sugar module. The administrator must download from it from SugarExchange using the Module Loader.

In case you've never visited a forum, I want to give you a bit of an idea about how they work. A database administrator — or the big kahuna — decides that he'd like to have an online area to discuss ideas. He starts the forum by creating several generic topics. For example, a company that manufactures software might have one topic pertaining to sales and another pertaining to software bugs. After the topics are established, end-users post forums to the topics, such as "anyone encountering a printing bug" or "tips for increasing end of the month sales." At that point, other users post *threads,* or comments, pertaining to the forums. Generally, several forums are going on at one time; moreover, forums eventually die out and new ones constantly spring up to take their place.

Creating a forum one topic at a time

The first step to creating a forum is to find a good topic. After you create a forum, members post threads of discussion. Over time, you'll find that some of your topics invoke a lot of response whereas other topics don't receive any at all.

Creating topics is a job for the administrator of the database — if that's not a part of your job description, then feel free to skip this section.

1. **Click the Admin link on the Sugar Home page.**

   The Forums Home page opens.

2. **Click Forum Topics in the Forum Topics subpanel.**

   The Forum Topic Home page opens.

3. **Click the Create button.**

   The Forum Topics Home page expands. If you've been following along at home, you should see a page similar to the one shown in Figure 11-3.

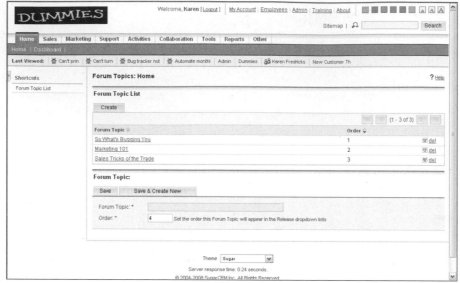

Figure 11-3:
The Forum
Topics
Home page.

4. **Enter Forum Topic title.**

   You want to create topics that are of general interest to your group that will elicit conversation.

5. **(Optional) Add an Order number.**

   If you don't supply a number, Sugar will assign the topic the next available one.

6. **Click Save to save the topic.**

Creating a forum

After the administrator creates some topics, it's time for the users to start creating forums by posting to the topics. Hopefully, after a user creates a forum, other users will chime in and start responding to the forum — or create new forums of their own.

1. **Click Forums on the Module Tab bar on the Sugar Home page.**

   The Forums Home page opens.

2. **Choose Create Forum from the Shortcuts menu on the Forums Home page.**

   The Forums form opens, as shown in Figure 11-4.

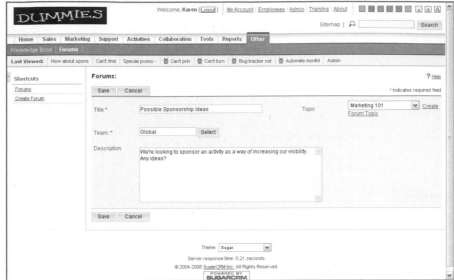

Figure 11-4:
Creating a
forum.

3. **Enter information into the following fields:**

- *Title (required):* Enter a name for the forum.

- *Team (required):* Click Select to select the team that has permission to view the forum.

- *Topic:* Specify a topic from the drop-down list; the list of topics was created by the administrator in the previous section.

- *Description:* Enter a brief description of the forum. Very often, this will be a problem you want some help with, or some cool trick you just discovered.

4. **Click Save to save the forum.**

The new forum is now listed on the Forums Home page under the topic name.

Threading your way through the forums

Now that you've decided on the topics and users have started to create forums, it's time for the real fun to start. Here's where users can post follow-up messages, or *threads.* Here's how to create a thread:

1. **Click Forums on the Module Tab bar on the Sugar Home page.**

   The Forums Home page opens, as shown in Figure 11-5.

2. **Click the title of the forum you want to respond to.**

   The Forums Detail view opens.

3. **Click the Create New Thread button.**

   The Threads page opens.

4. **Enter the thread information.**

   - *Title:* Enter a topic title for the thread.

   - *Sticky:* Select this check box to keep this thread at the top of the Thread List. When there are multiple stickies, the system lists the latest one at the top of the Thread List, followed by the others.

   - *Body:* Here's where you get to give your two cents worth. And those two cents can be formatted using the tools available on the Threads page.

5. **Click Save to save the thread.**

   The thread is now listed in the Threads List on the Forums Detail view.

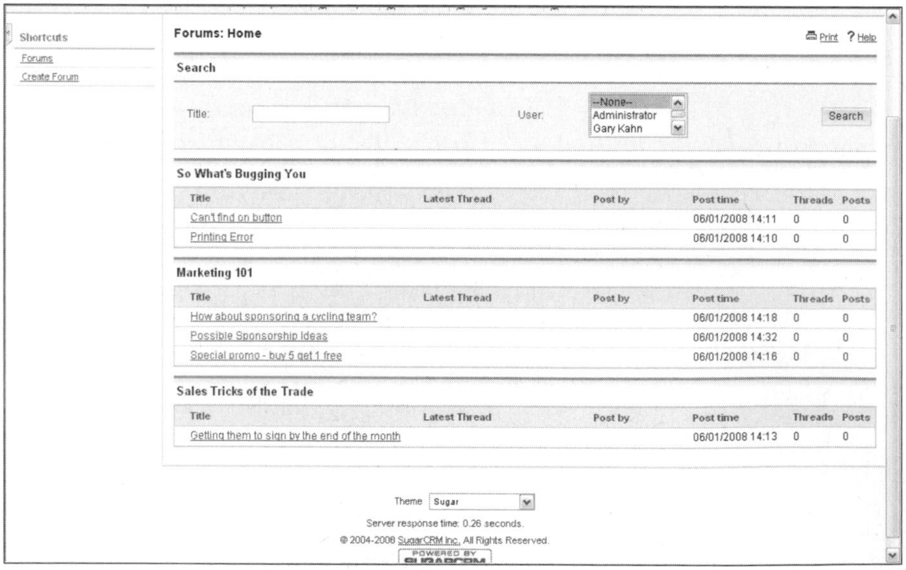

Figure 11-5:
The Forums
Home page.

Part IV
Sharing the Sugar Bowl

The 5th Wave   By Rich Tennant

"For 30 years I've put a hat and coat on to make sales calls and I'm not changing now just because I'm doing it on the Web in my living room."

In this part . . .

*E*very CRM product worth its sugar, er, salt has a way of managing e-mail, and Sugar is no exception. In this part, you discover how to send e-mail using e-mail templates — and earmark the important e-mail messages that you receive. Feel free to kick up your marketing efforts a notch by creating a full-scale marketing campaign — and tracking its progress. And, although they say you can't take it with you, you find out how to do just that by accessing Sugar from your PDA or by having an offline version.

Chapter 12

Adding Sugar to Your E-mail

• •

• •

*I*n this chapter, I show you how to configure Sugar so that you can send e-mail to an individual contact in your database, or to a selected group of contacts as part of a campaign. You also discover how easy it is to create e-mail templates to make your life even sweeter.

Getting Started with Sugar E-mail

An e-mail system consists of two separate but equal components: sending e-mail and receiving e-mail. Prior to sending e-mail from Sugar, you'll need to set up at least one outgoing e-mail account. However, with incoming e-mail, you have a few more options available to you:

⌐ **Continue to use your existing e-mail client.**

⌐ **Configure Sugar's e-mail module.**

⌐ **Use a plug-in to integrate Sugar and your existing e-mail client.**

You must configure the following areas in order to use any of Sugar's e-mail capabilities:

⌐ **Mail accounts:** You must set up at least one e-mail account in Sugar to be able to send e-mail. Additionally, you need to set up an e-mail account for every external e-mail account that you want to access through Sugar.

⌐ **General settings:** These are your e-mail preferences, such as your page layout. General settings apply to all of your e-mail accounts, but users can change these default settings.

⌐ **Folders:** You can create folders to help keep your incoming e-mail organized.

Setting up outbound e-mail accounts

The administrator must create an e-mail account in order to send e-mail. The first — and most important — e-mail account is one that will allow you to send e-mail from Sugar. After all, you can continue to use your existing e-mail client to *receive* mail, but you'll need to use Sugar if you plan to do cool things like e-mailing contracts, quotes, or campaigns.

Here's how you create an e-mail account in Sugar for outbound e-mail:

1. **Click the Admin link from any Sugar page and then click E-mail Settings in the E-mail subpanel.**

   The E-mail Settings Configure page opens, as shown in Figure 12-1.

2. **Enter information for the following fields:**

   - *From Name:* Enter a name to identify this e-mail account.

   - *From Address:* Enter the e-mail address associated with this account.

   - *SMTP Server:* Enter the outgoing (SMTP) server's address.

   - *SMTP Port:* Enter the e-mail server's port number; generally, it's 25.

   The e-mail procedure explained in this section applies to SMTP e-mail. The instructions will vary slightly if you are using a different e-mail system.

3. **(Optional) Add additional settings if your provider requires additional security settings.**

   Some providers require SSL or SMTP authentication; feel free to add them if needed.

4. **Click Save to save your settings.**

   You're now ready to start sending e-mail.

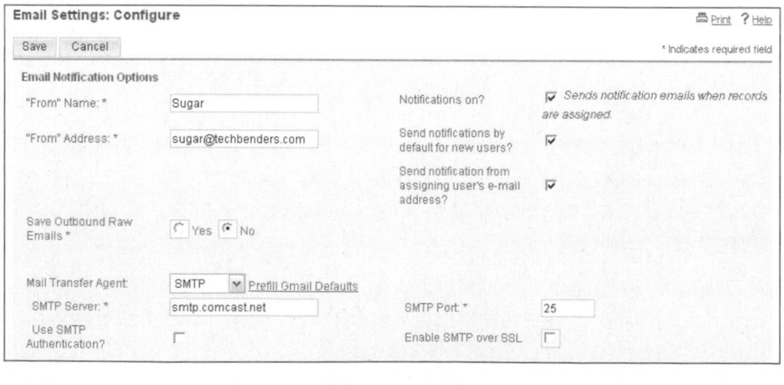

Figure 12-1: Configuring your outbound e-mail.

Email Settings: Configure				🖨 Print ❓ Help
Save Cancel				* Indicates required field
Email Notification Options				
"From" Name: *	Sugar	Notifications on?	☑	*Sends notification emails when records are assigned.*
"From" Address: *	sugar@techbenders.com	Send notifications by default for new users?	☑	
		Send notification from assigning user's e-mail address?	☑	
Save Outbound Raw Emails *	○ Yes ⦿ No			
Mail Transfer Agent:	SMTP ▾ Prefill Gmail Defaults			
SMTP Server: *	smtp.comcast.net	SMTP Port: *	25	
Use SMTP Authentication?	☐	Enable SMTP over SSL	☐	

Setting up inbound e-mail accounts

After you set up at least one outbound e-mail account, you're ready to create a few inbound e-mail accounts. Inbound e-mail accounts can be accessed by a specific user or a group of users; therefore, you can set up *group* mail accounts to handle e-mail that is more general and *individual* e-mail accounts for specific usage by a single user. As a user, you can subscribe to group e-mail accounts that your administrator has created. For example, you and several other people might have access to the info@yourcompany.com mail account.

Follow these steps to configure your incoming group e-mail accounts:

1. **Click the Admin link from any Sugar page and then click Inbound E-mail in the E-mail subpanel.**

   The Inbound E-mail Home page opens.

2. **Choose Monitor New Mail Account from the Shortcuts menu.**

   The Inbound E-mail Setup window shown in Figure 12-2 opens.

3. **Fill in the Basic Setup information for the incoming e-mail.** Your system administrator or your Internet service provider (ISP) will provide most of this information to you.

   • *Name:* Enter a name for the e-mail account.

   • *User Name:* Enter the username you need to access your e-mail.

   • *Mail Server Address:* Give the address of the incoming e-mail server.

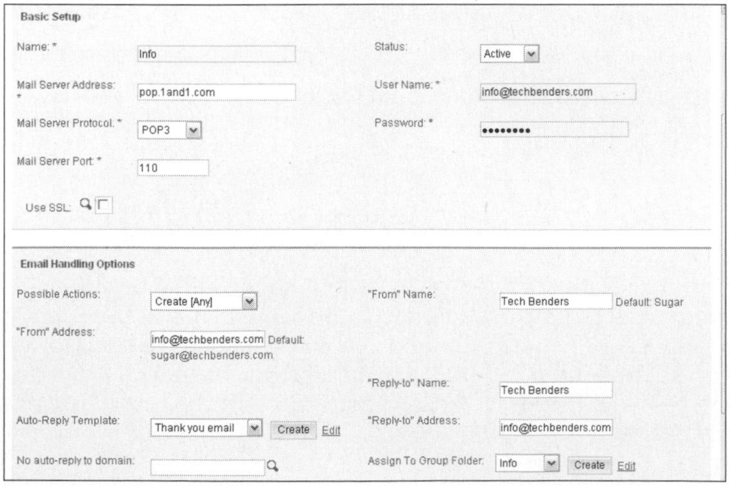

Figure 12-2:
Configuring the incoming e-mail account.

- • *Mail Server Protocol:* Choose either IMAP (normally used with an online e-mail client, such as Google or Yahoo!) or POP3 from the drop-down list.

- • *Password:* Enter your e-mail password.

- • *Mail Server Port:* The system automatically populates this field with the port number for the selected protocol.

- • *Use SSL:* Select this box if your external e-mail account requires SSL.

4. **Fill in the E-mail Handling Options section.**

   - • *Possible Actions:* Specify the action that the individual or team is permitted to perform from the drop-down list. For example, e-mails to this address can be used to create a lead or for bug handling.

   - • *From Name:* Fill in your name or the name of the group handling the e-mail.

   - • *From Address:* Provide your e-mail address.

   - • *Reply-to Name:* Enter the name that will be associated with reply e-mails.

   - • *Reply-to Address:* Enter the e-mail address that will be associated with reply e-mails.

   - • *Auto-Reply Template:* Choose an existing e-mail template from the drop-down list if you want an automatic response sent to any e-mails that arrive at this e-mail account.

   - • *No Auto-Reply to Domain:* You can include a domain name that should not receive the automatic response e-mails.

   - • *Assign To Group Folder:* Choose a group folder from the drop-down list, or click Create to create a new one. Adding a group folder will allow several people to access the group e-mail account.

5. **Click Save to save your changes.**

Working with the Emails Module

The administrator has the job of setting up the initial outbound e-mail account and the group inbound e-mail accounts for all the users. He'll most probably set up generic inbound accounts that will be used for general purposes, such as information, customer service, or technical support. At that point, he can bid adieu to e-mail setup and turn the rest of the project over to the end-users.

If you're a Sugar end-user, this section is for you because you're going to setup your personal incoming e-mail account — unless Mr. Administrator responds well to bribes — and tweak your e-mail preferences.

If you are using your own e-mail client, such as Outlook — or you have purchased a link between your e-mail client and Sugar — feel free to skip this section.

You begin your voyage into Sugar's Emails module by clicking Emails on the Module Tab bar. The Sugar Emails page shown in Figure 12-3 opens.

To understand the e-mail portion of SugarCRM fully, you must understand the concept of the e-mail client. An *e-mail client* is an `application` that runs on a `personal computer` or `workstation` and enables you to send, receive, and organize `e-mail`. Sugar's Emails module provides you with the following functionality:

- ✔ **Access e-mail without downloading them into your Sugar database.**

- ✔ **Import incoming e-mail into Sugar to the** *My E-mail* **folder.** Once imported, you can associate an imported e-mail with a Sugar record, such as a Bugs or an Accounts record.

- ✔ **Archive outgoing e-mail that you sent to Sugar.** For example, you might send an e-mail from Outlook and then use the Sugar Outlook Plug-in to create an e-mail record in Sugar.

- ✔ **Search for e-mail based on various criteria, such as keyword and subject.**

- ✔ **Create a related record, such as a Bugs or a Leads record, from an e-mail message.**

- ✔ **Create an address book of the users, contacts, and leads to whom you often send e-mail.**

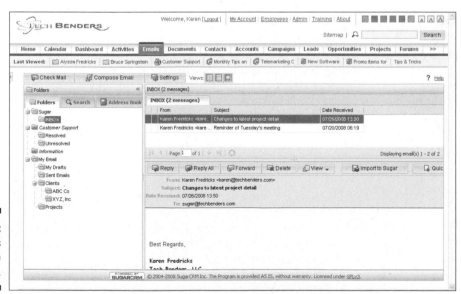

Figure 12-3:
The Emails module Home page.

The Check Email, Compose Email, and Settings options appear at the top of the page. The remainder of the Emails module Home page is divided into three panels: Shortcuts, Folders, and Inbox. The Folders panel includes the Folders tab, the Search tab, and the Address Book tab; you might want to flip to the Search tab to hunt down an old e-mail that you're having trouble locating (see Figure 12-4), or access the Address Book tab to find someone's e-mail address.

Figure 12-4:
Searching
for a lost
e-mail
message.

Any incoming e-mail accounts that your administrator has set up for you appear at the top of the Folders window along with an Inbox subfolder. Once received, you can organize your e-mail into folders that you create in the My Email folder.

You'll find three Views icons at the top of the Inbox panel, which unfortunately aren't labeled. The first icon displays a list of the messages in your Inbox. The second shows a list of your e-mail messages in the top panel and the contents of the currently selected message in the bottom panel. The third icon seems to display exactly the same view as the second icon; however, the e-mail viewing area is increased by removing access to the other Sugar module tabs.

Setting up inbound e-mail accounts: Part 2

Earlier in this chapter, you find that the administrator can set up an outgoing e-mail account and optionally configure incoming accounts as well. For those of you who don't have a nice administrator to do this work for you — or if you have numerous e-mail accounts that you monitor — you can set up additional accounts through the Emails module's Settings tab.

You must set up an e-mail account in Sugar for every external e-mail account that you want to access through Sugar. Sugar automatically creates an Inbox folder for every e-mail account that you configure. Additionally, you can create subfolders under that Inbox to help keep yourself — and your e-mail — organized.

To set up an e-mail account, follow these steps:

1. **Click the Emails module tab and then click the Settings tab.**

   The Emails Settings window opens.

2. **Click the Mail Accounts tab.**

   If you've been following along at home, the Mail Accounts tab should look like the window shown in Figure 12-5.

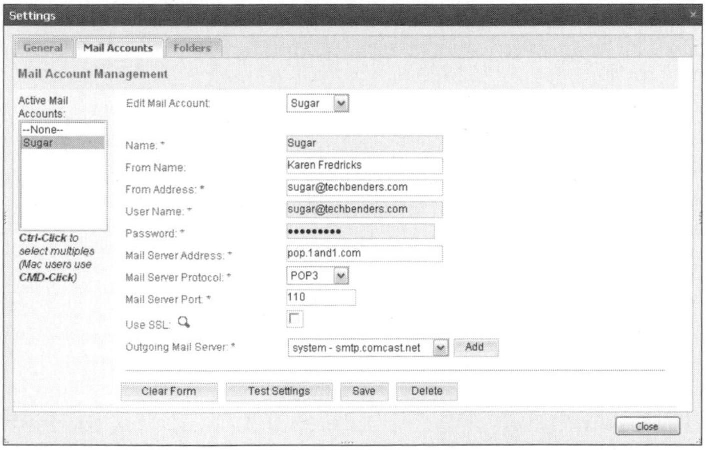

Figure 12-5: Configuring a personal incoming e-mail account.

3. **Choose None from the Active Mail Accounts field.**

   Alternatively, if you need to edit an existing incoming e-mail account, choose the name of the account from the drop-down list.

4. **Enter a name for the account in the Name field.**

   You'll probably want the name of the account to coincide with the name of the e-mail account that you are receiving, so name it something like Info or Tech Support — or your name.

5. **Enter information into the following fields:**

   • *From Name:* Your name.

   • *From Address (required):* The e-mail address that will be used on any outgoing correspondence.

- *User Name (required):* Your e-mail username for the account.

- *Password (required):* Your password for the account.

- *Mail Server Address, Mail Server Protocol,* and *Mail Server Port (all required):* Your ISP will provide the mail server address, protocol, and port number.

6. **Choose the Outgoing Mail Server from the drop-down list.**

   Specify the default e-mail server for your company from the drop-down list, or add a new one by clicking the Add button and filling in the appropriate SMTP information given to you by your ISP.

7. **Click the Test Settings button to ensure that all your settings are correct.**

   A little window will pop open requesting that you cool your jets while Sugar verifies your information. If all entries are correct, you're rewarded with a message telling you that your setup is correct.

8. **Click Save to create the e-mail account.**

   Sugar creates the e-mail account — and collects any e-mail waiting to be delivered.

9. **Click Close to return to the Emails module Home page.**

Personalizing your e-mail

You can set a number of e-mail preferences. These preferences include how you view your incoming e-mail and how others view e-mails you send.

1. **Click Emails on the Module Tab bar and then click the Settings tab.**

   The Emails Settings window opens.

2. **Click the General tab.**

   The Settings window opens, as shown in Figure 12-6.

3. **Configure your e-mail Preferences.**

   - *Check for New Mail:* Determines how often you want Sugar to check for incoming e-mail.

   - *Send Email as Plain Text:* Select this check box to send e-mails in plain-text format rather than as HTML.

   - *Copy to Sent Email:* Select this check box to store a copy of your outbound e-mail in the Sugar database.

   - *Signatures:* Click Create, enter your full name, and format your signature as HTML or plain text.

- *Character Set:* Here's where you can indicate a character set other than Western European if you are composing in a language that contains cool-looking characters and accent marks.

- *Signature Above Reply:* Select this check box to place your signature in your e-mail responses.

4. Configure your e-mail Visual Settings.

- *Layout Style:* You can view your e-mail in a two- or three-column format.

- *Place Tabs at Bottom:* Select this check box to display the tabs at the bottom of the page rather than at the top.

- *Number of Emails per Page:* Indicate how many e-mails you want to view per page in the Sugar Inbox.

- *Full Screen:* Select this check box for a full-screen display of the Emails page.

5. Click Save to save your preferences.

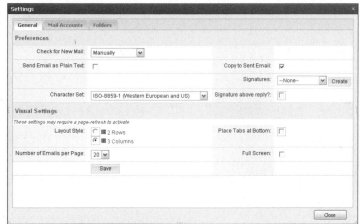

Figure 12-6:
Changing your e-mail preferences.

Filing e-mail in e-mail folders

In Sugar, the two types of e-mail folders are

- ✔ **Local folders:** Folders created by individual users to group and organize their own specific e-mail.

- ✔ **Group folders:** Folders set up by the administrator to organize incoming e-mail that is more department-specific.

In the earlier "Setting up inbound e-mail accounts" section, you saw how the administrator could set up group e-mail folders when he configured the group incoming e-mail addresses. In this section, you discover how to use the group folders — and make a few folders of your own.

Creating local folders

You create local folders directly on the Emails module Home page. The first time you access the Emails module, you'll notice several folders that Sugar automatically configured for you:

- ✔ **An Inbox for each of your personal e-mail accounts.** Mail in this folder is not stored in the Sugar database.

- ✔ **Group folders that the administrator has created.** Group folders are identified by an icon of three little people.

- ✔ **The My Email folder, which holds e-mail that is stored in the Sugar database.**

    The My Email folder is divided into two subfolders:

    - *My Drafts, which holds e-mail you've written but not sent.*

    - *Sent Emails, which is the folder that holds all your sent e-mail.*

You can create additional folders under the My Email folder to organize the e-mail that comes into your own specific account. You can also create subfolders under your group folders to help organize your departmental e-mail.

To create additional folders:

1. **Right-click the My Email folder on the Emails Home page and select Create Folder.**

    The Add New Folder dialog box displays.

2. **Enter a name for the folder and click OK.**

3. **(Optional) Right-click the new folder to create a subfolder, enter a name for the subfolder, and then click OK.**

You follow the exact same procedure to create a subfolder under a group folder. Refer to Figure 12-3 to get an idea of a typical folder structure.

Choosing your folders

Users have the option of determining which folders they would like to access. It's easy to decide which group folders you have access to — and which ones you want to access — by following these steps:

1. **Click the Emails module tab from any Sugar window and then select the Settings tab.**

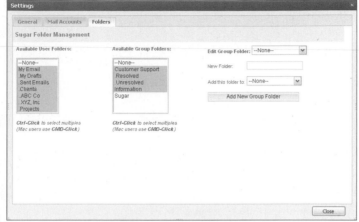

Figure 12-7:
Deciding
which folder
you want to
access.

2. **Select the Folders tab from the Settings window.**

   The Folders window opens, as shown in Figure 12-7.

3. **Make the desired folder changes.**

   • *To select your personal folders:* Hold down your Ctrl key and click the desired folders in the Available User Folders panel.

   • *To select group folders:* Hold down your Ctrl key and click the desired folders in the Available Group Folders panel.

   • *To rename a folder:* Select a folder name from the Edit Group Folder drop-down, modify the name in the New Folder field, and click save.

   Wondering how to rename local folders? Don't let the name Edit Group Folder fool you because all your folders are listed there and can be renamed.

   • *To create a new group folder:* Type a name in the New Folder field and then click the Add New Group Folder button.

4. **Click Close to save your changes.**

   Don't panic if you don't immediately see your new folders. They will magically appear the next time your browser refreshes.

Creating an Address Book

In the upcoming sections are a number of ways to generate outgoing e-mail in Sugar. One way is to use entries in Sugar's Address Book.

TIP

If you generate your e-mail using one of the other methods — or are using a plug-in to connect Sugar to your existing e-mail client — you can skip this section.

The idea here is to add the people you frequently e-mail to the Address Book. The benefit of the Address Book is that Address Book contacts will auto-populate when you type the first couple of letters of a recipient's name into a blank e-mail message.

Here's how to add entries to the e-mail Address Book:

1. **Click the Emails module tab from any Sugar window and then select the Address Book tab from the left panel of the Emails Home page.**

   You can see what the Address Book looks like in Figure 12-8.

2. **Click the Add Entries button.**

   The Select Address Book Entries window opens.

3. **Fill in the name of the person who you want to add to the Address Book and then click the Search button.**

   Although the Address Book is separate from the other modules, a person must already exist in a Contacts, Leads, Targets, or Users module in order to be added to the Address Book.

4. **Select the e-mail address of the person you want to add to the Address Book and then click Add.**

   Figure 12-9 shows you what the process looks like.

5. **Repeat Steps 3 and 4 if you want to add more names to the Address Book and then click Close.**

   The new entries appear in your Address Book.

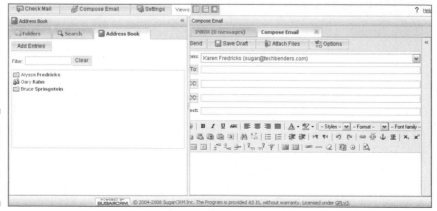

Figure 12-8:
Sugar's
e-mail
Address
Book.

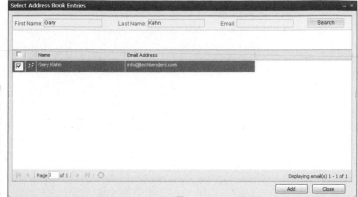

Figure 12-9:
Adding new
names to
the e-mail
Address
Book.

Creating E-mail Templates

Before you can win friends and influence prospects with your dazzling display of personalized e-mail documents, you need two things: the data and the
document template.

You're creating a *template,* not a *document.* A document is a plain old file that
you create, use once, and store for posterity. A template is a form that merges
with your contact information that is used over and over again.

A template is a form that contains placeholders that are filled with information from your database. Using Sugar to create e-mail templates enables you
to send personalized e-mail to each recipient. For example, you routinely
might want to send thank-you e-mails to your contacts and not have to reinvent the wheel each time.

You can create a template by following these steps:

1. **Click the Emails module tab from any Sugar window and then select
   the Create Email Template from the Shortcuts menu.**

   The Email Templates page (see Figure 12-10) opens.

2. **Give the template a name and optional description.**

   After all, if you go to all the effort of creating a template, you may as well
   be able to find it again!

3. **Supply a subject line and start filling in your message.**

   Nothing new under the sun here. The template editor includes all the standard formatting options, such as font, size, bold, and italics. For your added fun and enjoyment, you can also embed images and add URL links.

4. **Click the spot in your document where you want to insert a field.**

   You need to let Sugar know where you want to insert your data place-holders.

5. **Determine what type of field you want to insert into your template from the Insert Variable drop-down list.**

   Basically, you can insert either Account fields, or fields from your Contacts, Leads, Targets, and Users records.

6. **Select a field and then click Insert.**

   Your field choices will change depending on your variable type. Sugar will display the official field name and then place it into your template.

7. **Click Save to create the template.**

   You can use the template whenever you send an outgoing e-mail — and use it in your marketing campaigns.

The template editor

Figure 12-10:
Creating an
e-mail
template.

E-mailing Your Contacts

A benefit of sending e-mail from within SugarCRM is that a history of the event is added to your Contacts record's History subpanel each time you send an e-mail. E-mail is an increasingly popular form of communication, so having a record of all the e-mail that you send to each of your contacts helps you keep track of it all.

You can send e-mails to users, contacts, leads, and anyone else for whom you have an e-mail address. When you compose an e-mail, you can choose to send it using any of the e-mail accounts that you have configured. You can create your message from scratch using the e-mail editor, or you can use a pre-designed template.

Follow these steps to send an e-mail in Sugar:

1. **Create a new e-mail message using one of the following methods:**

   • *Click the contact's e-mail address in either the List or page Detail view.*

   • *Add the contact's e-mail address to the Address Book, click Compose Email in the Emails module, and have the address auto-populate in the To field.*

   • *Click Compose Email in the Emails module and manually fill in the e-mail address.*

   These methods all result in a new message (see Figure 12-11). Notice that if you used either of the first two methods, the contact's name already appears in the To field.

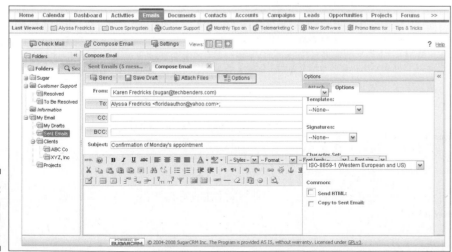

Figure 12-11:
Creating an
e-mail
message.

2. Choose an e-mail account from the From drop-down list if you created more than one e-mail account in Sugar.

3. (Optional) Add the names of additional individuals who will receive a copy of the e-mail.

4. Fill in the Subject field.

5. Create your message using one of the following methods:

    • *Enter the text in the body field.*

    • *Click Options and choose a template from the Templates drop-down list. While you're there, you might want to choose a signature from the Signatures drop-down list.*

6. (Optional) Click the Attach Files button to attach a file to the e-mail.

    The Attach options page appears in the right panel. Click Add File from File System to attach a file located on your computer, or click **Add Documents from Sugar Documents** to attach a file that's been saved to Sugar.

7. Click Send to send the e-mail or click Save Draft to save the e-mail as a draft.

    Off your e-mail goes, hurtling through cyberspace. You can see the message in the Sent Emails folder or by looking at the History subpanel of the Contacts record's Detail view.

Viewing and Managing E-mails

Sugar makes a distinction between incoming e-mail and incoming e-mail that is actually imported into the Sugar database. The distinction is even clearer when looking at the e-mail folders. The top set of folders contains the e-mail accounts that you've set up in Sugar; each account has a single Inbox. However, any e-mails that appear in the group or the My Email folders are e-mails that have been imported into Sugar. When a new e-mail message arrives, you have the option of either leaving it in the Inbox or importing it to Sugar.

Importing an e-mail message to Sugar

After you view an e-mail in the Sugar Inbox — and decide it's a keeper — follow these instructions to import it to your Sugar database:

1. **Check for new e-mail by clicking the Check Mail button in the Emails module.**

   Any new messages that arrive on the scene will appear in your Sugar Inbox. Alternatively, you can review the earlier "Personalizing your e-mail" section and request that Sugar automatically check for e-mail at regular intervals.

2. **Right-click the message you want to import to Sugar and choose Import to Sugar from the contextual menu.**

   The Import Settings window opens (see Figure 12-12).

Figure 12-12:
Importing an
e-mail into
Sugar.

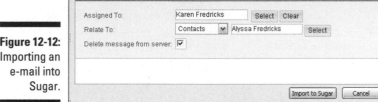

3. **(Optional) Assign the e-mail to another user.**

   By default, the e-mail is already assigned to you.

4. **Choose a record type from the Relate To drop-down list.**

   You can associate an e-mail with virtually any type of Sugar record, including Contacts, Accounts, Opportunities, or Bugs.

5. **Fill the name of the record that you want to link to the e-mail.**

   Alternatively, you can click the Select button and browse to the name.

6. **(Optional) Select the Delete Message from Server check box if you also want to delete the message from the external e-mail server and the Inbox.**

7. **Click the Import to Sugar button.**

   The imported e-mail will now appear in the My Email folder. From there you can drag it to one of your subfolders if you want. It will also appear in the History subpanel on the related record's Detail view. Once you place an e-mail on the History subpanel, any other Sugar users with access to that record will also have privy to the e-mail message.

Creating a record from an e-mail

In the above section, you take an incoming e-mail message and quickly associate it with an existing record. That method works great if the record already exists in Sugar, but how about times when you receive e-mail from a perfect stranger? And, more importantly, you want to archive that message as well.

One of the nicest features about Sugar is that it is just so darn accommodating — and tries to fulfill your every wish. Here's how you can create a new record on the fly from an incoming e-mail:

1. **In the Emails module, open the e-mail you want to associate with a new record.**

2. **Click Quick Create and choose Bugs, Cases, Contacts, Leads, or Tasks from the drop-down menu.**

   The appropriate Quick Create form displays. Figure 12-13 shows you what the new Contact form looks like.

3. **Fill in as much information as you can.**

   Sugar helps you a bit here by filling in the contact's name and e-mail address if the sender has included them in the header of the e-mail.

4. **Click Save to save the new record.**

   Like magic, the e-mail message will attach to Sugar and appear in the My Email folder. Better yet, you'll have a new record in your database — the e-mail message is accessible from the History subpanel.

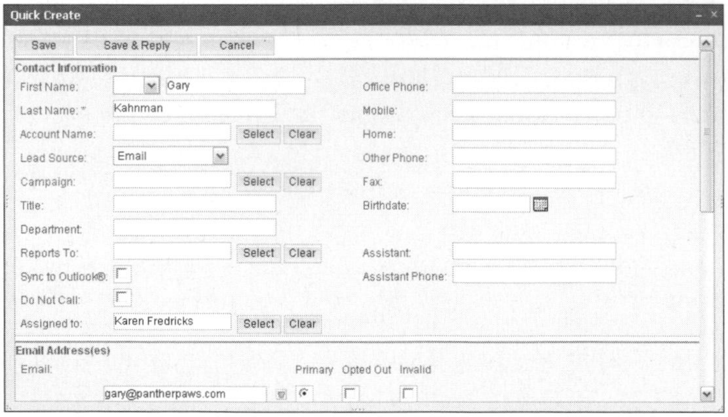

Figure 12-13:
Creating a new record from an incoming e-mail.

Working with group folders

You may have discovered numerous features in Sugar that help it live up to its CRM moniker. And, hopefully, you realize that Sugar can automate many of your routine business processes. For many of you, the group folders feature will be the proverbial icing on the Sugar cake.

Group folders are those folders that the administrator sets up to help process e-mail accounts that might be accessed by a department rather than by a specific individual. For example, most companies have an *info* e-mail account that might receive hundreds of e-mails a day. Thankfully, Sugar can make mincemeat of that large load if you follow these steps:

1. **Select a group folder from the Folders list on the Emails module Home page.**

   Any e-mails in the group folder display in the right panel.

2. **Select the message(s) you want to process, right-click the message(s), and choose Assign To from the contextual menu.**

   The cool thing here is that you can process more than one message at a time. Hold down the CTRL key and select as many messages as you need.

3. **Click the Users icon in the Assignment window.**

   Figure 12-14 shows the Assignment window.

   You can select a single person to assign the e-mail to, pick specific users, or assign it to everyone in the group.

4. **Choose a rule from the Rules drop-down list.**

   You have a few choices here:

   - *Direct Assign:* Assigns the e-mail to the specific user you selected.

   - *Round Robin:* Distributes the e-mails evenly between the selected users.

   - *Least Busy:* Assigns the e-mails to the user who has the shortest list of assigned e-mails.

5. **Click Assign.**

   Poof. The e-mail disappears from the group folder and magically reappears in the My Email folder of the assigned user(s). Talk about magic!

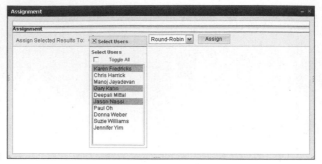

Figure 12-14:
Assigning
group
e-mails to
staff mem-
bers.

Changing Your Outlook on Sugar

Some Sugar users find themselves needing to use Outlook for a variety of reasons. For instance, your company might use Outlook to maintain the company calendar. Fortunately, you can use both Outlook and SugarCRM if you install the Sugar plug-in for Microsoft Outlook.

The plug-in is included with both the Professional and Enterprise versions of Sugar. If you're using the Community Edition, you can subscribe to it on a yearly basis.

If you are using the Sugar plug-in for Microsoft Outlook, you can synchronize your Outlook e-mail, contacts, calendar, and tasks to Sugar directly from Outlook. Synchronized e-mails will land in the My Email folder, tasks and appointments will land in your calendar, and your contacts will transform into Sugar accounts or contacts. Additionally, you can attach your Outlook e-mail to various record types, such as Accounts, Opportunities, or Bugs.

After you install the Sugar plug-in for Microsoft Outlook, you notice a Sugar toolbar in Outlook, as shown in Figure 12-15.

The SurgarCRM toolbar

Figure 12-15:
The
SugarCRM
toolbar that
appears in
Outlook.

The toolbar changes slightly when you wander into different areas of Sugar.

After you install the Outlook plug-in, you can change various Sugar options by accessing Tools⇨Sugar Options in Outlook. Here's where you'll enter your Sugar username, password, and the URL you use to access your Sugar database.

Archiving e-mail

The Sugar plug-in for Microsoft Outlook provides a quick way to attach an e-mail to a Sugar record. You can attach an e-mail to the following record types:

- ✔ **Accounts**
- ✔ **Contacts**
- ✔ **Leads**
- ✔ **Bugs**
- ✔ **Cases**
- ✔ **Opportunities**
- ✔ **Projects**

Once attached, the e-mail appears in the History subpanel of that record where you can click the e-mail link to view the details of the e-mail.

Archiving outgoing e-mail

The Sugar plug-in for Microsoft Outlook allows you to send an e-mail and attach it to a Sugar record in pretty much the click of a button if you follow these steps:

1. **Create a message in Outlook following your normal procedures.**

2. **Click the Send and Archive button in Outlook's message toolbar.**

    The Archiving Email window (see Figure 12-16) appears.

3. **Fill in the information about the record you're searching for.**

    By default, the e-mail address you're sending the e-mail to will already appear.

4. **Select the check box(es) for the record type(s) you're searching for and then click the Search button.**

    In the wink of an eye, Sugar finds the appropriate record(s).

Figure 12-16:
Attaching
an outgoing
message to
Sugar.

5. **(Optional) Click the Edit Email tab and change the information that will be attached to the Sugar record.**

   By default, your e-mail message will appear. However, you can add additional comments or remove extraneous information that you don't want to archive.

6. **Click Archive and then click Close.**

   The contents of your e-mail message will be attached to the appropriate Sugar record and then sent to the intended recipient.

Archiving incoming e-mail

The Sugar plug-in for Microsoft Outlook really shines when it comes to attaching incoming e-mail from Outlook to Sugar. The three methods for attaching an incoming e-mail are

- ✔ **Right-click the incoming message from Outlook's Inbox and choose the Archive to Sugar option.** As you can see in Figure 12-17, Sugar automatically identifies the sender and matches her to a record in your Sugar database. Click the sender's name, and the message is immediately attached to the record in Sugar.

- ✔ **Select the message from the Inbox and click the Archive to Sugar button on the Outlook toolbar.** This option opens the Archiving Email window (refer to Figure 12-16). By following the instructions discussed in the previous section, "Archiving outgoing e-mail," you can edit the message if necessary prior to attaching it to Sugar.

- ✔ **Open the message and click the Archive to Sugar button conveniently located in the message toolbar.** This also opens the Archiving Email window.

If Sugar can't find an appropriate matching record for an incoming message, you can create a new Sugar Contacts or Leads record by right-clicking the message and choosing one of those options. The Quick Create window (see Figure 12-18) appears, allowing you to fill in the basic record information. To speed the process even further, Sugar fills in as much information as it can garner from the header information of the incoming e-mail.

Need to attach several incoming messages from the same sender? Hold down the CTRL key, select the messages in your Inbox, right-click anywhere in the highlighted area, and select the record's name. The messages dispatch to Sugar immediately.

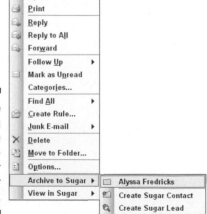

Figure 12-17: Giving a message a right-click for fast Sugar archiving.

Figure 12-18:
Quickly
adding a
new contact
record from
an incoming
e-mail.

Not sure whether you've archived a message to Sugar? There are a number of
ways to tell.

- **Right-click a message and choose Options; SugarCRM will display in
  the Categories field.**

- **The message's flag changes to red.**

- **You see the View in Sugar option when you right-click the message
  in Outlook.** Click it, and you're transported to the Details view of the
  record where you can see the e-mail in the History subpanel.

Connecting contacts to Sugar

The Sugar plug-in for Microsoft Outlook allows you to synchronize your
Outlook contacts with your Sugar records. Changes made to contacts in
either database are updated through the synchronization process.

Creating and maintaining two separate databases is very time-consuming —
and can very easily lead to unnecessary duplication.

Marking existing Outlook contacts for synchronization

Here's how you can begin the synchronization process:

1. **Navigate to the Contacts folder in Outlook and then select the contacts
   that you wish to synchronize to Sugar.**

You can hold down the CTRL key and "cherry pick" the contacts or hold down the CTRL key and tap the letter A to select all contacts.

When you first install the plug-in, none of your Outlook contacts synchronize to Sugar until you mark them for synchronization. You can double-check that an Outlook contact will synchronize to Sugar by opening the contact in Outlook where you'll see SugarCRM in the category field. In Sugar, a check mark will appear in the Sync to Outlook field on the record's Detail view.

You can't synchronize Outlook contacts that you've marked as Private.

2. **Click the Sync to Sugar button.**

   There is a moment of silence while Outlook checks your connection and sends your contacts to Sugar. If you look closely, a dialog box shows you the number of records being sent to Sugar.

   Sugar matches your Outlook and Sugar contacts based on the contact's e-mail address, first name, and last name. If no matches are found, Sugar will create a new Contacts record on the Sugar side; you'll be listed as both the creator and the person assigned to the record. Sugar will also attach the Contacts record to the appropriate Accounts record in Sugar; if it doesn't find a match, a new Accounts record will be automatically created.

   Only those Sugar Contacts records with the Sync to Outlook check box selected and Outlook contacts with SugarCRM showing in the category field will synchronize.

Working with new Outlook contacts

During the synchronization process, Sugar hunts through your database looking for Sugar records that match the information you've entered in Outlook. However, there is a little room for error. What happens if you forgot to mark an Outlook contact for synchronization? Comparatively, what if company names of two Outlook contacts are not an exact match and you end up with two separate — but equal — Accounts records in Sugar?

To avoid these unnecessary — and bothersome — problems, the Sugar plug-in for Microsoft Outlook installs a toolbar directly on the contact record's page in Outlook that allows you to do two things:

✔ **Save and Mark for Sugar Synch:** This saves you the trouble of having to go back and mark a new Outlook contact for Sugar synchronization.

✔ **Set Company to Sugar Account:** Here's where you can associate the contact with an existing Sugar Accounts record *now* to avoid duplication *later.*

Synchronizing your Outlook calendar and tasks

Attaching Outlook calendar items and tasks to Sugar uses pretty much the same methodology you use when attaching an Outlook contact to Sugar. You have the option of marking existing appointments or tasks to Sugar from an Outlook list showing those items, or you can opt to mark a new appointment or task during the creation process.

Because Outlook doesn't make a distinction between calls and meetings, the calls and meetings that you create in Sugar appear as appointments in Outlook.

To synchronize your existing Outlook appointments and tasks to Sugar:

1. **In Outlook, select the appointments or tasks that you want to synchronize to Sugar and then click the Mark to Sync button in the Outlook toolbar.**

   You can do this from just about any Sugar view. For example, hold down your CTRL key while selecting various appointments from Outlook's monthly calendar.

2. **Click Sync to Sugar in the Outlook toolbar.**

   A dialog box keeps you posted on how many activities or tasks are synching to Sugar.

To synchronize new appointments and tasks to Sugar, simply click the Save and Mark for Sugar Sync button that appears at the top of the scheduling window in Outlook. The next time you click the Sync to Sugar button, any of the changes you've made to those activities in either Outlook or Sugar will update in both programs.

Chapter 13

Campaigning Doesn't Just Occur in an Election Year

*O*n the simplest level, you can use SugarCRM as a glorified Rolodex and be quite happy with a place to find basic contact information. However, if you're at all interested in growing — or maintaining — the size of your business, you'll want to make use of the Campaigns module. You start by creating a Target List of the folks who will be the recipients of the campaign. Next, you decide exactly the type of collateral you'll be sending them. You test the campaign process — and figure out ways to measure the *ROI* (return on investment). Finally, should you find that your campaign stalls at the time of blast-off, you need a way to figure out exactly what's wrong.

Campaigns Module

Quite simply, a *campaign* is an activity — or series of activities — designed to accomplish a purpose. Just as a candidate campaigns to get elected, a sales manager campaigns to get products purchased. You measure the success of a political campaign by whether the candidate is elected; you measure the success of an advertising campaign by whether you see an increase in sales. And, to continue the analogy, should your campaign not attain the desired outcome, there's nothing to prevent you from trying again!

Typically, a mass marketing campaign *targets* a specific group of individuals or businesses. Therefore, the campaign process begins with identifying targets and grouping them into a Target List. In addition, you can associate

Contacts, Leads, and Opportunities records with an existing campaign to get a better understanding of your campaign's results. For example, you might want to know which specific Opportunities records were a direct result of a campaign.

Sugar gives you two options for creating a Campaigns record. You can find both options in the Shortcuts menu of the Campaigns module Home page:

- ✔ **Campaign Wizard:** This option steps you through the process of creating a campaign as well as all campaign-related tasks. Because so many steps are involved in creating a marketing campaign, it's probably best to complete the wizard as thoroughly as possible and then go back to add more information later.

- ✔ **Create Campaign (Classic):** This option creates a basic Campaigns record; however, you're responsible for completing the various other campaign-related tasks, such as specifying the e-mail settings all by your lonesome.

The Campaigns module is ideally suited for a variety of marketing efforts. Sugar excels with e-mail and e-newsletter campaigns; Sugar helps you by using merged documents, transmitting them to a Target List, and tracking their results. Sugar can also help automate snail-mail campaigns by merging a template with your Target List and creating labels. When you create other types of campaigns, such as radio, print ads, or telemarketing, you can't execute the campaign directly from Sugar; however, you can create a Campaigns record to help you manually track the results.

If you plan to create Campaigns records using snail mail, you need to purchase a license for the Sugar plug-in for Microsoft Word so that you can create personalized templates in Word and then merge them with your Sugar contact data. Chapter 8 shows you how to create mail merge templates.

The plug-in comes free with the Professional and Enterprise editions.

We're Off to See the Campaign Wizard

Whew! You might be thinking such a powerful feature must be confusing and complicated. Fortunately, the handy dandy Campaign Wizard guides you through the process.

Follow these steps to create a new Campaigns record using the Campaign Wizard:

1. **Click the Campaigns module tab from any Sugar window.**

   The Campaigns Home page opens.

2. Choose Campaign Wizard from the Shortcuts menu.

The Campaign Wizard displays. You'll probably find it easiest to use the wizard every time you create a new campaign, and then edit the various stages manually. And, as Figure 13-1 shows, creating a campaign involves a lot of stages.

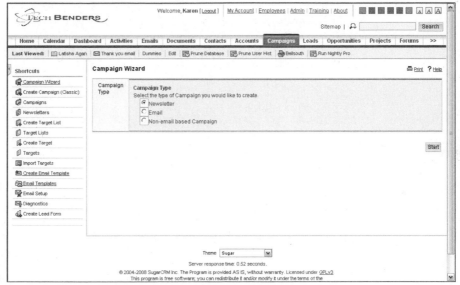

Figure 13-1: Launching the Campaign Wizard.

3. Select the type of campaign you want to create and then click Start.

The next screen of the Wizard opens; Figure 13-2 shows an example of a Newsletter campaign.

If you haven't done so already, Sugar will prompt you to set up an e-mail account to handle any potential bounced e-mails. This isn't a hard thing to do but must be performed by the database administrator; just make sure he knows the e-mail address you'll be using.

4. Enter the basic campaign information and then click Next.

You'll want to record a few minor pieces of housekeeping information:

- *Name:* Give the campaign a name.

- *Status:* Choose a status from the drop-down list to let others know how far along you are in the campaign process.

- *Assigned To:* Supply the name of the person who is in charge.

- *Frequency:* If you're creating a newsletter, you need to indicate how often you'll be sending it.

• *Start Date:* Click the calendar icon to select the campaign's start date.

• *End Date:* Click the calendar icon to select the campaign's end date.

• *Description:* Give a description of the campaign if you think it needs one.

5. (Optional) Enter the campaign budget information and then click Next.

This information is purely optional. However, if you'd like to calculate your ROI (return on investment), then you'll want to figure out your budget and how much money you hope to make from your marketing endeavor. Later, you might want to edit this information to include the actual cost of the campaign.

6. Enter the tracker URL information and then click Create Tracker.

A campaign e-mail can include text, images, and links directing your targets to other URLs. In case you wonder whether people are actually clicking the links in your e-blasts, you can set up a *tracker* URL to track the response to your campaign. The tracker URL keeps track of such information as the date, the time, and what domain the user was logged on to when she clicked the links.

Sugar can create trackers for you — as well as a specific opt-out tracker that supplies a link for anyone who wishes to opt out of your newsletter. If you choose to create an opt-out link, Sugar automatically selects the Email Opt Out option on the target's Detail view.

As you see in Figure 13-3, you just need to supply a name for the tracker and decide whether you want to have an opt-out link; Sugar does the rest of the work for you.

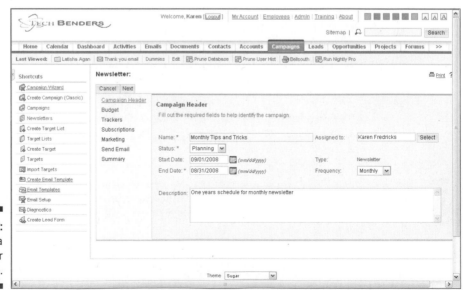

Figure 13-2:
Creating a
Newsletter
campaign.

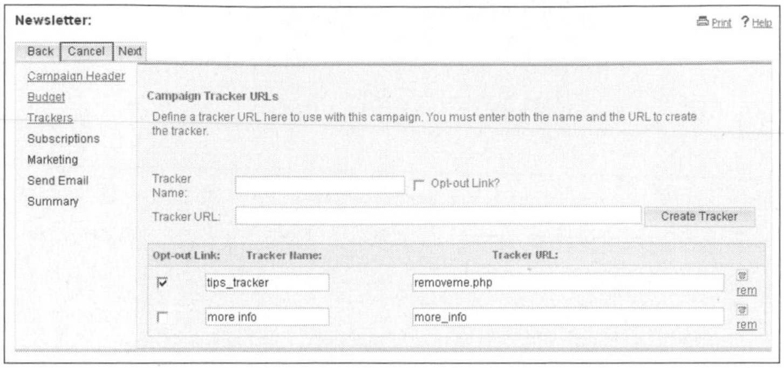

Figure 13-3:
Creating a URL tracking link is easier than you think.

If you want to create additional tracker URLs, click Create Tracker again and enter the new tracker information. Click Next when you finish adding URL trackers.

7. **Complete the Subscription Information page for your campaign.**

   The Subscription Information page of the Campaign Wizard opens. A Sugar campaign requires three lists of people, or *targets:*

   • *Subscription List Name:* These are the folks who you are either targeting for a marketing campaign or to whom you're sending a newsletter.

   • *Unsubscription List Name:* These are the people who no longer want to buy what you're selling — or at any rate, don't want to be bothered by future e-mails.

   • *Test List Name:* This list comprises all of your e-mail guinea pigs. Over the years, you've probably been the recipient of a mailing in which the sender hits the Send button a tad too early. Hopefully, by sending to a test list, you can circumvent problems now instead of later.

8. **Select your Target Lists and then click Save and Continue.**

   Click Allow Select and then click the Select button to use an existing Target List, or click Auto-Create to create a new Target List. If you choose the Auto-Create option, Sugar will suggest a snappy name for the list; you can add more names to that list later. Figure 13-4 gives you an idea of what the finished product looks like.

   You just gotta love software that unobtrusively makes life easier for you. When you choose to select an existing target list, Sugar displays just the right types. For example, if you want to select a test list, Sugar only shows you existing test target lists.

Newsletter: 🖶 Print   ? Help

Back | Cancel | Save and Continue | Finish

Campaign Header
Budget
Trackers
Subscriptions
Marketing
Send Email
Summary

Subscription Information

Each newsletter must have three target lists (Subscription, Unsubscription, and Test). You can assign an existing target list. If not, an empty target list will be created when you save the newsletter.

? Subscription List Name: ○ Auto-Create   Monthly Tips & Tricks Subscription Lis
                           ● Allow Select   [Select]

? Unsubscription List Name: ● Auto-Create   Monthly Tips and Tricks Unsubscripti
                            ○ Allow Select

? Test List Name: ○ Auto-Create   Test List
                            ● Allow Select   [Select]

Figure 13-4: Creating and choosing Target Lists.

9. **Fill in the information on the Marketing Email page.**

   The Marketing Email page you see in Figure 13-5 lets you specify how and when your newsletter or campaign is distributed. You want to indicate the From Name, From Address, when you want your campaign to be sent, and the name of the template you're using.

   Not sure how to create an e-mail template? A quick look at Chapter 12 will show you how.

   The Email Marketing record that you create is a mandatory part of an e-mail campaign. If necessary, you can create multiple Email Marketing records. For example, if you're sending a monthly newsletter, you'll want to create an Email Marketing record for each issue.

10. **Click Next to continue.**

    This is the moment you've been waiting for: the final page of the wizard! Whew! You made it. At this juncture, you can send a test e-mail or schedule the e-mail for a later transmission, as shown in Figure 13-6.

Newsletter: Monthly Tips and Tricks   🖶 Print   ? Help

Back | Cancel | Next

Campaign Header
Budget
Trackers
Subscriptions
Marketing
Send Email
Summary

Marketing Email

Fill out the form below to create an email instance for your newsletter. This will allow you to specify the information regarding when and how your newsletter should be distributed.

Name *	Tips & Tricks	Status: *	Active ▾
Use Mail Account:*	Karen Fredricks ▾	Start Date & Time: *	09/01/2008 🗓 2:00
			(mm/dd/yyyy) (23:00)
From Name: *	Sugar Guru	"From" Address *	sugarguru@sugar.com
"Reply-to" Name: *	Newsletter	"Reply-to" Address: *	Newsletter@sugar.com
Send This Message To: *	☐ All Target Lists in the Campaign.	Email Template: *	Tips and Tricks #1 ▾ [Create] [Edit]

Monthly Tips & Tricks Subscription List
Monthly Tips & Tricks Test List

Figure 13-5: Setting the e-mail parameters for the campaign.

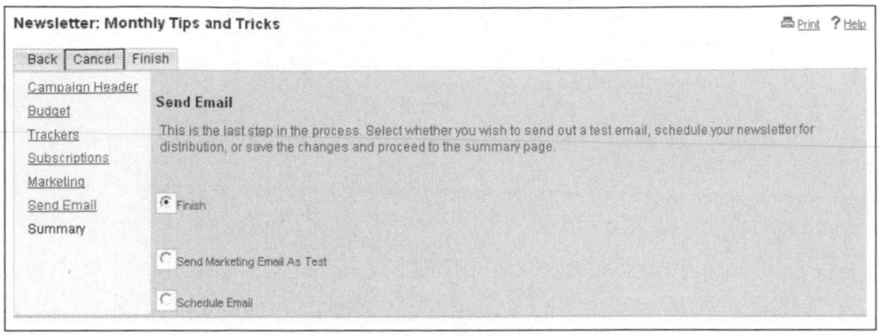

Figure 13-6:
Reaching
the end
of the
Campaign
Wizard.

Newsletter: Monthly Tips and Tricks   Print ? Help

Back | Cancel | Finish

Campaign Header
Budget
Trackers
Subscriptions
Marketing
Send Email
Summary

Send Email

This is the last step in the process. Select whether you wish to send out a test email, schedule your newsletter for distribution, or save the changes and proceed to the summary page.

⦿ Finish

○ Send Marketing Email As Test

○ Schedule Email

11. Click Finish to close the wizard.

Personally, I'd click Finish and go for a quick jog around the block, knowing that most of my work is complete and that I can tweak my campaign when I get back.

Creating Web-to-Lead Forms

If you surf the Internet, you've probably run across Web-to-lead forms. In general, a company's Web-to-lead form prompts you for your contact information in exchange for something you want. For example, you might have to fill out a Web-to-lead form to enter an online contest or to receive additional information about a product.

In essence, a Web-to-lead form is an easy way to harvest contact information. Typically, you place a link to a Web-to-lead form on your Web site. However, you can also place a link to a Web-to-Lead form in your campaign template. When the targets in your campaign click the link, they're prompted to fill in the form. Sugar will take that information and update the Lead record in your Sugar database or add a new lead in case the template finds its way to a new, unsuspecting target. You can then use this information in future campaigns.

Although this chapter focuses on using a Web-to-lead form as a part of your campaign, you can also create a link on your Web site to a Web-to-lead form. Hopefully, visitors to your site will click the link — and submit their contact information.

Here's how you easily create a Web-to-Lead form:

1. Click the Campaign module tab from any Sugar window and then choose Create Lead Form from the Shortcuts menu.

The Create Lead Form page displays, as shown in Figure 13-7.

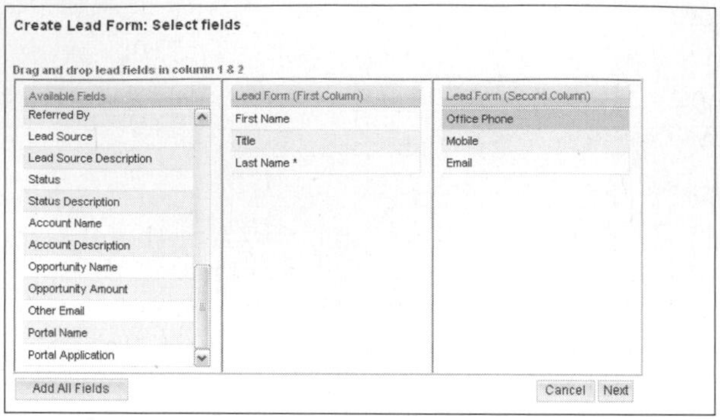

Figure 13-7:
Creating a
Web-to-lead
form.

> **Create Lead Form: Select fields**
>
> Drag and drop lead fields in column 1 & 2
>
> | Available Fields | Lead Form (First Column) | Lead Form (Second Column) |
> |---|---|---|
> | Referred By | First Name | Office Phone |
> | Lead Source | Title | Mobile |
> | Lead Source Description | Last Name * | Email |
> | Status | | |
> | Status Description | | |
> | Account Name | | |
> | Account Description | | |
> | Opportunity Name | | |
> | Opportunity Amount | | |
> | Other Email | | |
> | Portal Name | | |
> | Portal Application | | |
>
> Add All Fields   Cancel   Next

2. **Click and drag the desired fields from the Available Fields panel to either the First Column or the Second Column panels.**

   All the available Leads record fields appear in the Available Fields panel. If you would like to capture additional information, the administrator needs to go to Chapter 15 and read how to use the Sugar Studio to create new fields in the Leads module.

3. **Click Next to continue.**

   The Form Properties page opens.

4. **Enter the form information.**

   This is probably one of the easiest forms you ever have to contend with because most of the information is already filled in for you.

   - **Form Header:** Sugar automatically supplies a name; feel free to edit it.

   - **Form Description:** Again, Sugar fills this in, but you're free to change it at will.

   - **Submit Button Label:** This is the button that recipients click to transmit the Web-to-lead form. You can change the wording to Click Me, Sign Up Here, or any other cute phrase that crosses your mind.

   - **Post URL:** This is the location where the lead information is stored. If you want to change the URL, click Edit and change away.

   - **Redirect URL:** This is where the recipient lands after he submits the form; you might choose your Web site or some other landing page.

   - **Related Campaign:** Select the campaign that this form is linked to; this field is required.

     Not sure what to choose if the Web-to-lead form is placed on your Web site? Consider creating an ongoing campaign called something along the lines of "Web site Leads."

- **Assigned To:** By default, this is you, but you can click the Select button to select the name of another user if you prefer.

- **Form Footer:** Add a footer to the Web-to-lead form if you feel like there's something you want to say on the form.

5. **Click Generate Form.**

   After a momentary pause, the form opens in the editor, as shown in Figure 13-8. You can beautify the form by changing its color, or by adding additional information and/or hyperlinks. Required lead fields automatically appear with an asterisk. Notice that the header of the form corresponds to the header you assigned in the previous step.

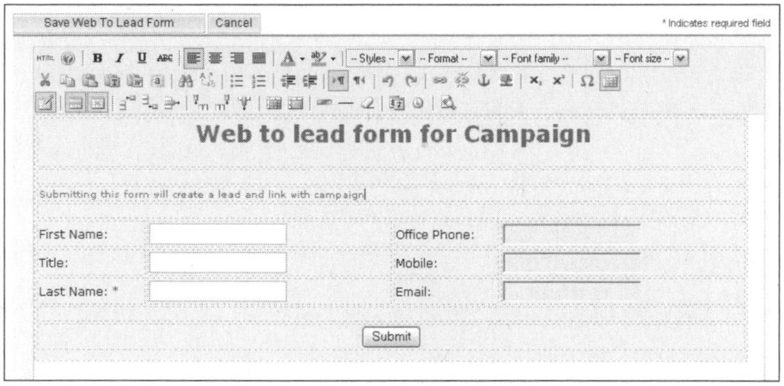

Figure 13-8: The Web-to-lead form generator.

6. **Click the Save Web To Lead Form button to save the form.**

   You receive a prompt to download your Web-to-lead form followed by a hyperlink to your form. Copy the hyperlink and paste it into a template or onto a part of your Web site.

Targeting Your Targets

Your campaign is fairly complete: You've associated an e-mail account with the campaign, you've determined the template to use with your campaign, and you've scheduled a start date and time for the campaign. But wait — you've overlooked one key element of the campaign. A campaign is only as good as the list of people to whom you're sending the campaign.

Keeping your eye on the Target List

If you start your campaign by using the Campaign Wizard, you have the opportunity to create three different types of Target Lists: campaign recipients, opt-outs, and test recipients. Once created, you can edit those Target

Lists to provide a few more details than what is available to you with the wizard. If you chose to create your campaign using the Create Campaign (Classic) method, you have to create the Target List from scratch.

Follow these steps to create a Target List.

1. **Click the Campaigns module tab from any Sugar screen and then choose Create Target List from the Shortcuts menu.**

   The Target Lists page opens.

2. **Enter the following information on the Target Lists page:**

   - *Name:* Give the Target List a name.

   - *Type:* Specify the Target List type from the drop-down list. I mentioned three Target List types: default, which consists of the people receiving the campaign; suppression list, which are the opt-outs; and test, which is the sample group you send to prior to sending the campaign. However, you can also designate a Target List as a *seed list* — usually, this is the head honchos who need to see and review the Target List before it's sent.

   - *Assigned To:* Add the name of the person in charge of the list; by default, that person is you.

   - *Description:* Optionally, enter a brief description of the Target List.

3. **Click Save to save the target list.**

Hitting the Target List with a few targets

In the previous section, you create a Target List, which is the list of recipients you want to reach with your campaign. Now you need to fill that list with contacts. A Target List can consist of four records:

- ✔ **Targets:** This is the low man on the totem pole. A *target* is a really cold prospect or lead. Targets are generally considered unqualified because you just don't have much information on them yet. You can convert a Targets record to a Leads record.

- ✔ **Leads:** Leads are the next step up from targets. You might have qualified a lead and have one or more opportunities associated with the lead. You can convert Leads records into Contacts, Opportunities, and/or Accounts records.

- ✔ **Contacts:** These are the folks that you've, well, made contact with — and have probably sold some of your wares to.

- ✔ **Users:** You might want to add database users to a test Target List so you can double-check the mechanics of your campaign before you set it loose on thousands of unsuspecting individuals.

Notice that an Accounts record can't be in a Target List. That's because you send marketing collateral or newsletters to specific people.

Follow these steps to add new targets to your Target List:

1. **Click the Campaigns module tab from any Sugar view and then click Create Target from the Shortcuts menu.**

   The Targets page opens.

   Unlike Contacts, Leads, and Users records, you can only access Targets directly from the Campaign module. Additionally, Targets are *stand-alone* records that can't be associated with other types of records. If you plan to send your campaign to only existing Contacts, Leads, and/or Users records, skip to Step 4.

2. **Enter any information that you have for the target.**

   If you have a text file containing a list of brand-new targets, you can import that list. Click the Import link on the Shortcuts menu and navigate to the saved file.

   By nature, you might not have much information about a target other than his name and e-mail address. You can add as many e-mail addresses as you want by clicking the Add Address link, filling in an address, and specifying whether the address is primary, opt-out, or invalid.

3. **Click Save to create the target.**

   When you save the target, the target's Detail view displays. You're now ready to add those targets — along with your existing Contacts, Leads, and Users records — to the campaign's Target Lists.

4. **Click Target Lists from the Shortcut menu and then click the name of the Target List you want to populate.**

   The Target List Details view opens.

   Make sure you select the correct Target List. Adding contacts to the wrong Target List can result in disastrous results. If you followed the wizard, you might see three lists for each campaign, as shown in Figure 13-9. The main recipient Target List displays Default in the Type column; test lists display Test as the type, and Suppression lists display Suppression List.

5. **Scroll to the appropriate subpanel and click the Select button.**

   For example, if you want to add existing contacts to the Target List, scroll to the Contacts subpanel. In any event, the Search window will open.

6. **Fill in your search parameters and click Search.**

   Alternatively, you can scroll through the contacts and place a check mark next to any contacts that you want to include. Figure 13-10 shows a search of all existing customers who are assigned to Karen Fredricks.

7. Select the check box to the left of the Name column to select all the contacts and then click Select.

The contacts are now included in your Target List.

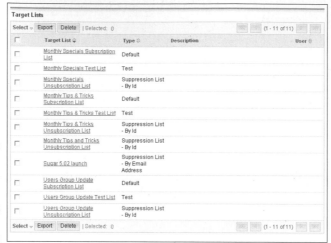

Figure 13-9: The rather confusing list of Target Lists.

Figure 13-10: Searching for contacts to add to a Target List.

Let the Campaigns Begin!

By now, you might have a mental picture of yourself at the starting line. You've gone through the *on your mark* and *get set* stages of the race, er, campaign. But hold on there — you need to attend to a few more housekeeping chores before hitting *Go!*

Look before you leap — or hit Send

Before you launch your e-mail or newsletter campaign, it's important that you test it to make sure the thing is going to work. Consider the following important points:

- **Test your e-mail preferences.** You should test your e-mail preferences before sending your message to thousands of people. If you don't, you might find yourself with a thousand e-mails in your Outbox that can't be sent. Make sure your test Target List includes contacts from both inside and outside of your office.

- **Test your e-mail template.** Again, testing your message before sending it across the universe is always a good idea. Having correct spelling and punctuation isn't a bad idea, either. Make sure the graphics can be viewed correctly through a variety of different e-mail clients.

    You might discover that although your templates look picture perfect when you first create them in Word, they look a bit *spacey* when you attempt to use them as e-mail templates. You might find that your message now appears to be double-spaced. Basically, something was lost in the translation from Word to HTML. You can correct this quite simply by returning to the scene of the crime — or in this case, the original template — and holding down Shift each time that you press Enter to create a new line.

- **Check with your ISP.** Many ISPs have implemented safeguards against *spam*. Before you send an e-mail to all the contacts in your database, call your ISP to find out how many e-mails you can send at a time. If your ISP limits the number of e-mails you can send at one time, you need to send your mailings in smaller groups or purchase an add-on product that sends your e-mail in batches. You discover more about these products in Chapter 18.

- **Read up on the Can Spam laws.** Laws are in place that require your e-mail to contain various elements, including your correct contact information and a way for recipients to opt out should they not want to hear from you.

Here's all you need to do to test your campaign:

1. **Click the Campaigns module tab from any Sugar view, click Campaigns from the Shortcuts menu, and then click your campaign.**

   The Campaign Detail view opens. You might want to take this opportunity to scroll down the page and make sure that a test Target List appears in the Target List subpanel, and that you have at least one record in the Email Marketing subpanel.

2. **Click the Send Test button.**

   The Send Test page opens. As shown in Figure 13-11, the test message will automatically send to your test list.

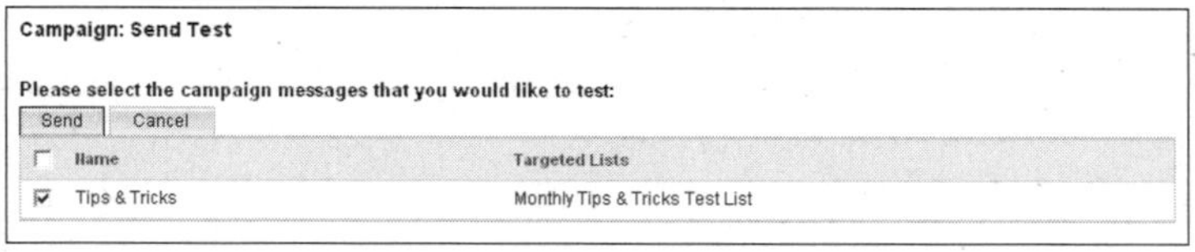

Figure 13-11:
Sending
a test
message.

Campaign: Send Test

Please select the campaign messages that you would like to test:

Send	Cancel

☐	Name	Targeted Lists
☑	Tips & Tricks	Monthly Tips & Tricks Test List

3. **Select the name of the campaign message you want to test.**

   When you're in the test mode, Sugar very cleverly disables your Suppression lists and then checks for duplicates. Therefore, you can send the test message multiple times until you get it right.

4. **Click Send.**

   This is a case of no news being good news. If all systems are go, you'll return to the Campaign Detail view. If there's a problem, Sugar rewards you with an error message. And, if you included yourself as one of the recipients in the test Target List, you can race over to your Inbox and take a look at the message.

Houston, we have a campaign problem

Running a campaign can seem a bit overwhelming. You have a template to produce. You have Target Lists to fill. You have tracker URLs to insert. You have Email Marketing records to create. You have a test to send. Holy guacamole — that's a lot of details to take care of! In the previous section, you create a test message that confirms whether you dotted all your Is and crossed all your Ts.

After all that effort, it would be fairly mind-blowing to have a technical glitch prevent the campaign from staying on schedule. Unfortunately, although a regular user can perform all the campaign tasks mentioned above, only an administrator can set up the actual e-mail handling portion of the campaign. Fortunately, Sugar comes with a neat Campaign Diagnostics tool that will put your mind at rest by confirming that the administrator has done her job — and you won't be left in a finger-pointing match should the campaign go off schedule.

Follow these steps to run the Campaign Diagnostics tool:

1. **Click the Campaigns module tab from any Sugar view and then choose Diagnostics from the Shortcuts menu.**

   The Campaign Diagnostics page displays on the screen.

   Warning messages like the one you see in Figure 13-12 appear if the administrator has not configured the e-mail settings and bounce-handling options correctly.

2. **(Optional) Contact your administrator to complete the necessary e-mail tasks.**

   You might alternate between using threats and bribes, depending on which method works best with your administrator. Printing the Campaign Diagnostics screen and posting it throughout the office often works well, too.

3. **Follow Step 1 above to return to the Campaign Diagnostics screen and then click the Re-Check button.**

   At this point, all systems should be good to go.

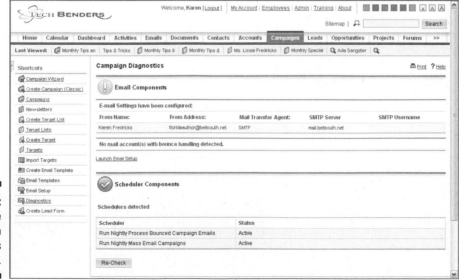

Figure 13-12:
The
Campaign
Diagnostics
screen.

Managing your non–e-mail campaigns

I mentioned earlier that there are basically two types of campaigns — those that use e-mail and those that don't. If you are using a non–e-mail campaign, such as a Telemarketing or a Mail campaign, you will need to make changes manually to the campaign to keep others updated on the status and success of the campaign.

Follow these steps to view the campaign's details so that you can make changes:

1. **Click the Campaigns module tab from any Sugar view, choose Campaigns from the Shortcuts menu, and then click the name of the campaign you wish to edit.**

   Seems like a whole lot of steps, but by now you should feel pretty comfortable with navigating to a Detail view.

2. **Click Edit to add additional campaign details and then click Save to save your changes.**

   In particular, you might need to adjust these fields to help calculate your ROI:

   • *Impressions:* This is the number of calls made, or items sent.

   • *Actual Cost:* This is the amount that the campaign cost you.

   Sugar uses this information to automatically calculate a Cost Per Impression figure.

3. **(Optional) Click Mail Merge to perform a mail merge.**

   You're now able to select the template you want to merge to your Target List.

   This option works only if you have the Sugar Mail Merge add-in for Microsoft Word.

4. **Mark as Sent after you launch the campaign.**

   You need to mark a non–e-mail campaign as sent to let other users know when the campaign has been launched. When you do this, the Campaigns subpanel on a target's Detail view will show the status as Active.

Measuring the success of a campaign

As you can see, creating a campaign requires a lot of planning and work. As the saying goes: no pain, no gain. However, all your work won't go unnoticed by the Sugar system — and hopefully not by your boss! After you launch a campaign, you can head to the pool, grab a drink, and float into the sunset with visions of dollar signs dancing in your head. Alternatively, you might want to check on the outcome of the campaign.

The campaign's Detail view allows you not only to view the current campaign status but the results as well. This information can help you plan future campaigns. For example, you might want to view the leads that came in as a result of the campaign and add them to a Target List for a future campaign, or add the opt-out records to a master unsubscribe Target List. You can even see the exact return on investment (ROI) of the campaign.

Because the campaign's Detail view supplies you with so much information about the results of your campaign, you'll want to head back there at least one more time:

1. **Click the Campaigns module tab from any Sugar view, choose Campaigns from the Shortcuts menu, and then click the name of the campaign you wish to analyze.**

   By now, you can probably open the campaign's Detail view in your sleep, but it's always nice to have instructions just in case!

2. **Click the View ROI button.**

   The ROI chart displays. Figure 13-13 shows you a sample of the data you'll find for your campaigns. The ROI chart shows the actual revenue versus the expected revenue generated from the campaign, and the actual and budgeted cost of the campaign. In case you're wondering, the revenue figure is a compilation of all new opportunities that users have attributed to the campaign; hopefully, that number will continue to increase every time you check the campaign's ROI.

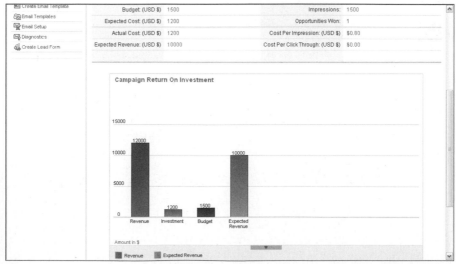

Figure 13-13:
Analyzing a campaign's ROI.

3. Click the View Status button.

If you've created an e-mail campaign, you're treated to a wide array of information. You'll see a tracking chart of responses from campaign targets. This includes seeing how many people viewed the message, how many opened any links that were included in the campaign e-mail, and how many people chose to opt out of the campaign. You'll even see the number of leads that were created as a result of your campaign. Talk about heavy-duty analysis!

If that's not enough, if you scroll to the bottom of the page, you'll find subpanels listing the people who are graphically represented in the chart. For example, you'll find lists of the people with bounced or invalid e-mail addresses as well as those who clicked through the various links in your campaign e-mail message. Most importantly, you'll see a list of the opportunities that were created as a result of your campaign.

Part V
Working with Extra-Strength Sugar

The 5th Wave   By Rich Tennant

VP Sales

"It's Web-based, on-demand, and customizable.
Still, I think I'm going to miss our old sales
incentive methods."

In this part . . .

You may think that Sugar offers you everything you could ever want right out of the box. However, you might be interested in adding a few special features that are a part of the Professional and Enterprise editions of Sugar. Those of you who are so inclined — or who didn't run fast enough — might want to add SugarCRM database administrator to your current job description. The database administrator is in charge of adding new fields to the database and making sure that they're properly placed onto your layout. Your job as administrator also includes managing all of those tricky settings and user permissions. And, when things go wrong, guess whom everyone will turn to? Not to worry, though — just turn to this part for help.

Chapter 14

Sweetening the Deal

- -

- -

Most of this book covers functionality that you can get free with the Community Edition of Sugar. However, you may want to consider upgrading to a fee-based version of Sugar — particularly if your business consists of many users and requires a bit more organization than does a smaller business. In this chapter, I focus on four features available only in the Professional and Enterprise versions of Sugar: Team Management, forecasting, reporting, and Workflow.

Being a Team Player

A *team* is a group of individuals who band together for a common goal. In Sugar, the Team Management option allows you to group users into teams — hopefully for the purpose of winning sales and satisfying customers. You can assign Sugar records, such as Accounts, Contracts, and Opportunities, to a specific team; once assigned, those records can only be accessed by members of that team.

Creating a team

By default, a *private* team is set up for each user and contains *only* that specific user. Sugar also sets up a *Global* team, which automatically includes *all* users. Any new records you create are automatically assigned to your team and, therefore, are visible only to you — unless you add other users to your private team or assign the record to a *different* team.

Because new records are assigned by default to your private team, it's good practice to set up teams prior to adding new records. However, should you find yourself with lots of records that need to be reassigned to a different team, don't forget about the mass update feature on the various Home pages that allows you to make all those changes en masse.

Here's how you can get the ball rolling and create a winning team:

1. **Click the Admin link from any Sugar screen and then click Team Management from the Users subpanel of the Administration Home page to open the Teams Home page.**

   Because creating and maintaining a team is a function of the coach, er, database administrator, it's only logical that you manage your teams from the Administration Home page.

2. **Choose Create Team from the Shortcuts menu of the Teams Home page.**

   The Teams page opens. See it for yourself in Figure 14-1.

3. **Fill in the team information.**

   There's really not much to do here other than to assign a team name and an optional description so don't rack your brain trying to come up with a mascot or team colors.

4. **Click Save.**

   The Teams Home page appears — with your team on the roster.

5. **Click the name of your team to open the Team Detail view.**

Figure 14-1:
Creating a winning team.

6. **Click the Select button at the top of the Users subpanel.**

   The User Search window opens. From here, you can search for a specific user or simply scroll through the list of users and select the one(s) you want to add to the team by selecting their check box.

7. **Click the Select button.**

   The selected users are now proud members of the team.

Being noticed by the team

E-mail is a great way to communicate. So great, in fact, that you might find yourself bombarded by lots and lots of e-mail — and lose an important message or two in the bargain. Using Team Notices, the database administrator can create broadcast messages to the members of the team. When the members log in to the database, they'll see the announcements on the Team Notices dashlets of their Home page.

Here's all you need to know to set up a team announcement:

1. **Click the Admin link on any Sugar screen and then click Team Management in the Users subpanel of the Administration Home page to open the Teams Home page.**

2. **Choose Team Notices from the Shortcuts menu of the Teams Home page.**

   The Team Notices Home page opens.

3. **Choose Create Team Notice from the Shortcuts menu of the Team Notices Home page.**

   The Team Notice form opens.

4. **Fill in the pertinent information.**

   You are, after all, creating an announcement so include all the appropriate who, what, when, where, and whys. Figure 14-2 gives you an idea of what a Team Notice form looks like.

5. **Click Save to save the announcement.**

   The announcement will be visible to all the group members the next time they access their Home page.

Sure beats the heck out of a bulletin board — and you don't have to search for a thumbtack!

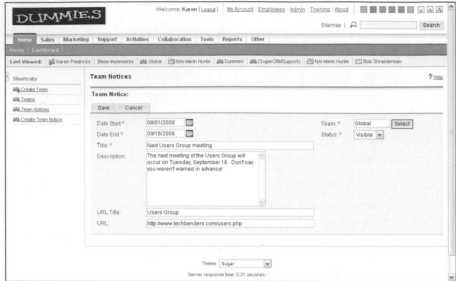

Figure 14-2:
Creating a
team notice.

Knowing which team to root for

Nothing's worse than hearing the entire office discuss an upcoming event — and not being sure if you're expected to attend! After your administrator has set up teams, check the roster to determine whether you made the cut.

If you find yourself unsure about your team status, there's an easy way to find out your eligibility. Click My Account from any Sugar view and then scroll to the My Teams subpanel. Any groups you're a member of are listed there. And, if you really want to feel like you're a member of the in-crowd, click a group name, and you'll be able to view a list of all the other group members.

The Forecast Is Looking Good

Chapter 7 focuses on the Opportunities module. The Forecasts module allows you to create quotas for your sales force — and measure its perfor-mance based on actual sales and opportunities.

Forecast records are based on sales opportunities. Only those users who are listed as the assigned user of an Opportunities record can include the oppor-tunity in a sales forecast.

A Forecast record consists of four parts:

- **Time Period:** A forecast is based on a time period. You can use traditional periods — months, quarters, or years — or you can define a custom period, such as a week or specific period.

- **Forecast Schedules:** After you set up a few time periods, you can create *schedules* by assigning a specific time period to various teams of users. For example, the region sales teams may have a monthly schedule, and the corporate sales team may have a quarterly schedule.

- **Sales Quotas:** The next step in the process is to set up sales *quotas,* or the amount of sales an individual is supposed to close during the given time period.

- **Forecast Worksheet:** The Forecast Worksheet reflects what sales people think they can produce in sales.

The first three steps of the forecasting process are performed by your friendly neighborhood database administrator. The final step — the Forecast Worksheet — is performed by the lowly worker ant.

After you create a Forecast record, you can add the My Forecast dashlet to your Home page so that you see it every time you log in to Sugar. You'll see a visual comparison of your quota along with your closed opportunities and committed forecast. Not sure how to add something to your Home page? Take a peek at Chapter 9.

Creating Time Periods

Time flies when you're having fun, and the administrator has the task of defining the Time Periods that will be used company-wide. For added fun and enjoyment, the administrator can also define the fiscal year for the company. After the administrator defines the time periods, the periods automatically appear in the Forecasts module where they can be attached to a forecasting schedule.

Follow these steps to create time periods:

1. **Click Admin from any Sugar view and then click Time Periods in the Forecast subpanel.**

    As you might expect, the Time Periods Home page opens.

2. **Choose Create Time Period on the Shortcuts menu.**

    The Time Period form page opens.

3. **Enter the appropriate information about the Time Period.**

   As shown in Figure 14-3, this doesn't involve much contemplation on your part. Enter a name for the Time Period, and then indicate a Start Date and End Date. If the Time Period corresponds with the Fiscal Year, feel free to select the Is Fiscal Year check box.

Figure 14-3: Defining a time period.

4. **Click Save to save the Time Period.**

   You are now free to roam around the cabin — or start working on those schedules.

I'm forecasting that there's a schedule on the horizon

After you create a Time Period or two, it's time to scurry around creating schedules. Fortunately for you, there's not much involved in the process so you should be able to perform this feat in a small amount of time.

To create a Forecast Schedule:

1. **Click Admin from any Sugar view and then click Time Periods in the Forecast subpanel.**

   The Time Periods Home page opens, this time with your Time Periods prominently displayed.

2. **Click the name of the Time Period you want to include in a schedule.**

   The Time Period Detail view opens with a chime. Okay, maybe I'm just hearing things, but all this talk about time might have you envisioning a row of ringing alarm clocks.

3. **Scroll to the Forecast Schedule subpanel and click Create.**

   The Forecast Schedule page opens.

4. **Fill in the timely information.**

   Again, it won't take you much time to create the schedule information. Indicate when the schedule will start, whether it's active, and specify the person for whom you're creating the schedule. Figure 14-4 shows you the finished product. You can select the Cascade option if you want this information to roll into other user's information that it relates to.

   The forecast start date determines the information you'll see in the Forecast Worksheet. Generally, you want to set a date prior to the actual period so users can access the Forecast Worksheet prior to the Time Period.

Figure 14-4: Creating a Forecast Schedule.

5. **Click Save to save the Forecast Schedule.**

   Any schedules that you create will appear in the Forecast Schedule sub-panel of the Time Periods Detail view, as shown in Figure 14-5.

Figure 14-5: The Time Periods Detail view.

Setting Quotas

After you create Time Periods and then use them to create Forecast Schedules, you're ready to start setting up sales quotas for your users.

Time passes — at times too quickly. As time goes by, you have to continue to create new Time Periods and schedules. An administrator's work is never finished!

Here's how to quickly set up a Quota:

1. **Select the Forecasts module from any Sugar screen.**

   The Forecasts Worksheet opens. If you're using the Forecasts module, you'll see quite a bit of this page in the future.

2. **Choose Quotas from the Shortcuts menu.**

   The Quotas Home page opens.

3. **Choose a Time Period from the drop-down list on the Quotas Home page.**

   You can see why you need to set up those Time Periods prior to setting Quotas. After you select a Time Period, any existing Quota records for that period will display in the Quota List subpanel.

4. **Fill in the new Quota information.**

   Although forecasting requires many steps, the steps are baby ones. In this case, you just need to choose a user from the drop-down list, fill in a quota amount and the currency you're using, and select the Commit Status check box to show that the Quota is Active. If you don't select Commit Status, the Quota will show as Pending. Figure 14-6 shows an example of a Quotas Home page.

5. **Click Save to save the Quota.**

   The Quota now appears in the Direct Report subpanel.

The cool part here is that various users can access different quota information. For example, a sales rep can only see his Quota record, whereas a manager can change the Quota record. Feel free to flip ahead to Chapter 16 for a bit more about role management.

Working through the Forecast Worksheet

The Forecast Worksheet is the icing on the cake — and the final stage of the Forecast process. Sugar automatically takes Amount, Probability, and Weighted Amount information from your opportunities and plunks them into the worksheet. You add your best-guess estimates for what you think you can sell and sit back and let Sugar calculate everything for you.

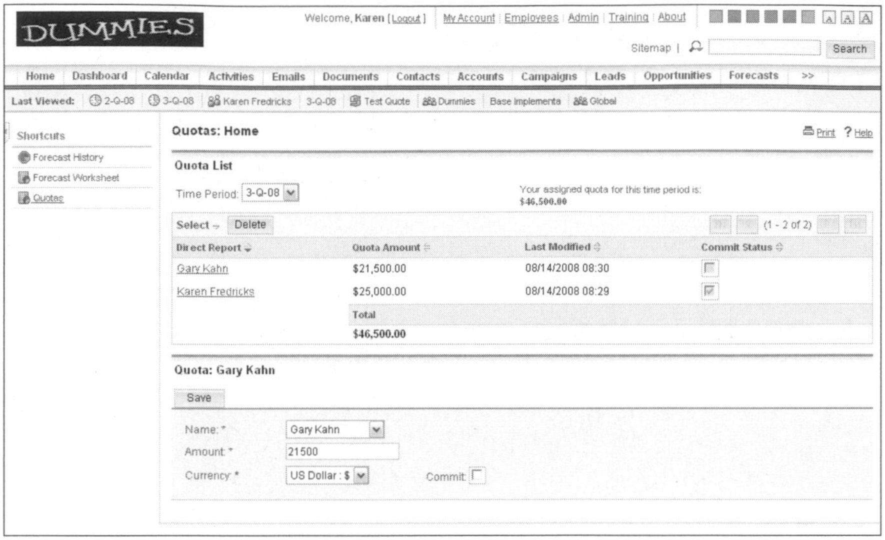

Figure 14-6:
The Quotas
Home page.

To edit the Forecast Worksheet:

1. **Click the Forecasts module tab from any Sugar view.**

   The Forecasts Worksheet appears.

2. **Choose the Time Period from the Time Periods drop-down list.**

   If you logged in as a regular user, you see only your data, and your Quota appears at the top of the page. If you logged in as a user with higher access privileges, you see data for the other users who report to you; you then have the option to view their specific information or a combined worksheet consisting of several users. Figure 14-7 shows you an example of a "rollup" worksheet that you'll see if you log in with higher access privileges.

3. **Enter the Estimated Best Case, Likely Case, and Worst Case forecasts.**

   Sugar follows along and updates the Totals row for you.

4. **Commit the amounts by clicking the Copy Values button, selecting Total Estimated Amounts, and then clicking the Commit button.**

5. **Click OK in the dialog box that appears.**

   The committed amounts appear at the bottom of the worksheet along with the date that you entered the totals.

6. **Click Save Worksheet to save your changes or Reset Worksheet if things don't look right and you want to try again.**

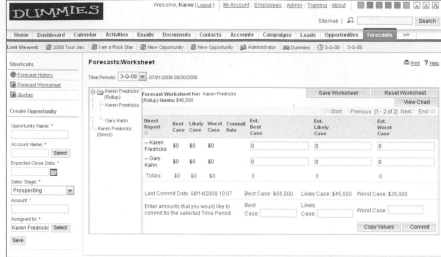

Figure 14-7:
The
Forecasts
Worksheet
in Rollup
view.

Viewing your Forecast Worksheet progress

The whole purpose of the Forecast Worksheet is to compare the actual sales to a pre-determined Quota. The worksheet enables sales managers to track sales for a specific Time Period by user, and allows users to see how they are measuring up to their Quota.

Charting your progress

The Rollup view accessed by a manager (refer to Figure 14-7) allows you to enter best- and worst-case sales scenarios. The manager can then click the View Chart button and view the chart, as shown in Figure 14-8.

The chart is a comparison of data that you've entered in a variety of Sugar modules:

- **Quota:** The sales goals set by the sales manager — or another power-to-be.
- **Committed Forecast:** The best-guess estimate for how likely the users are to achieve the Quota.
- **Closed Opportunities:** The total of all opportunities closed by the users during the given Time Period.

If you're in the Rollup view, the chart portrays the totals of all the users. If you click a specific user's name in the Forecast Worksheet, the chart displays only that user's information.

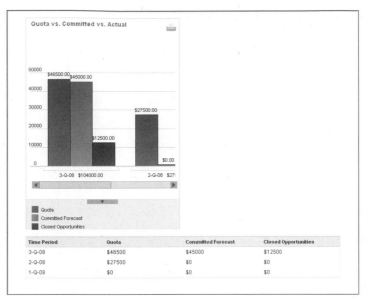

Figure 14-8:
Viewing
the Quota
versus
Committed
and Actual
sales.

Supercharging your Forecast Worksheet

At this point, most sales managers might think they've died and gone to heaven. However, Sugar has one more forecasting trick up its software sleeve — the ability to view more detail via the Forecast Worksheet.

If you are a manager, the Forecast Worksheet will list the various users in your sales department. And, you can drill down to garner more information on any one of them by simply clicking a name in the left pane of the Forecast Worksheet. The worksheet refreshes and provides you with a list of the user's current opportunities, similar to what's shown in Figure 14-9.

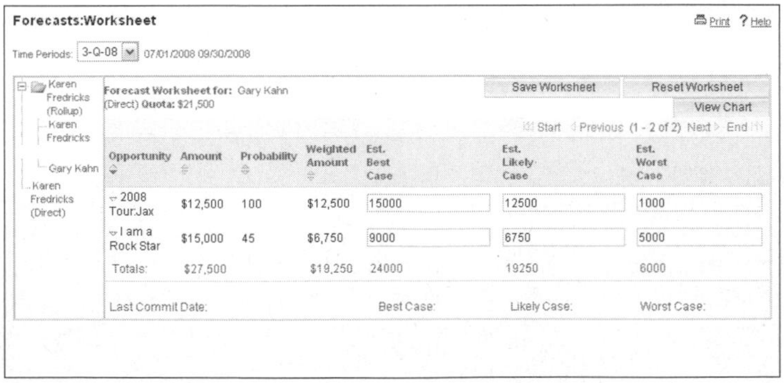

Figure 14-9:
Focusing on
one user's
informa-
tion in the
Forecast
Worksheet.

Optionally, you can provide estimated Best Case, Likely Case, and Worst Case figures, although they will not "roll up" into the estimated figures for the user as a whole. The manager can also drill down on any specific opportunity that he wants to edit or view by clicking the down arrow next to the Opportunity name. A pop-up window similar to the one shown in Figure 14-10 opens, displaying the Account name, probability percentage, and type; click the pencil icon to edit the opportunity if needed.

Figure 14-10:
Viewing a
bit more
informa-
tion on the
Forecast
Worksheet.

Additional Details	
Account Name: Stone Pony Productions, Inc.	
Probability (%): 100	
Type: Existing Business	

Forecasting your history

Although the thought of forecasting history is a bit of an oxymoron, Sugar does provide you with a way to view your forecast history from prior periods.

1. **Click the Forecasts module tab from any Sugar view and then choose Forecast History from the Shortcuts menu.**

   The Forecast History Home page opens. You'll notice a Committed Forecasts subpanel.

2. **Choose the Time Period you'd like to review from the Time Periods drop-down list.**

3. **Select either My Forecasts or My Team's Forecasts and then click Search.**

   A summary of the past forecast displays in the Committed Forecasts Search subpanel and shows the committed amounts, Time Period, and the number of opportunities for that period.

Creating Reports 101

The information that you *put into* a database is only as good as the information that you can *pull out* of it again. Although you might not be a proponent of using reams of paper to print out myriad reports, you'll probably want to at least view some simple information online.

The Reports module allows you to create, view, and edit reports on a variety of exciting topics including accounts, contacts, and opportunities.

Both the Professional and Enterprise versions come equipped with lots of reports. You might consider taking a peak at them before jumping in head-first and creating more reports "from scratch."

Need a new report in a hurry? You can always use an existing one, make your changes, and then click *Save As* to save the report with a different name.

It will come as no shock to you that you find the Sugar reports nestled away in the Reports module. Running existing reports from the Reports module is a great way to find out about the various report filtering and display options.

You might notice the Add to My Favorites button. This will allow you to select a report and designate it as a Favorite. You can access your favorite reports by choosing the My Favorite Reports shortcut from the Reports home page. You can also add a favorite report dashlet to your Home page for even easier access to the reports you run the most often. Chapter 9 shows you how to add items to your Home page.

The two basic types of reports are

- ✔ **Rows and Columns:** This is the typical report format; each column has a header reflecting one of your Sugar fields and the rows contain the corresponding data pulled from your records. For example, you might create a contact report with such columns as Name, Address, City, State, Phone, and E-mail, and then thousands of rows each containing the appropriate information from every one of your contacts.

- ✔ **Summation:** This type of report generally includes totals, such as sum, average, or count of the items reflected in the chart. Summation reports work particularly well when you're trying to group various data into individual categories. Optionally, a summation report can include a chart.

Running a Rows and Columns report

A Rows and Columns report displays information in rows and columns with the columns reflecting the fields that you choose to display in the report.

Here's how to take a look at an existing report:

1. **Click the Reports module tab from any Sugar view.**

   The Reports Home page opens, providing a list of the current Sugar reports. Notice in Figure 14-11 that the administrator created all the reports and assigned them to the Global team, which means that they are viewable by all the Sugar users.

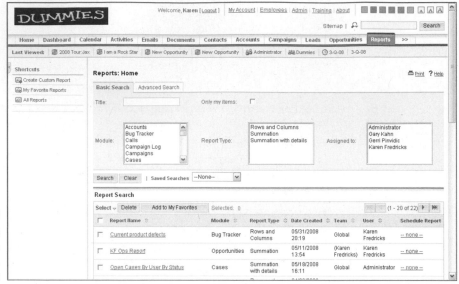

Figure 14-11:
The Reports
Home page.

2. **Choose the record type for which you want to create the report from the Module drop-down list.**

   Because many reports come with the Reports module and, over time, you might add lots more, you might want to narrow your options. You can also narrow your options to include a specific Report Type, such as Rows and Columns — the type of report you're focusing on.

3. **Click the name of the report you want to run.**

   Although this page is still labeled the Reports Home page, as you can see in Figure 14-12, it differs slightly from the *real* Reports Home page. This Home page includes three tabs that help you customize your report. The report information appears at the bottom of the screen.

4. **Select your basic report options and then click the Filter tab.**

   You have a number of options here:

   • *Report Name:* It's always a good idea to give a report a name that means something to you.

   • *Module:* Reports are based on a primary Sugar module; if necessary, you can add other related modules as well.

   • *Related:* Displays a list of the related modules, which you can then delete or change if necessary.

   • *Show Query:* Administrators can use this option to show the query on which the report is based.

- *Assigned To:* The person in charge of the report or the person you go to if the report doesn't work correctly.

- *Team:* The users who are allowed to view the report.

- *Rows and Columns or Summation:* Use this option only if you want to change the format of the report entirely.

5. **Select your filtering options and then click the Choose Display Columns tab.**

    You then specify additional filters to narrow the data based on the modules you select. For example, if your report is based on the Contacts module, you can filter the report to contacts that are located in a specific state.

6. **Choose the columns you want to display in the report.**

    Again, you can select columns based on the modules that you included in your report in Step 4. Select a field name from the Module column list and then click the left-pointing arrow to move the field to the Display Columns list.

    If you select a field in the Display Columns list, you'll see the column header that will appear on the report, which is generally way too long. For example, you might want to change the label *Contacts: Primary Address Postal Code* to a simpler *Zip,* like the example in Figure 14-13. To change it, delete the contents in the Label field and type the new and improved version.

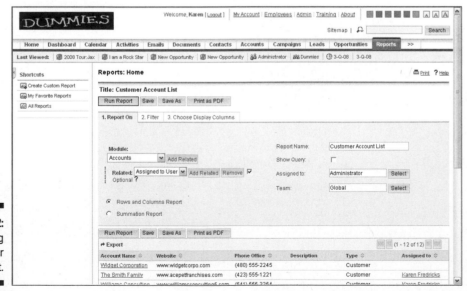

Figure 14-12:
Running
a Sugar
report.

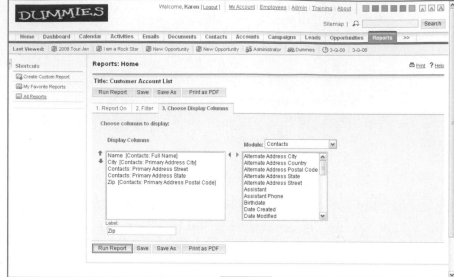

Figure 14-13:
Changing
the report
columns.

7. **Choose one of the following options when you're finished tweaking your report:**

   • *Run Report:* Click this button to refresh the report any time you change any of the reports options.

   • *Save:* Click this button to overwrite the previous version of the report.

   It's never a great idea to overwrite an "out of the box" report unless you're absolutely 100-percent positive that your version is superior to the original version. Using the Save As button is a much safer option.

   • *Save As:* Click this button to create a copy of the report with a new name.

   Need a new report in a hurry? You can always use an existing one, make your changes, and then click *Save As* to save the report with a different name.

   • *Print as PDF:* Click this button to print the report in PDF format.

Creating a Summation report

If you've ran a Rows and Columns report — and understand the various options — you're well on your way to running a Summation Report. The first several steps are identical, but I repeat them for you just in case:

1. **Click the Reports module tab from any Sugar view.**

2. **Choose the record type for which you want to create the report from the Module drop-down list.**

3. **Click the name of the report you want to run.**

   Because you're learning about Summation reports, your best option here is to pick a report that lists Summation as the report type.

4. **Select your basic report options and then click the Filter tab.**

   So far, so good — you're in fairly familiar territory here. You see the same options that you see for the Rows and Columns report — except that you'll notice that there are now five tabs to choose from: a Group tab appears after the Filter tab and a Chart Options tab appears on the end. You'll also notice a chart at the bottom of the screen.

5. **Select your filtering options and then click the Group tab.**

   Again, the filtering options are identical to what you see in the Rows and Columns report.

6. **Specify the data grouping on the Group tab and then click the Choose Display Columns tab.**

   A nice benefit of Summation reports is that they allow you to group information in sections. You can add grouping information by clicking the Add Column button, choosing a module option from the Group By drop-down list, and then choosing a field from the drop-down list to the right of the module type. The field information will depend on the modules you select in Step 2.

   Figure 14-14 shows an illustration of grouping case information by subject and then Account name, which would prove useful if you were trying to determine whether several people at the same company were all experiencing the same problems. If you select a date field, a third drop-down box appears that allows you to group by day, month, quarter, or year.

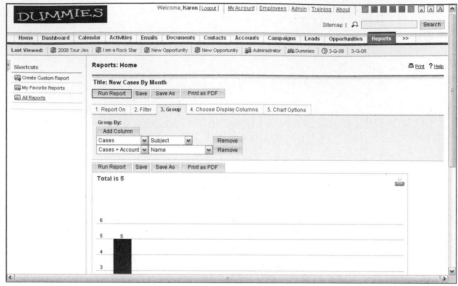

Figure 14-14:
Grouping
criteria for a
report.

7. Indicate your display Columns and then click the Chart Options tab.

Although the *process* for adding columns to a Summation report is the same as that for a Rows and Columns report, your options are slightly different. Because the whole idea of a Summation report is to group like items together, you see options like AVG and Quarter, meaning you can show an average of your data and/or group your data by quarter. You also notice a Show Details check box under the Label field, which displays the details of the report in addition to — or instead of — a chart.

8. Indicate your Chart Options.

You have three pertinent pieces of information to add here:

- *Chart Type:* You can have a horizontal bar, vertical bar, line chart, pie chart, or funnel chart type, or you can choose No Chart if you only want the summary information to appear.

- *Select Data Series for Chart:* Choose an available grouping function, such as Count or AVG (average), from the drop-down list. Your choices will depend on the Group-By and Display Columns options you select in Steps 6 and 7.

- *Chart Description:* Add a short description for the chart.

9. Choose an option to either Run, Save, or Print the report.

If you pick one of the chart options, the report displays as a chart complete with a legend. To hide the legend, click the down arrow. Place your cursor over a segment to see more information. If you chose the Show Details option, the details appear directly below the chart.

You can add custom charts to your Dashboard. For more information, head to Chapter 9.

Scheduling reports

After you have the hang of running and customizing reports, running them again is simple — just head back to the Reports Home page and select a report. However, if you want to automate the process even further, you can schedule to run a report at a specific time. Sugar runs the report and e-mails it to you. Talk about easy!

Here's how you can schedule e-mail delivery of your reports:

1. Click the Reports module tab from any Sugar view.

If you've already scheduled a report to run automatically, you will see the date and time that the report is scheduled to run. For now, you want to create a schedule, so *None* will appear next to any report not scheduled to run automatically.

2. Click None in the Schedule Report column of the report you want to schedule.

The Schedule Report dialog box opens, as shown in Figure 14-15.

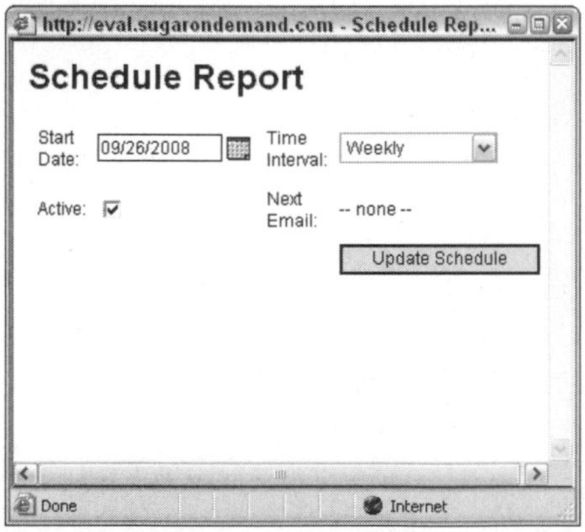

Figure 14-15:
Scheduling a report to run automatically.

> http://eval.sugarondemand.com - Schedule Rep...
>
> **Schedule Report**
>
> Start Date: 09/26/2008   Time Interval: Weekly
>
> Active: ☑   Next Email: -- none --
>
> Update Schedule
>
> Done   Internet

3. Enter the scheduling information.

You need to add only a few items to create such a powerful tool:

- *Start Date:* Select a date to begin the scheduling process.
- *Time Interval:* Choose an interval to run the report; you can pick durations, such as daily, weekly, and every four weeks.

- *Active:* Select the Active check box to get the show on the road. If you don't select this box, the schedule is not activated, and the Schedule Report column displays **None**.

- *Next Email:* If you're editing an existing schedule, the date and time that you previously specified appear here.

4. **Click the Update Schedule button.**

   You end up back at the Reports Home page where the next scheduled date and time appear in the Schedule Report column for that report. Sit back, relax, and wait to receive a copy of the report when it's scheduled to be delivered.

Working with Workflow

Workflow is the feature that sets apart the men from the boys. Workflow is the heart and soul of a true CRM product and probably the main reason you'll want to upgrade to the Professional or Enterprise version. Creating a *Workflow* allows you to track milestones, send out alerts, and take the appropriate action. For example, you might set up a Workflow to track warranty expiration dates; the customer will receive automatic notifications, which will stop when the customer either renews his contract or decides to discontinue the service.

The different stages of a Workflow can be assigned to different users of your organization. For example, in the above scenario, customer service might be in charge of sending the renewal notices, and accounting might be in charge of updating the customer's record. When one task is finished, the folks who are responsible for the next stage in the Workflow are notified.

A Workflow consists of five steps:

- Creating a *Workflow Definition,* which is the key element of the Workflow.

- Specifying the *Workflow Conditions* that trigger when the Workflow starts.

- *Creating an alert* to let your users or teams know exactly what is going on.

- *Creating an action* that you want to happen when an event triggers the Workflow.

- Optionally *specifying the Workflow Sequence* if you have several workflow processes that might overlap.

Although the process for creating a Workflow is a bit long and involved, you'll no doubt find the time you save to be well worth the effort. Not only will you be automating your processes, you'll also be assuring that nothing "falls through the cracks."

Creating a Workflow Definition

The database administrator is the person who starts the Workflow process. Be nice to this person because he is going to be saving the rest of the people in the organization a lot of time! The Workflow Definition is actually a record in your database; and, as is the case with other records, you can relate various elements to it after you create it.

Here's how the administrator can get the ball rolling:

1. **Click Admin from any Sugar view and then choose Workflow Management in the Developer Tools subpanel.**

   The Workflow Home page opens.

2. **Choose Create Workflow Definition from the Shortcuts menu.**

   The Workflow Definitions form opens.

3. **Fill in the Workflow Definition information.**

   When you finish, the final product looks similar to what you see in Figure 14-16.

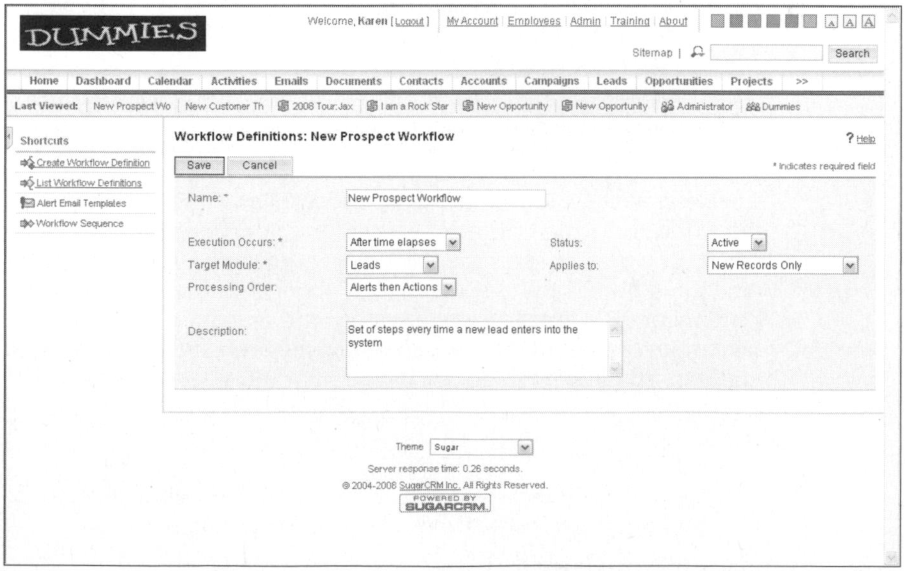

Figure 14-16:
Creating a Workflow Definition.

You have only a few pieces of information to fill out:

- *Name:* Enter a name for the Workflow.

- *Execution Occurs:* Indicate the event that will trigger the Workflow. Your choices are When Record Saved, which means when a change is made to a record, or After Time Elapses, which means the action is triggered by the passage of time.

- *Status:* Choose Active from the drop-down list to show that you want the Workflow to be usable. It's a good idea to set the status as Inactive until you've fully developed the Workflow to prevent it from triggering prematurely.

- *Target Module:* Select the module to which the Workflow applies.

- *Applies to:* Decide whether the Workflow will apply to new, existing, or both new and existing records. For example, a thank-you letter might apply to all Contacts records whereas a company introduction letter might only be sent to new Leads records.

- *Processing Order:* Decides which comes first: an alert or an action. The deciding factor is whether or not you want Workflow changes to be included in an alert. For example, let's say that changing the status of an opportunity will automatically create a task to follow up with the contact for that opportunity. You'll want to let the Workflow create that task *prior* to notifying your salesperson that the task exists.

- *Description:* Enter a brief description of the Workflow so you can remember what the darn thing is supposed to do.

4. **Click Save to create the workflow.**

   Congratulations! You land in the Detail view of the Workflow Definition where you can move on to the next step in the operation!

What condition is your condition in?

The second stage in the Workflow process is to add conditions to the Workflow. You might think of this in terms of *if* and *then;* for example, *if a new lead enters my database, then I am going to pester the heck out of him!* The nice thing here is that you can add a variety of conditions. For example, if the lead becomes a contact, you might want to send a thank-you letter and add her to your newsletter mailing list; if you never touch base with the lead, you might continue to include her in your marketing campaigns.

Here's how you can start adding a few conditions:

1. **Click Admin from any Sugar view and then choose Workflow Management in the Developer Tools subpanel.**

   The Workflow Home page opens.

2. **Click the Workflow Definition record you want to add conditions to.**

   The Workflow Detail view opens.

3. **Scroll to the Conditions subpanel and then click Create.**

   A pop-up window appears.

4. **Select the condition that you want to use to trigger the Workflow.**

   As you see in Figure 14-17, you have some nice options here. You might want something to happen when the contents of a field change — or when nothing changes during a given time period.

5. **Indicate the field or module that the Workflow depends on, fill in the time parameter, and then click Save.**

   The choices here vary slightly depending on the condition you pick in Step 4.

6. **Click Save to save your condition.**

   The condition now appears in the Conditions subpanel of the Workflow Detail view.

You can add as many conditions as you need to a Workflow. For example, you might want new leads in any one of six states to go to one salesperson, and new leads from a different set of states to go to a different salesperson.

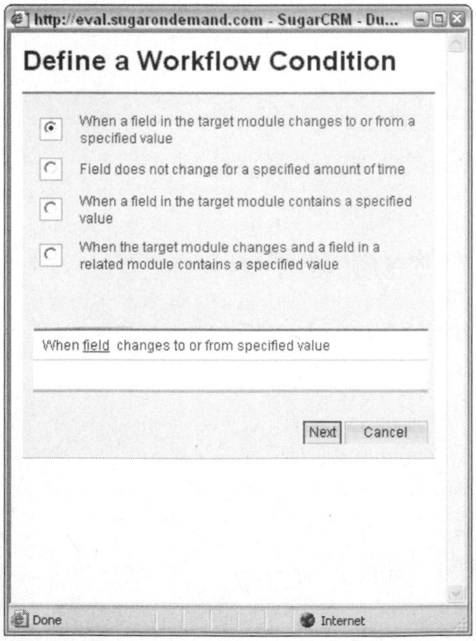

Figure 14-17: Adding conditions to a Workflow.

Alert! There's an alert ahead!

You can send alerts as part of the Workflow process. For example, you might want to let your co-workers know that you're going to start a marketing campaign so that they can prepare for all those new orders. Or, perhaps you want to alert someone when a contract is about to expire, or that one of his key customers hasn't made a purchase in six months. The possibilities are endless!

Alerts arrive in the form of an e-mail. An alert can be based on a template, or you can create your own unique message in the body of the alert. You also create a recipient list of the people who will receive the alert.

Creating an Alert Template

If you think your alert will take the form of a template, then you'll want to create the template prior to creating the alert. This prevents you from having to edit the alert to add the template to it.

The nice thing about Alert Templates is that they can be recycled and used in multiple Workflows. For example, you might have a variety of Workflows directed at specific users when their customer information changes. However, you can use the same Alert Template for each of these Workflows.

Follow these steps to create an Alert Template:

1. **Click Admin from any Sugar view and then choose Workflow Management in the Developer Tools subpanel.**

   Because Alert Templates are a part of the overall Workflow process, it's only natural that you return to the Workflow Home page to create one.

2. **Choose Alert Email Templates from the Shortcuts menu.**

   The Alerts Template page opens.

3. **Choose a module from the drop-down list and click Create.**

   The idea here is to tie the alert to the Workflow. If your Workflow revolves around new leads, select Leads as the module. If your Workflow involves contacting customers who haven't purchased from you in a while, select Contacts or Accounts.

4. **Fill in the basic information on the Alert Templates page.**

   Keep in mind that you're creating an e-mail message here so, as shown in Figure 14-18, the form looks somewhat like an e-mail message.

   The information you enter includes:

   - *Name:* Enter a name for the template.

   - *Description:* Enter a brief description of the template.

   - *Subject:* Enter the subject of the e-mail.

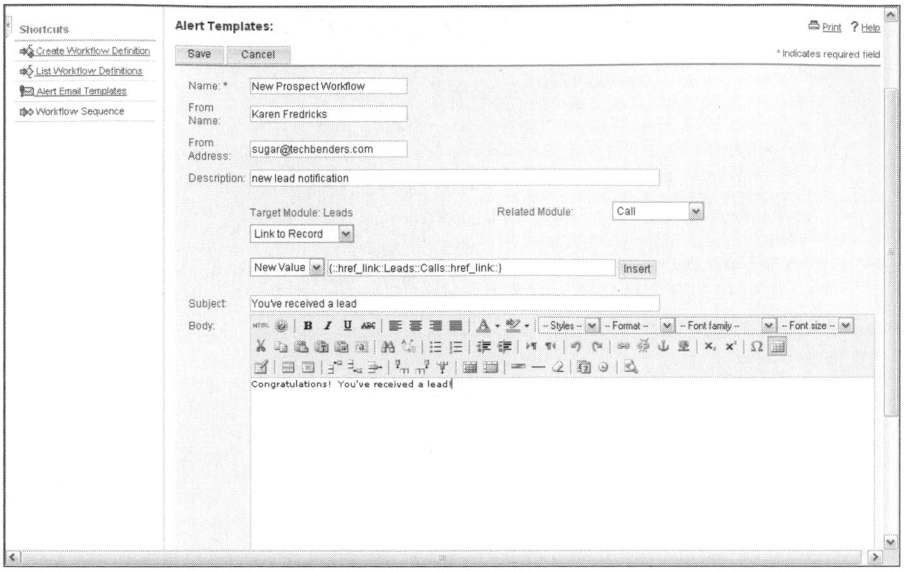

Figure 14-18:
Creating an
e-mail Alert
Template.

5. **Enter the body of the e-mail message.**

   The body of the e-mail message works like any other e-mail. You can format your text and write pretty much whatever you want. However, there's a neat trick here. If your alert depends on a change to a specific field, you can let the recipient of the alert know exactly what's changed. For example, you can choose a specific field from the Target module drop-down list, choose Old Value from the bottom drop-down list, and then click Insert so that the recipient knows exactly what information has changed. You can also choose New Value to see what the field has changed to.

6. **Click Save to save the template.**

Creating an alert

By now, your Workflow is really starting to take shape. You've even created a template that will automatically go to the users you need to notify of a Workflow-related event. You only have a few steps left, and fortunately, they're easy ones.

Now, you're going to set up the actual Alert process, which is easy if you follow these instructions:

1. **Click Admin from any Sugar view and then choose Workflow Management in the Developer Tools subpanel.**

   The Workflow Home page opens.

2. **Select the Workflow that you've been busily creating, scroll to the Alerts subpanel, and click Create.**

   The Alerts page opens, as shown in Figure 14-19.

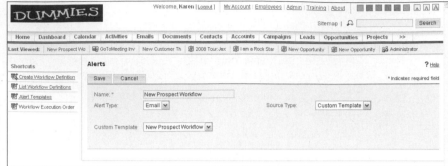

Figure 14-19:
Creating an
alert.

3. **Fill in the alert information.**

   I told you this was easy; there are only a handful of fields:

   • *Name:* Enter a name for the alert. You might choose a name that corresponds to the name of the Workflow to avoid confusion.

   • *Alert Type:* You can send the alert in the form of an e-mail or an invitation.

   • *Source Type:* You have two options here. If you choose Normal Message, an Alert Text box will appear for you to type in the message. If you select Custom Template, the Custom Template field will appear, and you can choose a custom template from the drop-down list.

   • *Custom Template:* This field displays existing Alert Templates if you select Custom Template as the source type. Choose the template from the drop-down list.

4. **Click Save to save the alert.**

   Your alert appears in the Alerts subpanel of your Workflow; look closely, and you'll notice a cute Recipients icon. Stay tuned — you'll be clicking that icon in a minute.

Sending an alert to those that need 'em

At this point, you might feel like you're working on a giant jigsaw puzzle. Fortunately, you only have a few more pieces to add. The Alert Recipient List allows you to determine who is supposed to get the alert — an important part of the entire Workflow process.

1. **Click Admin from any Sugar view and then choose Workflow Management in the Developer Tools subpanel.**

The Workflow Home page opens. If you just added an alert, you were already in the Workflow Detail view. However, it's always a good idea to start from the top to make sure that no one gets lost along the way.

2. **Select the Workflow that you've been busily creating, scroll to the Alerts subpanel, and click the Recipients link.**

   The Alerts Detail view opens. Notice that it includes an Alert Recipient List subpanel.

3. **Click Create.**

   A pop-up window opens.

4. **Select the option for the user(s) who are to receive the alert.**

   Sugar creates hyperlinks depending on your selection. For example, if you want to send the alert to a team of users, Sugar will furnish the message you see along the bottom of Figure 14-20. Click the hyperlink to select the users, teams, or recipients of the alert.

5. **Click Save to save the recipients list.**

   The selected users appear in the Alert Recipient List subpanel.

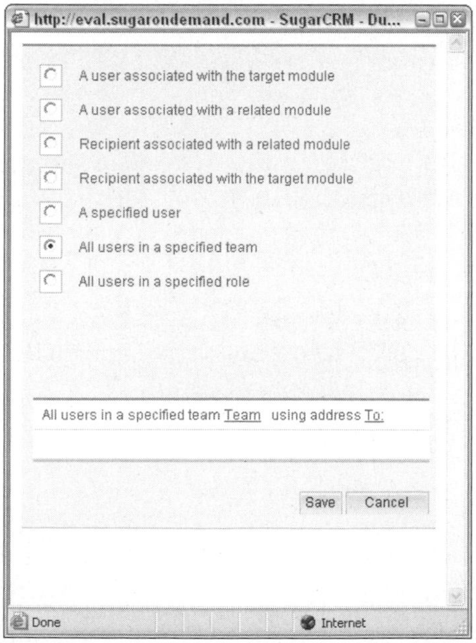

Figure 14-20: Deciding who is to receive an alert.

Actions speak louder than words

You're now ready to put the last piece into the Workflow puzzle. You can schedule actions to occur automatically when the Workflow is triggered. For example, you might set up a Workflow to notify a sales rep when a new lead in his territory is added to the Sugar database. Then, when the Workflow starts, you can have Sugar automatically change the lead's status. Cooler yet, you can add multiple actions to a Workflow. For example, you might have Sugar create a new opportunity for the lead and add the lead to your newsletter recipients.

Here's how you can set up those actions.

1. **Click Admin from any Sugar view and then choose Workflow Management in the Developer Tools subpanel.**

   The Workflow Home page opens.

2. **Select the Workflow that you've been working on, scroll down to the Actions subpanel, and click Create.**

   A pop-up window appears.

3. **Select as many actions as you want and then click Next.**

   • *Update fields in the Targets module:* Change information in the Target record.

   • *Update fields in a related record:* This updates information on one of the subpanels. For example, if you're working with the Leads module, you might want to add a note to the record.

   • *Create a record associated with a module related to the Targets module:* Create an entirely new record.

4. **Fill in your response and then click Save to save the action.**

   As shown in Figure 14-21, here's where you hone the information you indicate in Step 3. For example, if you opt to update fields in the Targets module, here's where you supply the fields you want to update and provide a value for those fields.

5. **Click Save to create the action.**

   You land on the Workflow Detail view where you can view the Workflow in its entirety, as shown in Figure 14-22.

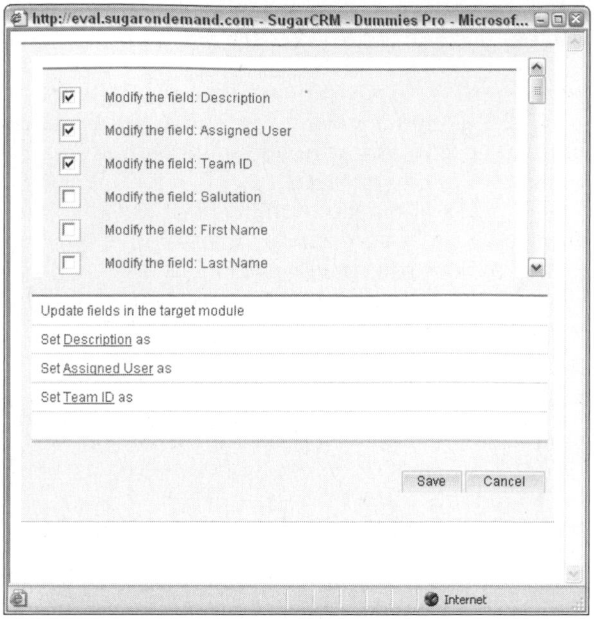

Figure 14-21:
Creating an
action.

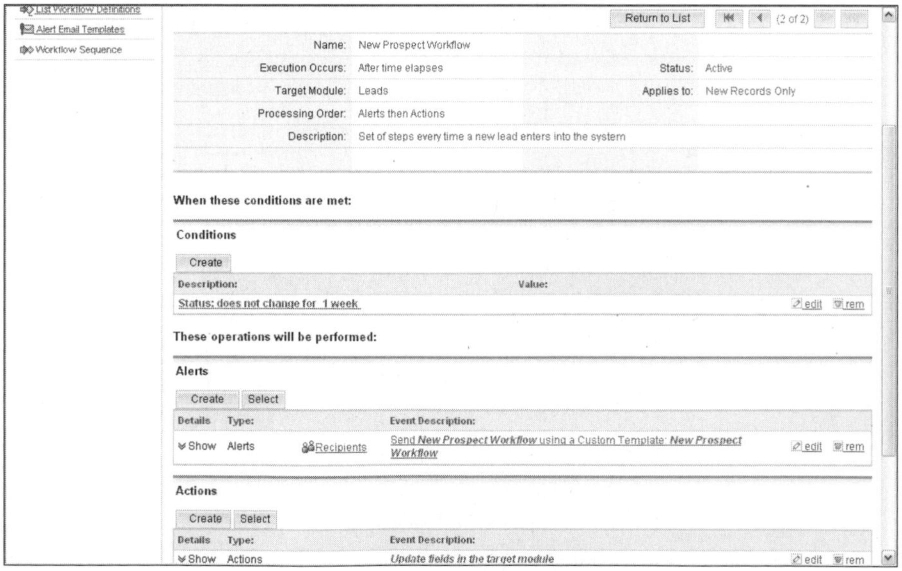

Figure 14-22:
At last! The
Workflow is
finished.

Two optional but useful Workflow steps

At last! You've come to the end step of the Workflow process. You should be proud of yourself — you definitely deserve a well-earned pat on the back. At this point, the Workflow is finished, although you might still want to tweak it a bit. You can go back and edit any part you want by following all of the above directions, looking for the pencil/Edit icon as you go.

Although you're finished with the actual process of creating a Workflow, you might want to add two optional — albeit important — steps to your Workflow checklist.

Specifying the Workflow Sequence

If you create more than one Workflow for the same module, you might run into a conflict down the road. For example, suppose you have one Workflow process that includes sending a welcoming e-mail to new leads and another process that sends out a thank you to any leads that place an order. The lead might be confused if he receives that thank-you letter prior to buying anything.

You can arrange the order of related Workflow items to ensure that your Workflows don't conflict with one another and run in an orderly fashion. To do so, simply follow these steps:

1. **Click Admin from any Sugar view and then choose Workflow Management in the Developer Tools subpanel.**

   The Workflow Home page opens.

2. **Choose Workflow Sequence from the Shortcuts menu.**

   The Workflow Sequence page opens.

3. **Select the module that contains the conflicting workflows and then click Select.**

   To make life easy, Sugar only gives you a choice of the modules that contain Workflows.

4. **Arrange the order of the Workflows on the Workflow Sequence page.**

   As Figure 14-23 illustrates, you can rearrange the order of the processes by selecting the up and down arrows next to each process. Your changes will save automatically.

Testing the Workflow

With so many steps involved in the process of creating a Workflow, it's only natural that you might get lost along the way. You might want to think of yourself as a rocket scientist — you'd be very disappointed if nothing happened when you yelled, *"Blast-off!"*

Again, Sugar has your back. Testing the Workflow prior to implementation will allow you to rest comfortably, knowing that all your Ts are crossed and your Is are dotted. Plus, you won't have to hide the next time the boss comes roaring around the corner.

If you had set the Workflow status to Inactive while creating the Workflow, you'll need to change it to Active prior to testing the Workflow.

You test the Workflow by actually recreating the process. This includes adding or making changes to the Workflow that correspond to the conditions you created for the Workflow, making sure that the appropriate alerts are sent and the specified actions are taken.

1. **Click Admin from any Sugar view and then choose Email Settings in the Email subpanel.**

   Verify that all your basic e-mail settings are correct.

2. **Make sure that there is a check mark in the Notifications On? check box.**

3. **Log in to Sugar as a different user and click My Account.**

   Verify that your e-mail settings are correct.

4. **Access the module around which the Workflow is built and create or edit a record.**

   For example, if you want to test that you'll receive a notification every time a new lead from Florida is created, then create a new lead who just happens to be located in Florida.

   You should now receive an e-mail informing you that a new lead was just created, at which point you can let out a loud whoop and dance around the office. If not, it's back to the drawing board.

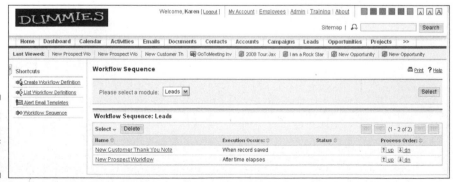

Figure 14-23: Changing the order of Workflows.

Chapter 15

Adding an Extra Lump of Sugar

*I*n this chapter, I show you (that is, all of you who have Administrator rights to your databases) not only how to add new fields to a SugarCRM database, but also how to set the various field parameters to help users use the database more effectively and efficiently. After you add a field, you want to put it somewhere so that it's visible to all of your users. I show you how to maintain consistency in your database by using drop-down lists. Finally, if you have a specific need that isn't addressed by the existing Sugar modules, I show you how to add one.

Creating Your Own Unique Database

For many of you, the modules and their fields that come with Sugar are more than enough to run your business. If that's the case, feel free to skip this chapter. However, many of you like to do things in your own unique fashion. Fortunately for you, Sugar includes the ability to make changes to modules, fields, drop-down lists, and even layouts directly from within the Sugar program. And, by doing so, you can create a customized solution for your business that would probably cost you tens of thousands of dollars if you were to hire an outside programmer to create the whole thing "from scratch."

To make structural changes, you must be a database administrator; the makers of Sugar made this a requirement so that you understand the importance of this responsibility. So, unless you have those rights to the database, you don't even have to read this chapter! I suppose you still could just for curiosity's sake, but it isn't necessary.

Sugar is *Open Source software,* which means that you have access to the entire source code. Therefore, if you have a good, working knowledge of PHP, you can change any aspects of Sugar. This chapter focuses on the areas you can change by using the Developer Tools you find in Sugar; however, feel free to explore other changes that are beyond the scope of this book.

Doing your homework

I am a firm believer that a little knowledge is a dangerous thing. Although making structural changes to your Sugar database isn't hard, it is something that should be well thought out and planned. This is particularly true if you plan to share your database with other users. Planning is important because you usually have a goal in mind for your database. For example, if your goal is to create a report with three columns — contact name, birthday, and Social Security number — you need to make sure all those fields exist in your database. Planning also prevents you from adding thousands of contacts to your database, only to find that you have to modify each record to include information that was omitted the first time around!

Okay, I admit it — I'm a former secondary school teacher, and I guess that background just naturally spills over into my Sugar consulting. Well, class, pretend you're back in school because you're going to be assigned some homework. I consider it important homework that you must complete prior to jumping in and making major changes to the structure of your database, so your assignment is as follows:

1. **Jot down all the fields that you want to add to your database.**

   Most of the fields you want to see, such as company, name, phone number, and address, are already included in Sugar. What you need to decide here is what fields, if any, are specific to your business.

   Dust off your thinking cap while you create your list. Sometimes one field will do the job, and other times you might need multiple fields. For example, suppose you sell widgets that are red, white, or blue. In one scenario, a customer needs to buy only one widget; in this case, you create a product field with three choices in the drop-down list — red, white, or blue. Or, perhaps you manufacture a different kind of widget; in this case, a customer would hopefully buy one of each color. This time, your purposes would be better served by creating three fields — one for each type of widget.

2. **Scurry around the office and collect any documents that you want Sugar to create for you. This includes both forms and form letters.**

   You have to get a little high-tech here, but I think you can handle it. Get out your trusty highlighter and highlight any of the information in each document that is contact specific. For example, each contact has its own unique address. Maybe you're thanking particular contacts for purchasing widgets (as opposed to gadgets, which you also sell). This means that you need a Product field.

3. **Think how to populate the fields with drop-down lists. Then, on the list that you start in Step 1, jot them down to the side of each of the fields.**

For example, if you run a modeling agency, you might need a field for hair color. The drop-down choices could contain red, blonde, black, and punk pink.

4. **Visualize where you'd like your new fields to appear.**

Adding a field is half the fun. The other half comes from deciding where you want that new field to appear.

5. **Sketch out any reports that you want to create from Sugar and add the column headings to the now rather long list that you created in Step 1.**

The idea here is to get your thoughts down on paper so that you can visualize how you want your reports to look. If you already have a sample of your report in Excel, you can use that. If not, get out your trusty pencil and outline on a piece of paper what you want your report to actually look like.

6. **Identify your pain points.**

We're not talking about a stubbed toe here. Rather, think about areas of your business that Sugar could help you manage. Maybe you're a travel agent and would love to add a module that lists itineraries. Or, perhaps you're selling yachts and need a place to track the specs on each vessel. Put Sugar to use to help manage any or all data.

7. **Jot down even your smallest wish.**

You may as well take advantage of Sugar's customization capabilities. For example, you might deal only with hospitals and would like to rename the Accounts module the Hospital module.

8. **Get out a red pen. At the top of your paper, write *100%, Well Done*, and then draw a smiley face. Hang your list on your refrigerator.**

Okay, that last step isn't really necessary, but now you're well on your way to having the database of your dreams!

Knowing your Developer Tools

After you've done your homework, you're probably chomping at the bit to jump in and start creating. Although I admire your enthusiasm this might be a great time to take a quick peek at the design tools that you'll be using.

The tools are easy to access — just click the Admin link on the Home page and scroll to the Developer Tools subpanel. Figure 15-1 shows you what you're getting in to.

Figure 15-1:
The
Developer
Tools
subpanel.

Developer Tools

Create and edit modules and module layouts, manage standard and custom fields, configure tabs, and define workflows.

Studio	Edit Dropdowns, Custom Fields, Layouts and Labels	Portal	Add tabs which can display any web site
Module Builder	Build new modules to expand the functionality of SugarCRM	Module Loader	Add or remove Sugar modules, themes, and language packs
Configure Tabs	Choose which tabs are displayed system-wide	Dropdown Editor	Add, delete, or change the dropdown lists in the application
Configure Group Tabs	Create and edit groupings of tabs	Rename Tabs	Change the label of the tabs

Although the elements are logical, it doesn't hurt to take a fast tour:

- ✔ **Studio:** You might think of the Studio as a playground for nerdy grown-ups; this is where you can add fields, change a label, rearrange your layouts, and edit a subpanel on your existing modules.

- ✔ **Module Builder:** Like a fancy set of building blocks, here's where you can build new modules to customize Sugar exactly to your liking.

- ✔ **Configure Tabs:** If you're overwhelmed by the number of tabs that display across the top of Sugar, here's the place to remove the ones you aren't using.

- ✔ **Configure Group Tabs:** You might want to swap the module format for a menu-based system grouping.

- ✔ **Portal:** Select this option to add tabs to other Web sites.

- ✔ **Module Loader:** Use this option to load Sugar modules, themes, and language packs that you've purchased or downloaded.

- ✔ **Dropdown Editor:** Click this option to add and edit the contents of your drop-down lists.

- ✔ **Rename Tabs:** Select this option to rename a module tab.

Stepping into the Studio

You might think of the Studio as the heart and soul of your design efforts. This is where you change the data that is displayed — and determine how that data can be viewed — for the basic Sugar modules as well as any modules that you might have created. Figure 15-2 shows the Sugar Studio Home page.

Need a little more room to spread out? Click a double left arrow to close a section that you're not using, such as the Help or Shortcuts menu section. Want to get them back? Click the double right arrows.

Figure 15-2:
The Sugar
Studio
Home page.

The Studio Home page lists all the existing modules in the left panel. The middle panel displays the exact same information in the form of icons. If you like working from a list, click the plus sign (+) to expand the module to show the Labels, Fields, Layouts, and Subpanels associated with the module. If you prefer icons, clicking them will reveal the view you see in Figure 15-3.

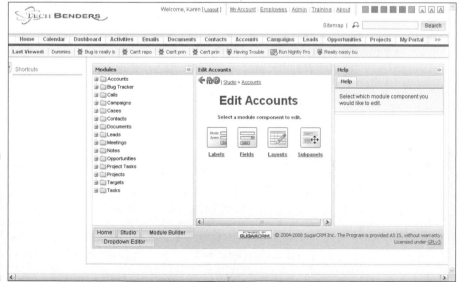

Figure 15-3:
Drilling
down on
a module
icon from
the Studio
Home page.

You'll also notice that the right panel offers you helpful hints; these hints will change to reflect the area of the Studio you're in. And, should you get lost wandering around the Studio, the buttons that run along the bottom of the page will get you back on track.

Adding a field to the database

Before getting started, I want to outline briefly the three steps involved with adding fields to a database:

1. Understand why you want to add fields and what purpose these fields will serve. And, if you did your homework earlier in this chapter, you're already done!

2. Determine what fields you're going to add and what type of data will be stored in them (dates, numbers, drop-down items, and so on). If you're creating a drop-down list, decide on the drop-down items.

3. Add the fields to your layouts and subpanels.

For most of you, adding a field to your database will be easy. After all, you're good at following directions. However, for some of you, knowing *why* to enter a field can prove to be more challenging.

To explore the question of why, I first want to reiterate the basic concept of fields. What the heck is a field? A *field* is a single piece of information. In general, a field contains just one piece of information. For example, you have only one business zip code; therefore, you have one business Zip Code field. Alternatively, you probably have several phone numbers: home, business, toll-free, cellular, fax, beeper . . . and the list goes on. Each of these phone numbers requires a separate field.

A good field holds one fairly specific piece of information. A bad field contains too much information. For example, having a separate field for your street address, city, state, and zip code is a good thing. These separate fields allow you to perform a lookup based on any of the criteria: You could find clients by zip code, city, or state. An example of creating a bad field is lumping all the address information into a single field; in this example, you'd then lose your ability to search by zip code, city, or state. (Need a refresher on searching? Head to Chapter 9.)

You can add custom fields to any module in Sugar. The actual addition of fields is relatively easy; just follow these steps:

1. **Click Admin on the Sugar Home page and then click Studio in the Developer Tools subpanel.**

   The Sugar Studio opens.

2. **Expand the module that you want to edit from the Modules panel and then click Fields.**

   The Edit Fields panel opens, as shown in Figure 15-4.

3. **Click the Add Field button.**

   The Field Editor panel (shown in Figure 15-5) opens on the right side of the screen, replacing the Help panel. If you still need a bit of help, click the Help tab.

   If you're attempting to create a new field that is identical to an existing field, click the name of the existing field in the Edit Fields panel and then click the Clone button on the Field Editor. Make any necessary changes and then click the Save button.

4. **Choose one of the data types from the drop-down list.**

   • *Text Field:* This is probably the most common of the field type choices; a *character field* can contain both numbers and characters.

   • *Address:* Talk about a timesaver! When you designate a field as an address field, Sugar automatically creates five fields: street address, city, state, zip code, and country.

   • *Checkbox:* Creates a check box field.

   • *Currency:* This field comes equipped with a dollar sign, appropriate commas, optional decimal places, and a sunroof (optional).

Figure 15-4: Making field changes.

Figure 15-5:
Creating a
new field.

- *Date:* When the time comes for you to enter information into a Date field, you see a tiny little calendar that enables you to select a date. The calendar supplies a useful purpose. If you create a field for a birthday and make it a character field, the other local yokels using the database might get creative and input anything from Jan 1 and January 1st to 01/01 and 1/1. Finding all birth dates in the month of January would become an exercise in futility.

- *Dropdown:* When you choose this data type, you pick an existing drop-down list to associate with the field or create a new one. I cover creating drop-down lists in the upcoming "Creating a drop-down list" section.

- *Decimal:* This field accepts only numbers, a decimal point, and more numbers.

- *Integer:* This will create a field specifying positive or negative numbers. You can specify a range with the Min and Max value fields. This option enables you to enter only numbers into a field. Say you want to find all your customers that have more than 30 employees. You can easily search for a number greater than *30,* whereas you can't possibly search for a number greater than *thirty.*

- *MultiSelect:* This is a special type of drop-down list field that allows you to select multiple items from the drop-down list.

  You cannot create a MultiSelect field in the Module Builder.

- *Flex Relate:* This is kind of a wild card field; with a Flex Relate field, you can choose a record type from a drop-down list, select a record, and then link that record to the current record.

  You can add only one Flex Relate field to a module.

- *Phone:* If you designate a field to be a Phone field, you automatically get a year's supply of dashes.

- *Radio:* Creates a radio button, which will allow you to pick only one of the drop-down list options.

- *Relate:* Creates a field to associate a record with another record. You can add multiple Relate fields to a module.

- *TextArea:* Where you can store a large amount of information you don't want to bury among your other notes. For example, you might want to include your driving directions in this area.

- *Link:* Use this field type if you need to associate another Web address with your record.

5. **Specify a Field Name**. Enter a name for the field.

   The field name can't include any spaces so use a name like FieldName or Field_Name rather than Field Name.

6. **Add the remaining field properties.**

   The remainder of these fields is optional but it's always nice to know what they mean just in case you decide to use them:

   - *Display Label:* The label you will see to help you identify the field.

   - *System Label:* This is the official "system" name for the field label.

   - *Help Text:* Like a little set of training wheels, this information will appear when a user places their cursor over a field.

   - *Default Value:* Add a default value for the field. For example, if you sell most of your products in the state of *confusion,* add confusion as the default value for the state field.

   - *Max Size:* Enter the maximum number of characters that the field can have.

   - *Required Field:* Select this check box to ensure that the users will enter information into this field.

   - *Audit:* Select this check box if you want changes to this field to appear in the Audit Log for a record.

   - *Duplicate Merge:* Select an option from the drop-down list to indicate whether you want to use the field as a way of finding duplicate records.

7. **(Optional) Fill in any remaining field values.**

   Some fields appear depending on the value you use in the Data Type field. For example, a Decimal field will ask for a Precision (number of decimal places) and an Integer field will ask for a minimum and maximum value.

8. **Click Save to create the field.**

   The new fields are listed above the core fields in the Edit Fields panel. Notice that a tiny "c" was added to the end of each one indicating that it is a custom field.

Deleting a field

If you delete a field from a database, all data in that field is deleted. Forever. Permanently. Delete a field only if you're sure that you no longer need that data.

The *core* fields that come with Sugar are so important that Sugar won't allow you to delete them. As an alternative, you can delete those fields from your layout so that they can't be accessed.

Ironically, the monumental task of deleting a field is ridiculously easy to fulfill. To do so, just follow these steps:

1. **Click Admin on the Sugar Home page and then click Studio from the Developer Tools subpanel.**

   The Sugar Studio opens.

2. **Expand the module that contains the field you want to delete, and then click Fields.**

   The Edit Fields panel opens.

3. **Select the field you want to delete.**

   I don't think I need to mention how important it is that you click the field you want to delete and not one you mean to keep.

   You can only delete customized fields; you can identify them by the "c" that appears after their names.

4. **Click the Delete button in the Properties panel to delete the field.**

   Click OK to confirm the deletion, as shown in Figure 15-6.

5. **Click OK to the warning prompt.**

   That's all, folks. If you're waiting for a second reminder to ask whether you're really, positively, 100 percent sure that you want to delete the field, you'll be waiting for a very long time because it's not going to happen. Any information associated with the field will be gone permanently.

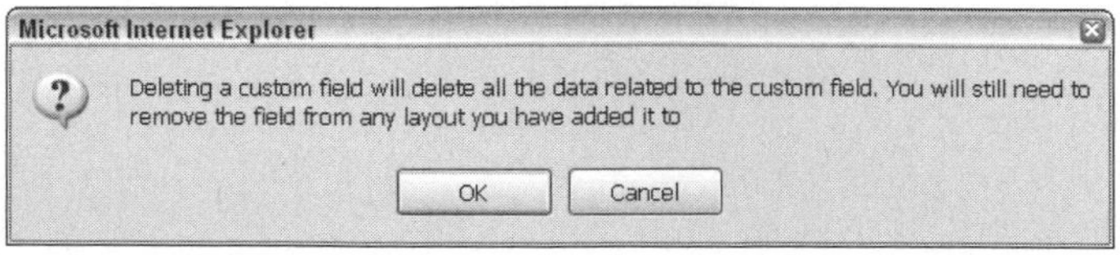

Figure 15-6:
The scary
warning
you receive
when delet-
ing a field.

Microsoft Internet Explorer

Deleting a custom field will delete all the data related to the custom field. You will still need to remove the field from any layout you have added it to

OK   Cancel

Editing fields

After you create a field, you might find that you need to tweak it later on down the road. Unlike many programs that are very difficult — if not impossible — to edit, you can edit your newly created, *customized* fields to your heart's content. However, the only part of a *core* field that you can edit is the label.

To edit a field:

1. **Click Admin on the Sugar Home page and then click Studio in the Developer Tools subpanel.**

   The Sugar Studio opens.

2. **Expand the module that contains the field you want to edit and then click Fields.**

   The Edit Fields panel opens.

3. **Select the field you want to change.**

4. **Click Save to save your changes.**

The only portion of a core field that you can change is its label.

What you see is what you get

Arranging fields the way you want them might sound like a no-brainer, but many SugarCRM users never realize the importance of changing the field locations in the various Sugar views. For example, after you add more fields you might end up with the main business phone number on the top portion of your layout, the toll-free number somewhere in the middle, and the direct-line phone number in a third location. If you're constantly scrolling through your layout to find phone numbers, you'll want to move them together into one strategic place on your layout. This organization might not make your layout *look* better, but you'll certainly *work* better! The point is to design your layout in such a way that data input becomes easy.

You can edit where a field appears — or doesn't appear. In addition, you can change the order in which the fields appear. You can make those changes to a number of locations throughout Sugar:

✔ **Layouts:** You can edit the Edit, Detail, and List views of any record type. In addition, you can edit the QuickCreate menus.

The Detail layout is what you see when you view a specific record; the Edit layout is what you get when you edit *a* record. Although you can modify those layouts to be very different from one another it would prove to be very confusing.

✔ **Search pages:** You can change the search fields in both the Basic Search and Advanced Search windows.

✔ **Subpanels:** You can add your new fields to a subpanel. For example, if you add an Account Number field to the Accounts module, you might want to see it on the Accounts subpanel for all the associated Contacts records.

The good news here is that it's very easy to add and remove fields from any page. The bad news is because there are so many places to customize, it's easy to add a field and then forget to make it visible throughout the various areas of Sugar.

As an example, say you add a toll-free phone number to the Contacts module. At the very least, you'll need to add that field to the Edit view (so you can add the number) and to the Detail view (so that you can see it). You might even decide to include it in the QuickCreate menu and on the Advanced Search window if you might want to find a contact by his phone number. As if that weren't enough choices, you might include the number on the Contacts subpanel of the Accounts and Leads module. Whew! You have your work cut out for you.

Changing the List view is a drag

The technique for adding fields and editing their position differs slightly between the various views. Here's how you can edit the various list-type views including the List view, Basic and Advanced Search pages, and the subpanels.

1. **Click Admin on the Sugar Home page and then click Studio in the Developer Tools subpanel.**

   The Sugar Studio opens.

2. **Expand the module for which you want to change the view, expand the Layouts section, and then click the List view you want to edit.**

   If you've been following along at home, the Edit Layout page opens. Figure 15-7 shows you an example of the page you see when editing the ListView.

   You might want to close the Help panel on the right side of the screen to free up a bit more space to see the Studio fields.

   The Edit Layout panel consists of three columns if you're editing the ListView:

- *Default:* Contains the fields that are displayed in a List view by default.

- *Available:* Contains fields that the users can choose to create a custom List view.

- *Hidden:* Contains fields that the users won't be able to see until the administrator makes them available.

If you're editing Search windows or subpanels, you only see the Default and Hidden columns.

3. **Make your changes by dragging fields to the desired location.**

You can move fields around to get just the look you're looking for. For example, you might want to add a new field to the QuickCreate menu and remove an existing one.

- *To add a field:* Select and drag the field from the Available or Hidden column and drop it into the Default column.

- *To remove a field:* Select and drag the field from the Default column to the Available column.

- *To hide a field from users:* Select and drag the field from the Default or Available column to the Hidden column.

4. **Click the Save & Deploy button to save your changes.**

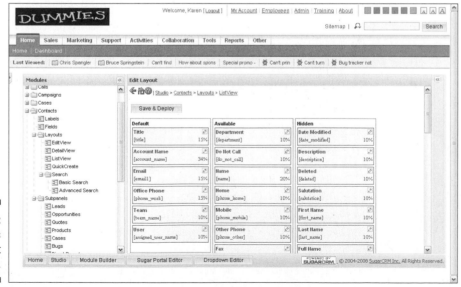

Figure 15-7:
Sugar's
Edit Layout
page.

Changing the page views

When you modify the Edit view or Detail view, things look a bit different. Studio shows the separate sections of the layout and the fields they contain. You can edit, create, rename, and/or move the sections. Talk about having things just the way you like them!

1. **Click Admin on the Sugar Home page and then click Studio in the Developer Tools subpanel.**

   The Sugar Studio opens.

2. **Expand the module for which you want to change the view, expand the Layouts section, and then click the DetailView or ListView.**

   The Edit Layout page opens, as shown in Figure 15-8. Notice that it comes equipped with a Toolbox.

3. **Make your editing changes.**

   Notice the pencil icon in the top-right corner of each field; to drag a field, you need to place your mouse pointer directly on that icon.

   - *Remove an existing field:* Select the field and drag it to the Recycle bin. The field will appear in the list of fields under the Recycle bin where you can retrieve it at any time.

   - *Replace a field:* Select the field from the list of available fields under the Recycle bin, drag it to the new location, and drop it on the field that you want to replace.

   - *To add a field:* Drag the New Row icon from under the Recycle bin and drop it on the layout where you want it to appear. The field will display (filler). You can then replace the filler field with an available field.

   - *To move a field:* Drag the field to the desired location on the layout.

   - *To expand the width of a field:* Drag the field next to it to the Recycle bin.

   - *To decrease the width of an expanded field:* Click the minus sign on the left corner of an expanded field; the field will contract and a filler field will be left in the open space.

4. **(Optional) Click a field's pencil icon and then replace the existing field name with a new field name in the dialog box that opens.**

   In most cases, the field name and the field label are exactly the same. Having a field label differ too radically from the name of the actual field proves to be quite confusing when you wander into the area of template and report creation. However, sometimes you might want to tweak the field label so that it fits your layout better. For example, a field named *Cellular Telephone Number* might be shortened to a more readable *Cell.*

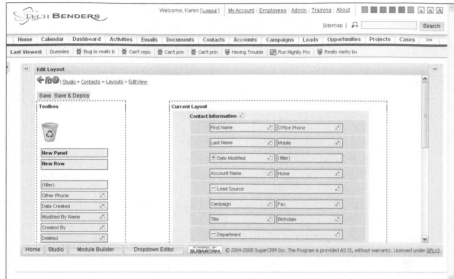

Figure 15-8:
Changing
the
DetailView
or ListView.

5. **(Optional) Drag the New Panel icon to the layout to create a new panel.**

   You can then create a label for the panel by clicking its pencil icon and giving it a name. Once created, you can start adding fields to it.

6. **(Optional) Drag a panel to a new location on the layout to move it.**

   You can drag a panel — and all the fields it contains — to a new location on your layout.

7. **Select a save option when you're finished editing the layout.**

   • *Save:* Allows you to save your changes without making them visible to your users.

   • *Save & Deploy:* Displays the updated view to the Sugar users.

Working with Drop-down Lists

The sure-fire way to destroy a database is by adding information in an inconsistent manner. Drop-down lists help ensure that users input data in a uniform way. As an added bonus, drop-down lists also save you time: When you type the first several letters of an item in your drop-down list, Sugar responds by completing the word for you.

As the administrator, you can create and edit values in all of the existing drop-down fields. Better yet, you can create new drop-down lists for Dropdown and MultiSelect field types.

Creating a drop-down list requires two steps:

- ✔ **Building a drop-down list.**
- ✔ **Specifying that the field is to contain a drop-down list.**

Creating a drop-down list

Although you can start by creating a field first, it's probably better to start by creating the drop-down list. It will save you from having to edit a new field to associate it with a drop-down list.

1. **Click Admin on the Sugar Home page and then click Dropdown Editor in the Developer Tools subpanel.**

   The Dropdown Editor panel opens, as shown in Figure 15-9.

2. **Click the name of the drop-down list you want to edit or click the Add Dropdown button.**

   Because the names of the drop-down lists are a bit confusing, selecting an existing drop-down list can be a bit tricky and may take you a few tries before you select the correct one. In any event, the panel shown in Figure 15-10 opens.

3. **Give the drop-down list a name in the Name field.**

   To make life easier for you, provide a name that coincides with the field that is going to use the drop-down list.

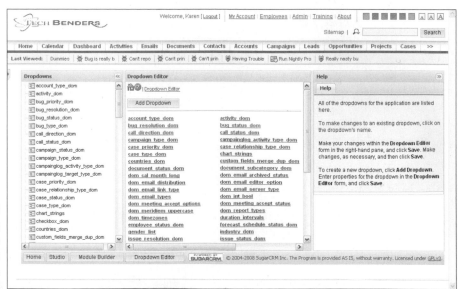

Figure 15-9:
Sugar's
Dropdown
Editor.

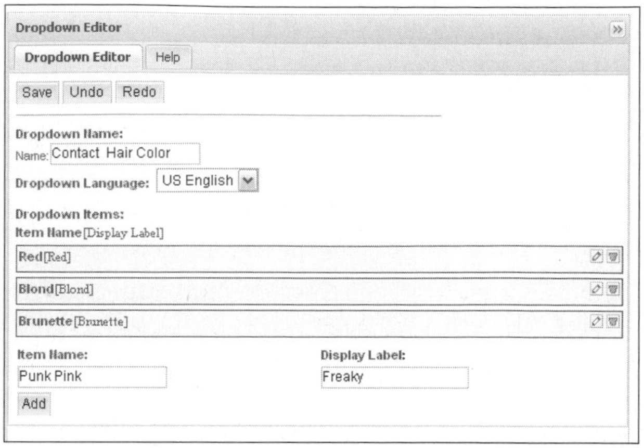

Figure 15-10:
Creating a
drop-down
list.

4. **Add the first drop-down item in the Item Name field and add its label to the Display Label field.**

   Generally, the Item Name and the Display Label are the same.

5. **Click the Add button.**

   Your new drop-down value appears at the bottom of the Dropdown Editor.

6. **Continue adding new drop-down values by repeating Steps 4 and 5.**

7. **Click Save to save the drop-down list.**

   The new drop-down list displays under the module name in the center panel.

Adding the drop-down list to a field

This might seem like a case of "Which came first, the chicken or the egg?" In the preceding section, I tell you how to create a drop-down list. Typically, your next step is to create a field and associate the drop-down list with it. In other cases, you might create a field, create the drop-down list, and then *edit* the field to associate the drop-down list with the field.

Here's what you need to do to edit an existing field and associate it with a drop-down list:

1. **Click Admin on the Sugar Home page and then click Studio in the Developer Tools subpanel.**

   The Sugar Studio opens.

2. **Expand the module that contains the field you want to add the drop-down list to and then click the name of the field.**

   The Field Editor panel opens.

   You can only add drop-down lists to Dropdown and MultiSelect field types.

3. **Choose the name of the drop-down list from the Dropdown List drop down menu.**

   Whew! You might want to reread that sentence a few times. Basically, Sugar provides you with a list containing all your drop-downs. And, if the name of the drop-down list matches the name of your field, Sugar cleverly makes the association for you automatically.

4. **Click Save to save the changes to the field.**

Manufacturing a Module

Just as you can add fields to your database, you can also add modules. Using modules is a great way to organize the information in your database. Once created, a module can appear as a subpanel on other records.

There are a number of great scenarios for creating a custom module. For example, you might create a Products module that lists the various products you're tracking that includes the serial number and a link to the Accounts or Contacts record(s) that purchased that specific product. Or, if most of your business comes from specific individuals, you might create a Referrals module and then link the referral source to each Accounts record that they send you.

Before you begin to reinvent the wheel, you might want to check out SugarForge (www.sugarforge.org) and SugarExchange (www.sugar exchange.com) where you can either download lots of modules for a slight fee or free.

Packing up a package

The first step to creating a new module is to create a package. In Sugar, a *package* holds your custom module(s). Although a package can contain modules that are unrelated to each other, generally you create a package for a project you're working on.

After you create a package, you can begin creating modules for it, or you can return to the Module Builder later to finish the project.

The process of creating a Package is a very easy one:

1. **Click Admin on the Sugar Home page and then click Module Builder in the Developer Tools subpanel.**

   Module Builder opens. If this is your first foray into the Module Builder, there won't be much to see except a rather large icon that reads New Package.

2. **Click the New Package icon.**

   Module Builder's Package panel changes to allow you to enter information about the new module.

3. **Enter the basic module information.**

   As you can see in Figure 15-11, there's not much information that you need to enter:

   • *Package Name:* Give the package a name.

   • *Author:* You may as well get credit for your work.

   • *Key:* Enter an alphanumeric key to help Sugar with its housekeeping, as Sugar will append this key to various directories and tables. In general, it's a good idea to keep the key name as short as possible — but long enough so that you can still identify it.

   • *Description:* Enter a description of the package.

   • *Readme:* If there's something else about the module that you want other users to know, feel free to give them some reading material.

4. **Click Save to create the `module` package.**

   The Package page refreshes and displays a couple of new options. You're now free to roam around the cabin — or start to build your module.

Making a module

After you create a package, you're ready to fill it with a module — or two or three. And of course, you'll want to edit the module — which you already know how to do if you read the section, "Stepping into the Studio," earlier in this chapter.

1. **Click Admin on the Sugar Home page and then click Module Builder in the Developer Tools subpanel.**

   Alternatively, if you just finished creating a package, you can start by clicking the New Module icon that appears when you save a package.

2. **Click the name of your package and then click the New Module icon.**

   The Module page opens, as shown in Figure 15-12.

3. **Fill in the basic module information:**

- **Name:** Enter a name for the module.

- **Label:** Enter the name that the users will use to identify the module.

- **Navigation Tab:** Select this option if you want to create a tab for the module on the Module bar.

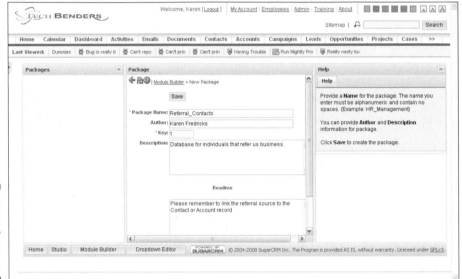

Figure 15-11:
Creating a new package in Sugar.

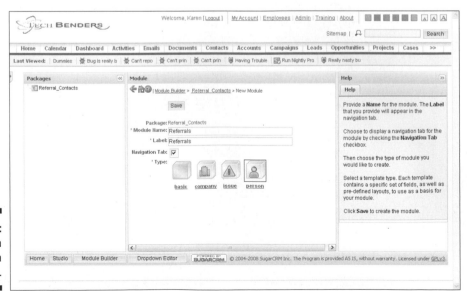

Figure 15-12:
Adding a module to a package.

4. **Select the type of module you want to create by selecting its icon.**

   Each module template contains a set of fields; picking the right module type *now* will save you from having to add a bunch of fields later.

   - *Basic:* Creates the basic fields used in most modules, such as Name, Assigned to, Team, Date Created, and Description.

   - *Company:* Provides such fields as Company Name, Industry, and Billing Address. Think of this as the Accounts module clone.

   - *Issue:* This Cases and Bug Tracker clone includes such fields as Number, Status, Priority, and Description.

   - *Person:* Gives you basic contact fields, such as Name, Title, Address, and Phone Number.

   Choosing a module type is just a starting point. After you create a module, you can edit any of the field labels or create new custom fields.

5. **Click Save to save the module.**

   The Packages page refreshes and shows you a hierarchy in the Packages panel on the left side of the page. This hierarchy should give you a feeling of déjà vu because it's the same type of hierarchy that appears in the Studio.

6. **Expand the name of your project from the Packages panel and then expand the name of your module.**

7. **Click an element to start editing the module.**

   You'll probably want to start by looking at the fields that Sugar created for you and tweaking them. You can then move on to your layouts and customize the ListView, EditView, DetailView, and Search fields if needed.

You can't delete any of the default fields that come with a module but you can hide them from within the Layouts pages.

Building a relationship

Like a family tree, a Sugar module can have multiple relationships with other modules. For example, the Accounts module is related to the Contacts, Leads, and Opportunities modules. After you establish a relationship between modules, the related modules will appear as subpanels in a record's Detail view. In the example of the Accounts module, the Contacts, Leads, and Opportunities subpanels are in an Accounts record's Detail view because they are *related* to the Accounts module.

When you create a module, you need to specify its relationship to other modules. A Sugar module can have multiple relationships with other Sugar modules. You can also specify the modules in which you want to display the custom module as a subpanel.

1. **Click Admin on the Sugar Home page and then click Module Builder in the Developer Tools subpanel.**

2. **Click the name of the package and then click the name of the module that you want to relate to another module.**

   The Module's page opens.

3. **Click the View Relationships button.**

   Any existing relationships display on the page.

4. **Click Add Relationship to create a relationship.**

   The relationship fields display in the Properties tab in the right panel. You might take a look at Figure 15-13 just to make sure you're on the right track.

5. **Add the following information about the relationship:**

   • *Relate To:* Choose the module that you want to associate with your new module from the drop-down list.

   • *Label:* Enter a name for the relationship.

   • *Subpanel:* Choose Default from the drop-down list if you want to display the associated module as a subpanel on the Detail view of the custom module.

   • *Record Subpanel:* Choose Default from the second drop-down list if you want to display the custom module as a subpanel on the Detail view of the related module.

Figure 15-13:
Creating a
relationship.

6. **Click Save to create the relationship.**

   The new relationship displays under the Add Relationship button in the middle panel.

Deploying the module

Neither Rome — nor a Sugar module — is built in a day. Now, maybe you see why it's so important to plan your Sugar implementation before you dive off the customization deep-end.

Knowing that it can often take several days — or even a month — to create a new module from start to finish, Sugar offers you a "create now, use later" scenario. Here's how you can get that module to your users:

1. **Click Admin on the Sugar Home page and then click Module Builder in the Developer Tools subpanel.**

   Alternatively, if you just finished creating a package, you can start by clicking the New Module icon that appears when you save a package.

2. **Click the name of your package and then click the name of your module.**

   Sugar offers you three options for getting your newly created module into the hands of your end-user:

   • *Publish:* Use this option when you only want to give the module to *specific* users. Sugar creates a zip file, and then the users upload it by using the Module Loader. Further customization can be done by using the Studio.

   • *Deploy:* This option makes the module available to *all* the users in your organization. Further customization can be done by using the Studio.

   • *Export:* This option is used to share the module with other developers. Sugar creates a zip file that a developer can save and install with the Module Loader. Further customization can be done by using the Module Builder.

   For now, concentrate on deploying your new module to all your users.

3. **Click Deploy.**

   Sugar begins loading the module into your Sugar instance and indicates that something wonderful is happening. Any smoke that emanates from your computer is temporary.

When Sugar finishes deploying your module, the Package page will refresh. If you want to make further changes to the module, you can do so from the Sugar Studio where the new module appears along with all the existing ones. Your users can access the module by clicking the corresponding tab on the Module Tab bar.

Configuring Module Tabs

By default, all the module tabs are displayed when a user logs in to Sugar. However, if you're the administrator you can decide which module tabs to display — and which ones to hide. You can even choose the order in which these tabs are arranged.

When you decide which tabs you want your users to access, the users can go into the My Account page and make further modification (see Chapter 9). However, users can't add module tabs that the administrator removed. And, if the administrator has an ax to grind with the users — or is afraid that they might wreak a bit of havoc — the administrator can prevent the users from making any changes to the module tabs.

Although it's been said that you can't go home again, this adage doesn't hold true in Sugar. Nobody — not even Mr. Administrator — can hide the Home tab.

Renaming the module tabs

You can rename the module tabs that display in Sugar:

1. **Click Admin on the Sugar Home page and then click Rename Tabs in the Developer Tools subpanel.**

   The Administration: Rename Tabs page opens. As shown in Figure 15-14, it's a simple page consisting of the name of the official tab name (Database Value) and its label (Display Value).

2. **Click the label that you want to edit and replace it with the new value.**

   You can't change the name of the Database Value; it remains constant just in case you want to return to the original tab name.

3. **Click Save to save your changes.**

   The new tab name appears in the module tab menu.

Figure 15-14:
Renaming a
tab.

Playing hide and seek with the tabs

By now you're acquainted with the basic modules and are probably in awe of their functionality. However, sometimes less is more — particularly when you are dealing with computer-challenged database users. For example, you might not use the Quoting module that you'll find in the Professional and Enterprise versions, or you might use Outlook for your activities and not want to confuse your users with the Activities module. Or perhaps you just want to start out slowly and introduce new modules as your users become more proficient Sugar users.

Sugar makes it easy to hide a module tab. The operative word here is *hide*; it's an easy matter to *unhide* a module should you decide you'd like to use the module.

Follow these steps to hide a module tab — or to bring it back to life if you've already hidden it:

1. **Click Admin on the Sugar Home page and then click Configure Tabs in the Developer Tools subpanel.**

   The Configure Tabs page shown in Figure 15-15 opens. Like the Rename Tabs page, this is a simple page consisting of two columns: Display Tabs and Hide Tabs.

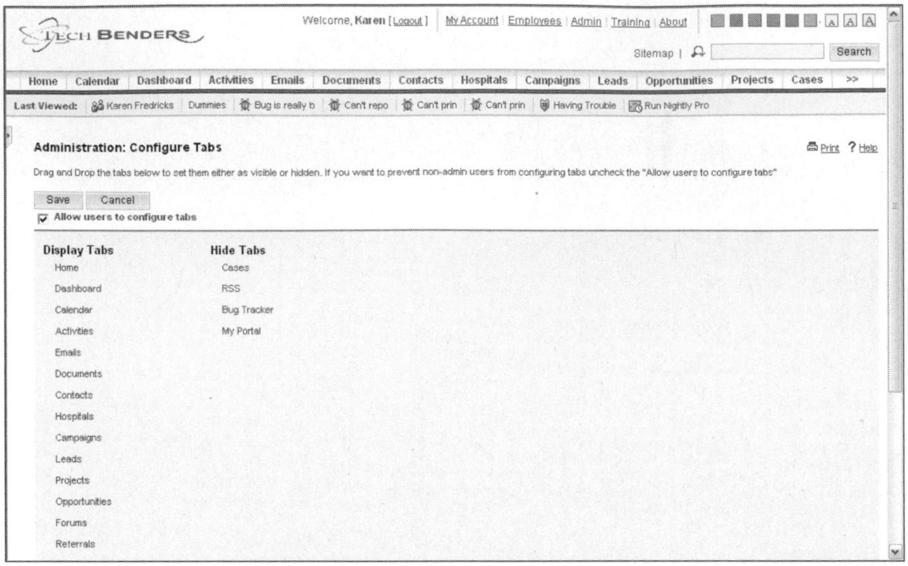

Figure 15-15:
Hiding tabs
from the
users.

2. **Drag any tabs you don't want the users to have access to from the Display Tabs column to the Hide Tabs column.**

3. **(Optional) Remove the check mark in the Allow Users to Configure Tabs check box if you don't want the users to make changes to the tabs that they're allowed to access.**

4. **Click Save to save your changes.**

Chapter 16

The Administrator's Recipe Book

*I*f you're the Master Chef . . . er, I mean database administrator, you need to make sure that your soufflés don't flop — and that your database purrs along. As the administrator, you have the sole access to the Administration module where you perform great feats of daring, including updating Sugar and setting system settings. You also set up users — and decide which areas of Sugar they can access.

Setting up the System

If you're the database administrator, becoming familiar with the system configuration is good practice. If you're the sole user of the database, these settings will likely save your sanity. If you share the database with other users, these settings can probably save you all a lot of head scratching.

You can access Sugar's System Settings by clicking the Admin link on your Home page and then scrolling to the System subpanel of the Administration Home page. The System subpanel (shown in Figure 16-1) is divided into nine areas; although I only cover the most basic ones, feel free to flip through the other settings.

System

Configure the system-wide settings according to the specifications of your organization. Users can override some of the default locale settings within their My Accounts page.

System Settings	Configure system-wide settings	Backups	Perform a backup
Scheduler	Set up scheduled events	Repair	Check and repair Sugar
Diagnostic Tool	Capture system configuration for diagnostics and analysis	Currencies	Set up currencies and currency rates
Upgrade Wizard	Upload and install Sugar upgrades	Module Loader	Add or remove Sugar modules, themes, and language packs
Locale Settings	Set default localization settings for your system		

Figure 16-1:
The System
subpanel.

Fiddling with the System settings

Clicking the System Settings link on the System subpanel opens the System Settings page shown in Figure 16-2. Here's where you can configure various default settings that will apply to all your users.

You have a number of options to change including:

- ✔ **User Interface:** This subpanel configures how users will view Sugar. You can set the number of records they'll see in a List view or the number of subpanels they'll see in a record's Detail view.

  Worried that your users won't like your choices? Don't be — users can specify different settings for many of the options in their My Accounts page. Worried that they will change so many things that they'll get confused? You can opt to keep them from customizing their Home page and subpanel layouts by checking those options.

- ✔ **Logos:** Here's where you can upload your logo to give Sugar a piece of your corporate identity.

- ✔ **LDAP Authentication Support:** If your organization is using LDAP or authentication, you can also enable LDAP authentication in Sugar.

- ✔ **Proxy Settings:** If you're using a proxy server to connect to the Internet, you'll need to enter the settings.

- ✔ **Customer Self-Service Portal:** This option enables your customers to access their Bugs, Notes, and Cases information.

- ✔ **SkypeOut:** Allows your users to make calls through Skype.

- ✔ **Mail Merge:** Click this if you have the Sugar plug-in for Microsoft Word.

- ✔ **Export:** By default, both users and administrators can export files from Sugar. However, here's where you can prevent users from exporting data.

Click the Save button after you select your System Settings options to make sure they're saved.

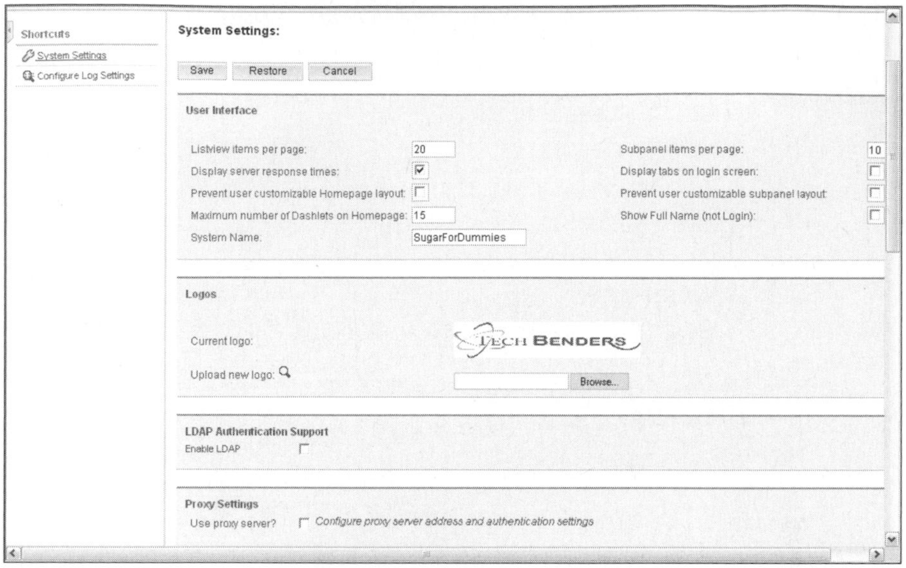

Figure 16-2:
Changing
the System
Settings.

Sticking to a Scheduler

You might nickname Sugar's Scheduler "Set it and Forget it" because that's exactly what it does. You can schedule a variety of *jobs* that will automatically run based on your pre-determined time schedule. The benefit is the peace of mind you have in knowing that various scheduled maintenance tasks will run without any further intervention. It's a wonderful thing — set up a task and have Scheduler complete the job for you.

The Scheduler allows you to automate several key jobs. The small amount of time you need to set up a job in the Scheduler will save you plenty of time — and possible heartache — in the future.

1. **Click Admin on the Home page and then click Scheduler in the System subpanel.**

   The Schedulers Home page opens. As shown in Figure 16-3, the Scheduler comes equipped with several pre-programmed jobs. Feel free to edit them to make them behave the way you want, or continue to create your own unique task:

   • *Process Workflow Tasks:* Chapter 14 talks about Sugar's Workflow feature that triggers an activity based on an event. This process runs those triggers.

   • *Run Report Generation Scheduled Tasks:* Runs reports and e-mails them to a specific user.

   • *Check Inbound Mail Accounts:* Checks for activity in your Inbox.

- *Run Nightly Process Bounced Campaign E-mails:* Checks your mass e-mail campaigns to look for any bounced e-mails.
- *Run Nightly Mass E-mail Campaigns:* Sends the outbound e-mail for your mass e-mail campaigns.
- *Prune Database on 1st of Month:* Similar to the Windows Defragmenter, this permanently deletes any records that your users have deleted to improve performance.

2. **Click Create Scheduler in the Shortcuts menu of the Scheduler Home page.**

   The new Schedulers form opens, as shown in Figure 16-4.

3. **Fill in the Scheduler information:**

   - *Job Name:* Give the job a name.
   - *Status:* Select Active when you're ready to go live with the job.
   - *Job:* Select a job type from the drop-down list. The job names correspond with the pre-programmed jobs listed above.
   - *Interval:* Specify the time intervals to check for new scheduled jobs.
   - *Execute If Missed:* If for some reason the job didn't run, select this check box to run it manually — just give yourself a minute or two because it might take a while to run the job.
   - *Date & Time Start:* Give a date for the job to start running.
   - *Date & Time End:* Specify a date to stop running the job.

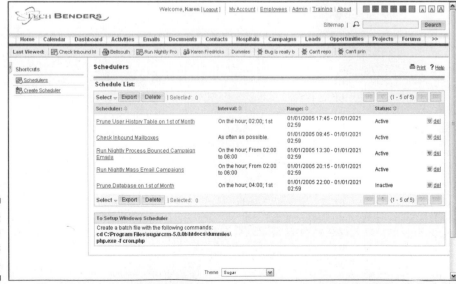

Figure 16-3:
The Schedulers Home page.

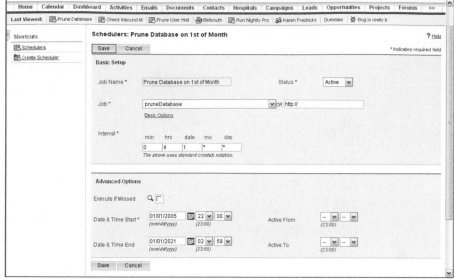

Figure 16-4:
Creating
a new
Scheduler
job.

4. **Click Save to create the job.**

   If you're using UNIX or Linux, you need to add a new Cronjob to your Crontab. If you're using Microsoft Windows, you can add the tasks to the Task Scheduler.

   The new job appears on the Schedule List.

Applying Sugar updates

Nobody's perfect. Although it might seem that Sugar comes pretty darned close, from time to time, a few of those dreaded bugs slip by the programmers and annoy the heck out of you. Or, you run out to purchase the latest and greatest version of Microsoft Office only to find that it won't work with your existing version of Sugar. Enter the update.

Sugar's *Upgrade Wizard* provides a quick way to upload and install Sugar upgrades. During the upgrade process, Sugar automatically converts all customizations implemented through the Sugar Studio. And, although the database administrator is the only one who can update Sugar, she can do it from the luxury of her desktop rather than needing direct access to the server.

As you can see in Figure 16-5, Sugar makes it abundantly clear when a new update arrives on the scene by placing a notification at the top of just about any window you wander to.

Figure 16-5:
It's time
to update
Sugar.

Here's what you need to do to make sure you have the latest and greatest Sugar version:

1. **Download the appropriate Sugar Upgrade zip file from the Sugar Web site.**

   For your convenience, `www.sugarcrm.com` has a download link that takes you to the Download Wizard that walks you through the process of finding the correct upgrade file.

2. **Click Admin on the Sugar Home page.**

3. **Click Upgrade Wizard in the System subpanel of the Administration Home page.**

   The Upgrade Wizard displays, as shown in Figure 16-6. The wizard will hold your hand while you continue to upgrade your Sugar installation.

4. **Click Next to continue.**

   A progress window appears while Sugar checks your system to make sure you're good to go. When it finishes, the System Checks page appears.

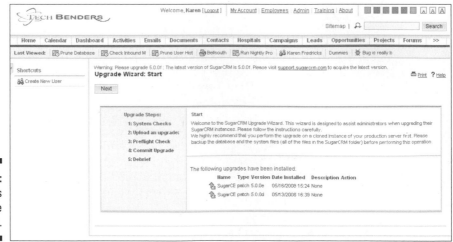

Figure 16-6:
Sugar's
Upgrade
Wizard.

5. **Click Next.**

   The Upload an Upgrade page appears.

6. **Click the Browse button, navigate to the location where you saved the Upgrade zip file, and then select the file.**

   The path and filename conveniently appear in the Upload an Upgrade box.

7. **Click the Upload Upgrade button to upload the package to your installation of Sugar.**

   An indicator window appears while Sugar uploads the package and displays it on the page. Feeling lost? Take a look at Figure 16-7 which should help clear things up.

8. **Click Next to continue.**

   Again, you have to wait a minute as Sugar performs a preflight check. At this time, you just might feel like you're in a spaceship hurtling towards Mars. At any rate, the Commit Upgrade window appears.

9. **Click Next to continue.**

   Like most wizards, the Upgrade Wizard contains many Next buttons. However, this is the final one because if all systems are go, you'll see the Debrief window.

10. **Click Done.**

    Aren't you glad I didn't tell you to click Next? At any rate, you're treated to a page verifying that yes, indeedy, you have officially upgraded to the latest Sugar version.

Figure 16-7:
Uploading the upgrade file to Sugar.

Getting Locale with the locals

Clicking the Locale Settings link on the System subpanel opens the System Locale Settings page you see in Figure 16-8. Here's where you can configure various default settings that apply to all your users. Use this page to specify the default system-wide locale settings, such as the language, date and time format, and even the type of currency that your company uses. Changing these settings ensures consistency for users when they access Sugar; these settings appear throughout Sugar in various documents including Quotes and Contracts.

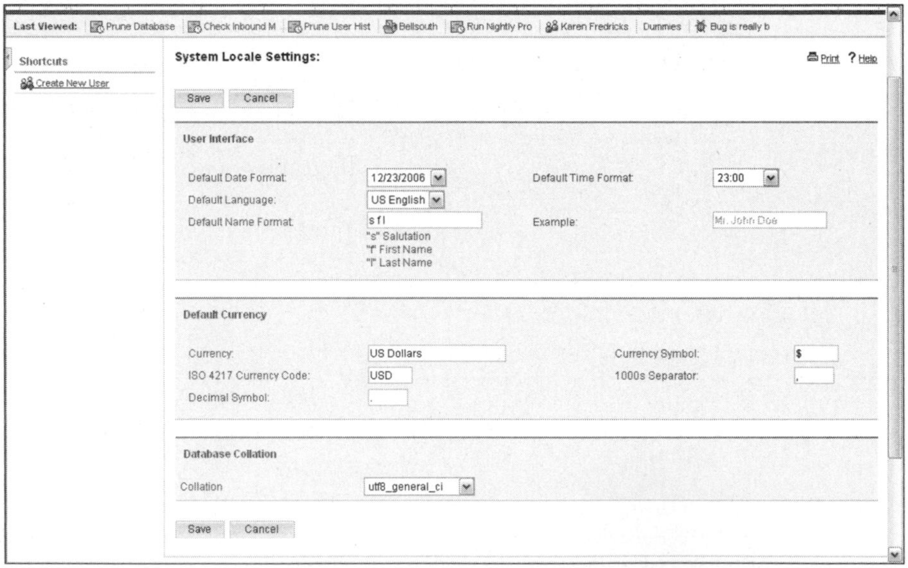

Figure 16-8:
Changing the system-wide locale settings.

Dealing with Database Users

A *user* is a special contact in your database who logs in to your database. If several people enter data into your Sugar database, I highly recommend setting up each person as a separate user. If you and Jane are both set up as users of the database, make sure that you log in as you and Jane logs in as herself. Sugar automatically enters several key pieces of information based on how you log in to the database. For example, you're recognized as the record creator of each new Contacts record that you add to the database. Your name is automatically associated with any meetings, calls, or other activities that you schedule. Having unique, identifiable users in a database allows you to view your activities on a calendar. Otherwise, you might find yourself driving to Podunk to visit Jane's mom on her birthday!

After you assign the players to the teams, get ready to rumble! The purpose of the game is to decide exactly what each user can do within Sugar. You can do this on a user-by-user basis. This works out well if you assign access rights to each new contact when you create it. Or, as the administrator, you can assign users a *role*. Roles determine which modules a user has access to — and the type of activities he can perform within that module.

Adding a new user to the mix

Although creating new users is an easy process, take your time and fill in as much pertinent information as possible. In addition to simply creating users, the administrator can — and should — include contact information about the users.

1. **Click Admin on the Home page.**

   It's only logical that because only an administrator can create new users, you start the process on the Administration Home page.

2. **Choose Create New User from the Shortcuts menu.**

   The Users page shown in Figure 16-9 opens.

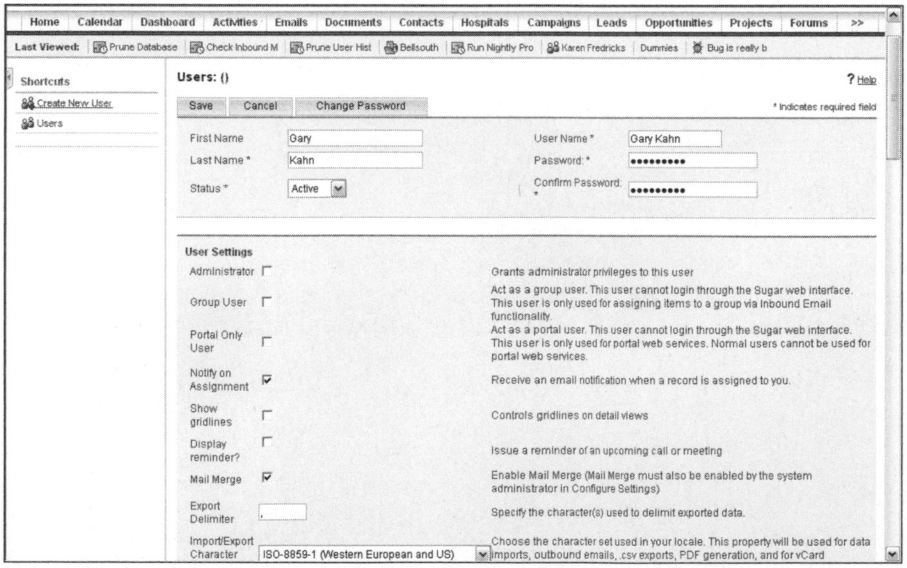

Figure 16-9: Adding a new Sugar user.

3. **Add the user's first and last name, their login name and password, and the user status in the top subpanel.**

   The user name is the name the user will use to log in to the database. Although it's not case sensitive, make sure you remember what name you decide on. If you set up multiple users for the same database, consider sticking to a set naming convention: *Gary Kahn* or *gkahn* are good choices; you might want to avoid *Gary B. Kahn* or *Gary Kahn, Esq.*

   You can't *delete* users but you can stop someone from accessing the database by changing their status to *inactive.* This is done so that you can still see what records have been assigned to them, or what fields they've changed.

4. **Select the appropriate options in the User Settings subpanel.**

   You can specify whether you want the new user to have Mail Merge privileges (if the user has access to the Sugar plug-in for Microsoft Word), and how you want his name to appear at the top of the various Sugar views. You can enable e-mail notifications to the user when a record is assigned to him.

   Most importantly, you can specify the *type* of user you wish to create. In Sugar, there are three different kinds of users in addition to the basic end-user. By default, Sugar assumes you're creating an end-user unless you specify otherwise.

   • *Administrator:* Finding the job of database administrator to be overwhelming? You can assign another user to be your partner in crime.

     Assigning two users as the database administrator is always a good idea. Not only do those two people feel extra special, but it can also save your little rear end. As hard as it might be to believe, the administrator might leave the company suddenly and without warning — taking the keys for the restroom and the password for the database with him. This means you might not be able to access the database, add users, or make field changes. You might also find yourself looking for a new job. *Remember:* No password, no entry!

   • *Group user:* A group user can't log in to the database. The function of a group user is to receive general inbound e-mails that might pertain to a department as a whole instead of a specific individual. For example, you might create a group user named Complaints to handle customer service issues. You can then assign them to the appropriate users from the group Inbox.

   • *Portal-only user:* A portal user can log in to portals created in Sugar but can't log in to the Sugar database. For example, you might create a user record for one of your top customers so that he can access general portal information, such as FAQ's and the Knowledge Base.

5. **Set the values in the Locale Settings subpanel.**

   Although you can set default locale settings (see the earlier "Getting Locale with the locals" section), you can change these values for individual users if necessary. For example, your company may be headquartered in New York, thus you've set default locale values to EST and US Dollar. However, you may have a user located in California who works on PST, or maybe a user in London who works in a different time zone and uses a different currency.

6. **Specify the information in the User Information subpanel.**

   Here's where you can supply work-related details including the user's title, department, phone numbers, who he reports to, and any other pertinent info. You can even add a comment in the Notes field if necessary.

7. **Supply the user's home address in the Address Information subpanel.**

8. **(Optional) Enter a Publish Key in the Calendar Options subpanel to prevent others from publishing the user's calendar.**

9. **Change the modules that the user can see in the Layout Options subpanel.**

   By default, a new user has access to all the Sugar modules. As the administrator, you decide which of those modules the user can access.

   As shown in Figure 16-10, the Layout Options subpanel contains three lists:

   - *Display Tabs:* Lists the tabs that the user can see.

   - *Hide Tabs:* Shows the tabs that the user can't see.

   - *Admin Remove Tabs:* Lists the tabs that *none* of the users can see.

   You can move a tab from one list to another by selecting it and then clicking the appropriate right or left arrow. To change the order of the modules, select the module and then click the up or down arrow.

   Chapter 3 shows the end-user how to configure the tabs that she sees. Chapter 15, on the other hand, shows you how the administrator can prevent the end-user from doing exactly that.

10. **Add the user's e-mail address in the Email options subpanel.**

    You can set up an e-mail address — or two or three — for each user.

11. **Click Save to create the user.**

    You land with a plop on the Users Home page where the new user is listed right along with all the other Sugar users. They also appear on the Employees List, which you can access by clicking the Employees link from any of the Sugar views.

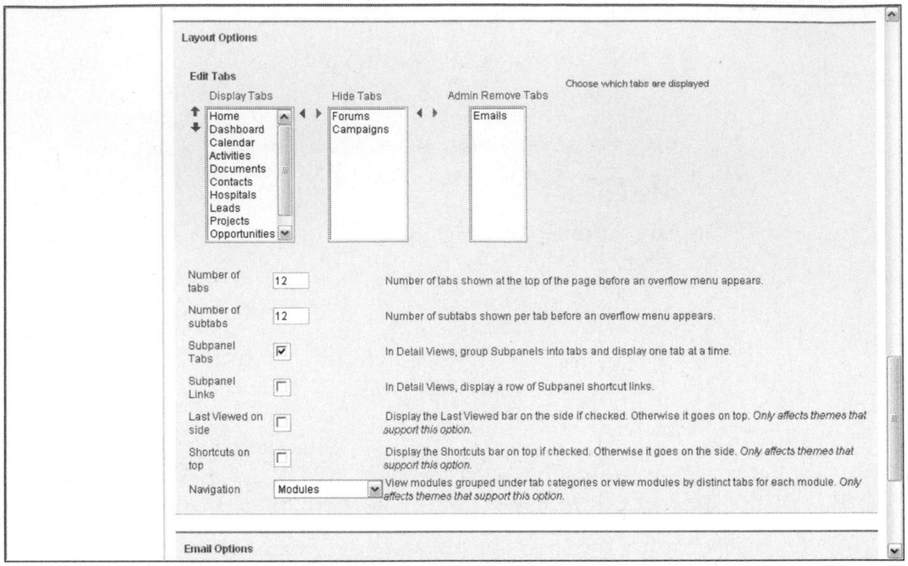

Figure 16-10: Determining which tabs a user may access.

Doing the rock 'n role

After you create your users, you assign them roles depending on the tasks they perform within your organization. By default, users have access to all Sugar modules. Roles enable the administrator to limit access to specific modules. Additionally, roles allow the administrator to decide the functionality the users have within a module.

For example, you may decide that your customer service folks don't need to access the Opportunities module; you can create a role that restricts their access to this module and assign that role to everyone in the customer service department. Or, you may want to allow your sales staff the ability to view and edit Accounts, Contacts, and Leads records but not the ability to delete or export records.

Users who aren't assigned a role can, by default, access and take any action in any module they want. The only way you can change that access is by assigning them a role that limits access to a module. The same role can be assigned to multiple users, and a user can be assigned multiple roles.

An administrator, by default, has permission to access all modules and records. And, the only way you can deny him those permissions is to edit his user record so that he is no longer an administrator.

Creating a starring role

Follow these steps to create a role:

1. **Click Admin on the Home page.**

2. **Click Role Management in the Users subpanel.**

   The Roles Home page opens.

3. **Choose Create Role from the Shortcuts menu.**

   The Roles page opens.

4. **Supply a name for the role, give it an optional description, and then click Save.**

   All the Sugar modules — along with the basic functions — are listed in table format. You use this table to grant permission to access modules or perform specific actions.

   As shown in Figure 16-11, the edit view appears a bit intimidating at first.

   You might think of this as a giant Bingo board. The column on the left lists all the Sugar modules. The top row shows you the various functions:

   - *Access:* Determines whether the users assigned that role can access a module.

     If you deny users access to a module, you automatically deny the users all the functionality listed in the rest of the columns in that row.

   - *Delete:* Authorizes the user to delete records (Contacts, Accounts, Leads, Opportunities, and so on). By default, the administrator already has permission to delete at will.

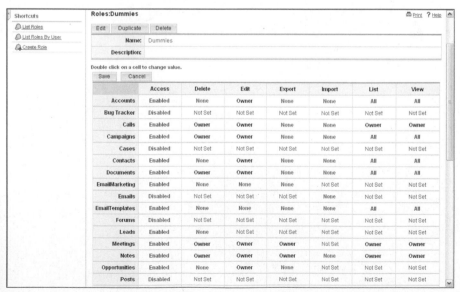

Figure 16-11:
Creating a
user role.

Roles:Dummies

Shortcuts
- List Roles
- List Roles By User
- Create Role

Edit | Duplicate | Delete

Name: Dummies
Description:

Double click on a cell to change value.

Save | Cancel

	Access	Delete	Edit	Export	Import	List	View
Accounts	Enabled	None	Owner	None	None	All	All
Bug Tracker	Disabled	Not Set	Not Set	Not Set	Not Set	Not Set	Not Set
Calls	Enabled	Owner	Owner	None	None	Owner	Owner
Campaigns	Enabled	Owner	Owner	None	None	All	All
Cases	Disabled	Not Set	Not Set	Not Set	Not Set	Not Set	Not Set
Contacts	Enabled	None	Owner	None	None	All	All
Documents	Enabled	Owner	Owner	None	None	All	All
EmailMarketing	Enabled	None	None	None	Not Set	Not Set	Not Set
Emails	Disabled	Not Set	Not Set	Not Set	None	Not Set	Not Set
EmailTemplates	Enabled	None	None	None	None	All	All
Forums	Disabled	Not Set	Not Set	Not Set	Not Set	Not Set	Not Set
Leads	Enabled	None	Not Set	Not Set	Not Set	Not Set	Not Set
Meetings	Enabled	Owner	Owner	Owner	Not Set	Owner	Owner
Notes	Enabled	Owner	Owner	Owner	None	Owner	Owner
Opportunities	Enabled	None	Owner	None	Not Set	Not Set	Not Set
Posts	Disabled	Not Set	Not Set	Not Set	Not Set	Not Set	Not Set

- *Edit:* Lets users edit records in the module through the Edit page, List view, or the Mass Update panel in the List view.

- *Export:* Permits the user to export any List view information to a file.

- *Import:* Users can import record data in the module.

- *List:* Users can view lists of records in the module or in a subpanel but can't edit them unless they have editing permissions.

- *View:* Users can see the Details view of module records.

5. **Double-click a cell to change its value.**

   Here's where the Bingo board concept comes into play. If you want to disable a module, double-click the cell in which the Access column and the module row intersect. Depending on the cell you're modifying, you have a number of options available:

   - *All:* All users who are assigned to the role can perform the action.

   - *Owner:* Only the user who either created or is assigned to the record can perform the action.

   - *None:* None of the users assigned to the role get to play — or perform the action.

   - *Enabled:* Allows the user to view the module.

   - *Disabled:* Hides the module from the users' view.

   - *Not Set:* This leaves the setting unchanged. This can be because you haven't gotten to the setting yet or you left the function unset knowing that another role covers that particular function.

If you assign more than one role to a user, the most restrictive setting prevails. For example, if a user is assigned to two roles — one allowing him to access a module and one disabling the module — he won't be able to access the module.

6. **Click Save when you finish defining the role.**

Rolling out roles to the users

By now, if you're following along at home, you've added a couple of new users to your database. You've also created a role that will both let the users carry out their day-to-day business and leave you with the security of knowing they can't abscond with the entirety of your database should they decide to seek employment elsewhere. Your next step is to tie the two together. Fortunately for you, the hard work is over; assigning a role to a user is very easy.

1. **Click Admin on the Home page.**

2. **Click Role Management in the Users subpanel.**

   The Roles Home page opens. The role you created is listed there.

3. **Click the name of the role to which you want to assign a few users.**

   The Roles page opens.

4. **Scroll to the Users subpanel (see Figure 16-12).**

Figure 16-12:
The Users
sub-panel
of the Roles
Home page.

5. **Click the Select button.**

   The Select Users window opens, revealing a list of all your database users.

6. **Select the corresponding check box for all the users you want to assign to the role and then click Select.**

   The user(s) that you assign to the role appear in the Users subpanel.

7. **(Optional) Click the Rem icon corresponding to a username to remove a user if you no longer want him to abide by the role.**

Viewing roles for a user

Because so many options are available to you when creating a role, it's only natural that you might get lost along the way, particularly if you assign several roles to a user. Fear not, dear reader. Sugar again has your back, allowing you to view the finished work — or in this case the final role settings — on a user-by-user basis.

Follow these steps to view the permissions you set for each user:

1. **Click Admin on the Home page.**

2. **Click Role Management in the Users subpanel.**

3. **Choose List Roles by User in the Shortcuts menu.**

   The Roles page opens, looking slightly different than you've seen it before.

4. **Choose the user in question from the drop-down list.**

   Sugar responds by displaying a table detailing the user's permissions for each module. The bad news is that you can't change any of the permissions for the user. The good news is that you can click the List Roles shortcut and edit the role if you need to.

Part VI
The Part of Tens

The 5th Wave   By Rich Tennant

"Somebody got through our dead-end Web links, past the firewalls, and around the phone prompt loops. Before you know it, the kid here picks up the phone and he's talking one-on-one to a customer."

In this part . . .

*E*very *For Dummies* book has a Part of Tens. By golly, this book is no exception to that rule. Think of this as the icing on your Sugar cake. Here's where I answer a few of your more burning questions:

- ✔ What in the world is the difference between Sugar Community Edition and the subscription-based Professional and Enterprise versions?

- ✔ Is there a way that I sweeten the deal even more — or at least add a few items to make Sugar work even "more better?"

- ✔ Where do I go from here if I want to learn even *more* about Sugar?

Chapter 17

Ten Reasons to Upgrade to the Professional or Enterprise Version

As I mention throughout this book, SugarCRM has three flavors: Community, Professional, and Enterprise. Each version builds on the previous version: Professional contains all the features you find in the Community edition; and Enterprise has all the features you find in SugarCRM Professional. I sprinkle references to the Pro and Enterprise features throughout the book. And, in Chapter 14, I devote an entire chapter to a few of the Professional features. In this chapter, I list my ten favorite Pro and Enterprise features.

Sugar created the Professional and Enterprise editions to support companies with many users and teams. Hopefully, customers with less than five users find that the Sugar Community Edition meets their needs because both the Professional and Enterprise versions require a minimum of five users.

Users of a shared database must all use the same version of Sugar. A user of the Sugar Community Edition (CE) can't open a database created with Sugar Pro. However, you can upgrade a Sugar CE database if you decide to move up to Sugar Pro or Enterprise.

You can use any of the Sugar versions in a network environment.

Becoming a Team Player

You find references to teams sprinkled throughout the Pro and Enterprise editions. The administrator can create and manage teams based on job type, division, geography, or any other criteria he can think of. After the administrator creates a team — and assigns users to it — he can assign access rights to the team.

You can assign most of the record types that you create in Sugar to both an individual user and a team. For example, Opportunities, Contacts, Accounts, and Cases can all become the shared responsibility of a team of users.

I Want that Report on My Desk First Thing in the Morning!

Putting information into Sugar is only half the fun; the other half comes from being able to mine and manipulate the data to give you a good feel for what's working in your business — and what's not.

If you're a single user running your business from a tree house in your backyard, you probably have most of the facts and figures about your company whirling around in your head. The amount of data in your database grows proportionally with your number of employees; relying on your memory is no longer a viable solution.

The Reports module (see Chapter 14) transforms piles of data into organized knowledge. Managers can evaluate performance by running reports on salespeople, marketing campaigns, and customer service issues. Reports are *drillable* which means managers can double-click the information in a report to see the underlying data.

The Reports module includes a basic report writer, so managers can develop new reports based on customized queries. Customized reports can also take the form of a chart or graph so they can appear on the Dashboard module. Reports can be printed in PDF format and you can schedule them to be sent to your Inbox on a regular basis.

You Can Quote Me on That

Although a handshake is binding in some parts of the world, most of us would prefer to have our business dealings committed to in writing. Sugar Professional allows you to create Quotes (Chapter 7) and Contracts, which you can deliver to customers via e-mail, Word, or PDF format.

Sales reps can generate quotes that calculate line items, currencies, and taxes — saving you the worry of having to double-check their math. Version control makes it easier to manage the myriad versions of quotes and contracts that your users have issued.

The Quotes module integrates with the Products module so that you can create a Product Catalog designed to arm your sales reps with product information ranging from the amount of inventory on hand to discounted pricing available to preferred customers.

The Forecast Is Always Sunny

Large companies — especially those with lots of cubicles and a large sales force — live and die by quotas. The Forecasting module (refer to Chapter 14) allows sales managers to view the committed sale amounts of individual sales people as well as sales teams.

Forecasts are based on opportunities. The module includes a forecasting worksheet that allows you to set a quota and predict the best- and worst-case scenarios for that quota. At the end of the sales period, you can then see who is meeting or beating their quota — and who's not.

Becoming a Road Warrior

Who says you can't take it with you? Certainly not the folks at Sugar who give you an option for accessing your database when away from the office — and possibly away from an Internet connection.

The Sugar Offline Client enables users and administrators to use the Sugar application on their local machines without connecting to the Sugar server. This allows users to work in locations where it's not possible to access the Sugar server. They can then synchronize the data on their PC with the data on the Sugar server to make the updated information available to all users in the organization.

You can use the Sugar Offline Client, which is only supported on the Microsoft Windows platform, for the following subset of Sugar modules:

- ✔ Home
- ✔ Calendar
- ✔ Activities
- ✔ Accounts
- ✔ Contacts
- ✔ Emails

- ✔ Leads
- ✔ Opportunities
- ✔ Quotes
- ✔ Products
- ✔ Forecasts

The Offline Client does not synchronize information from any custom modules that you create.

Keep Up with the Folks at Microsoft

Face it. Microsoft is everywhere. Most likely, you're running more than one of its products on your computer. Like many other software products, Sugar takes the "if you can't beat 'em, join 'em" philosophy. Sugar Professional and Enterprise includes plug-ins to two of the most popular Microsoft products — Outlook and Word (refer to Chapters 12 and 8, respectively).

Both Microsoft plug-ins are also available to Community Edition users for a slight fee.

A word about Word

The Sugar plug-in for Microsoft Word enables you to merge data, such as names and addresses, from Sugar Professional or Enterprise with form letter templates created in Word.

With the Sugar plug-in for Word, you can

- ✔ **Perform a mail merge from Sugar using a Microsoft Word template.**
- ✔ **Perform a mail merge from Microsoft Word using Sugar data.**

Changing your Outlook on Sugar

For many Sugar users, Microsoft Outlook represents their first foray into the world of CRM. Because old habits are hard to break, new Sugar users often encounter Outlook anxiety pains. The Outlook plug-in connects Sugar to Outlook. Outlook addicts synchronize Outlook e-mail, contacts, and calendar information into the appropriate Sugar modules.

With the Sugar plug-in for Outlook, you can

- ✔ **Synchronize contacts, appointments, and tasks between Outlook and Sugar.**

- ✔ **Archive e-mail items from Outlook with Sugar Accounts, Bugs, Cases, Contacts, Leads, Opportunities, and Projects records.**

- ✔ **View Sugar records from within Outlook.**

- ✔ **Create Sugar Accounts, Bugs, Cases, Contacts, Leads, and Opportunities records from within Outlook.**

Portals

Sugar's Customer Self-Service Portal module allows companies to provide marketing, sales, and support services via the Internet. Customers with a problem can create a case, upload relevant information, and track the case to its resolution without ever having to pick up a phone. All cases automatically appear within the Sugar Cases module.

Using the customer portal reduces the time your customer service and tech support people spend on the phone — and this typically helps your bottom line.

In addition to creating a case, the Sugar portals allow additional functionality:

- ✔ **Account Updates:** Customers can update their contact information.

- ✔ **Subscription Management:** Customers can select the subscriptions to newsletters that they want to receive; their selections are automatically registered in the Campaigns module.

- ✔ **Knowledge Search:** Customers can search for information found within the Knowledge Base, FAQs, and Bug Tracker.

Flow through Your Work with Ease

A *workflow* (see Chapter 14) is a defined series of tasks to produce an outcome. Sugar Professional and Enterprise editions include a Workflow module that allows you to define different workflows for different types of jobs. Defining workflows has several benefits: it allows the company to standardize their business processes, it automates the procedure, and it insures follow-through.

In Sugar, a workflow consists of four parts:

- **Templates:** You define workflow templates based on the process you want to follow.
- **Alerts:** You create alerts based on changes to records or a time lapse.
- **Triggers:** You define what action sets the wheels in motion.
- **Define actions:** You define what you want to happen when a trigger is set off.

Access Control

If you are the only user of your Sugar database, your security might be limited to the password that allows you access to your entire database. In the Community Edition of Sugar, the administrator can create roles (refer to Chapter 16) that determine the access level of each user to the various modules and what they can change and/or see when they access that module.

Sugar Professional and Enterprise editions take the issue of security a bit further by giving you a few more options:

- **Field-Level Access Controls:** You can limit access to specific field information.
- **Role Management:** You can create roles based on user types (Administrator and Normal).

Building a Bigger Database

MySQL and PHP are both *Open Source* (meaning they are free to download and use) software products. The PHP/MySQL combination has become a popular choice for database-driven Web sites and the combination that Sugar supplies with all three versions. Although MySQL can be used for a variety of applications, it is most commonly found on Web servers.

For most of you, the MySQL database is powerful enough to run your business — and your database software. However, larger corporations often require beefier database software to run their various business processes. The two most popular database applications are Oracle and Microsoft SQL Server.

SugarCRM Enterprise allows you to connect Sugar to either an Oracle or SQL Standard Server database. This is enticing to large companies for a number of reasons:

- ✔ **ROI:** Oracle and SQL Server are expensive databases. When a company has forked over a sizeable amount of cash for these solutions, they want to be able to use these powerful databases with all of their applications.

- ✔ **Smaller learning curve:** All databases need an administrator and Sugar is no exception. And, chances are good that the over-worked and underpaid IT guy is going to inherit that position. Using a database that he's already familiar with means he already has the advanced knowledge needed to keep the database in good, working order.

- ✔ **Advanced Reporting Capabilities:** Larger, more powerful databases come with design tools to create reports accommodating just about any need. Administrators can design complex reports by using familiar design tools.

Chapter 18

Ten Ways to Make Your Life Even Sweeter

*I*t's only natural that Sugar, an Open Source product, has captured the imagination of developer types who love to program. Literally hundreds of add-on products work with Sugar. The products range from little things like changing the screen colors to robust solutions for your HR department. In this chapter, I highlight my favorites.

You can go to two areas to find the products listed in this chapter — as well as investigate hundreds of other products on your own:

▶ **SugarExchange** (www.sugarexchange.com): Only those developers who are "certified" by Sugar can post products to this site; developers pay to list their products here.

▶ **SugarForge** (www.sugarforge.org): A Web site where anyone can post embellishments to Sugar.

There is a bit of "good and bad" news that goes along with SugarForge. The good news is that many of the products listed here are either free or very inexpensive. The bad news is that sometimes you get what you pay for — and you might find that some of these products are "handyman specials" that require a bit of tweaking. Many of the products mentioned here come with free trial versions — you might want to *try* these products before you *buy*.

Parlez-vous Francais?

If there is any question as to the worldwide popularity of Sugar then check out the fact that Sugar has been translated to over 75 languages. Called *language packs,* you find these translations on both SugarForge and SugarExchange by clicking the Language Packs category on the left edge of both sites.

In addition to typical languages, such as French and Spanish, you find Sugar language packs in everything from Hebrew and Hungarian to Thai and Turkish.

I Think I Need a Change of Theme

Out of the box, Sugar comes with a number of themes (Chapter 3) that change the color of your Sugar installation as well as the look of the Module tabs. Although changing the theme won't make you *work* better — it just might make you feel a bit more at home in Sugar.

Some of the themes are designed to be very functional. For example, the Enhanced Notes theme gives you the ability to attach notes to your various records that include a username. Other themes, such as the Golf theme and the Love theme, are a bit more whimsical. There are even RTL themes that — you guessed it — work with languages that read from right to left.

Have BlackBerry, Will Travel

Who doesn't use a smartphone these days? And more and more of those phones are a BlackBerry. Although Sugar can be accessed directly from the browser of any smartphone, there are a few limitations:

- ✔ **The screen on a handheld device is much smaller than on your laptop or desktop machine.** Therefore, although you can see Sugar on your phone, you'll be doing a lot of scrolling to see an entire record.

- ✔ **Pulling up links on a handheld is much slower than on a computer.**

- ✔ **If you don't have connectivity — such as when you're traveling on an airplane — you don't have a database.**

Mobile Edge is a monthly subscription guaranteed to keep you up-to-date with your Sugar database. Quite simply, it installs a mini version of Sugar on your BlackBerry. You can view all the basic Sugar modules — Accounts, Contacts, Activities, Opportunities, and so on. Any changes you make are instantly available to the home office, and vice versa.

Grabbing Tidbits of Information

You might have a love/hate relationship with Sugar: You love having a CRM database but hate entering all of that information. If that's the case, then Contact Capture by Broadlook Technologies should rank high on your list of must have add-ons.

Contact Capture can capture information from a variety of sources including e-mail signatures and Web site directories. The procedure is simple: highlight the information, press a hotkey, and indicate where you want the information to go (Contacts, Leads, and/or Accounts records). For example, you can highlight contact information from the signature area of an incoming e-mail and within seconds add a new record to Sugar. Better yet, you can find a list of contacts from virtually any source and export the entire list to Sugar.

Broadlook is so sure that you'll become addicted to Constant Capture that they provide it free for the first year.

Plugging in to Microsoft Office

Face it. Microsoft is everywhere. Most likely, you're running more than one of its products on your computer. Like many other software products, Sugar takes the "if you can't beat 'em, join 'em" philosophy. Sugar offers plug-ins to two of the most popular Microsoft products: Outlook and Word. You can download the plug-ins free if you are using either the Professional or Enterprise versions of Sugar; you'll have to pay for them if you're using Sugar Community Edition.

Even though the following two products are mentioned in Chapters 8 and 12, they are so useful that they bear repeating in this chapter.

Plugging in to Outlook

A common misconception I hear from potential CRM users is that they don't need CRM because they're using Outlook. I like to think of SugarCRM as Outlook on steroids because of all the powerful tools you can find in

Sugar that aren't available in Outlook. However, many Sugar users continue to use Outlook as their e-mail client yet want to have those e-mails linked to Sugar.

The Outlook plug-in (refer to Chapter 12) installs a Sugar toolbar in Outlook. From there you have a number of options:

- **Archive to Sugar:** Attach the e-mail — or edit the e-mail content on the fly — to Bugs, Accounts, Contacts, or other Sugar records.
- **Create a new Sugar record:** Create a new Accounts, Bugs, or Contacts record from an incoming e-mail.
- **Sync to Sugar:** Synchronize your Outlook contacts, appointments, and tasks to Sugar at the click of a button.

What's in a Word

Chapter 12 shows you how to create e-mail templates using Sugar's template editor. However, many of you would probably prefer to use Word because you're already familiar with it. With the Word plug-in, you can create templates in Word. The process is quite simple. You start by creating a document in Word — or editing an existing one. Anytime you want Sugar data to fill the template, you select the appropriate Sugar field name from the SugarCRM toolbar that appears in Word. Once completed, you can perform a mail merge on the fly by selecting Sugar Contacts, Accounts, or Opportunities records.

Chapter 8 talks about creating a document library in Sugar. The Word plug-in takes the concept one step further by allowing any of the documents you create in Word to be uploaded directly into Sugar. Once loaded, they're available in the Documents module — or any other module that uses templates.

Using a Talended Piece of Software

A new business has it fairly easy. They can download a copy of SugarCRM and have their marketing, service, and support needs met instantly. Throw in a piece of accounting software and they're ready to go.

However, the plot thickens with larger or more established companies. First, they might have information floating around in a variety of *legacy* systems that Sugar is replacing; these products can range from Outlook and Excel to Access and SQL or even Salesforce.com. Although you can import information into Sugar fairly easily, the process becomes very cumbersome if you have to bring in multiple data sources — many of which include multiple tables of information.

The process gets even more complicated. Some of your systems may contain data that you need to keep in both Sugar *and* the other, existing system. For example, you might have proprietary inventory-tracking software that includes customer contact information that must be updated on an ongoing basis. It's enough to make most of us wave the white flag and admit defeat.

But wait, the cavalry — or in this case Talend — arrives to save the day. Talend software will

- ✔ **Help with your data migration.**
- ✔ **Synchronize the data among your various systems.**
- ✔ **Give you a 360-degree look at all of your data.**

Talend includes connectors to over 250 different data source types for purposes of migrating and synchronize your data. You can "click and pick" to define very complicated mapping systems between your various databases. In addition, Talend helps you clean data and even eliminate your duplicates.

But wait — there's more! After you synchronize your data, you need a way to analyze it. You might want to identify trends or target a certain class of customer. For example, you might want to focus on your customers who have placed the biggest orders — and logged the fewest support calls. Using Talend, you can run just such a report.

Talend is available in both Open Source (free) and Enterprise (subscription) editions.

Connecting QuickBooks to Sugar

Most business owners need at least two pieces of software to run a business: database software like Sugar to keep track of customers (and to market to potential customers) and accounting software to help keep an eye on the bottom line. Unfortunately, software that does it all often comes with a whopping price tag — and a very steep learning curve. As a result, you might have chosen Sugar for you CRM needs and QuickBooks for your accounting needs.

QConnector, by RPS Technology, lets you have the best of both worlds. It eliminates the need to enter your information into both sets of software because it *synchronizes* your QuickBooks data with your Sugar data. The synchronization includes your account, invoice, payment, and product data so that you can bid adieu to double-entry data input.

Getting Organized with Sales Folders

Chapter 8 shows you how to attach a document to the Documents module. However, if you're attaching a lot of documents, you might find this feature to be somewhat limited because there's no way to organize these documents into a file system.

If you plan to attach lots of documents to Sugar, check out SalesFolders by InvisibleCRM. Here's a few of the things it does to make your life easier:

- ✔ **Creates a desktop application that allows you to drag a document directly into Sugar.**

- ✔ **Lets you create a file structure for the documents you store in Sugar.**

- ✔ **Automatically synchronizes your new or changed documents between your desktop and Sugar.**

- ✔ **Allows you to save documents in Word or Excel directly into Sugar.**

Being Alerted by SalesAlerts

Unlike many other CRM products, Sugar does not contain "pop-up" alarms that appear shortly before your scheduled activities. Enter SalesAlerts.

Using SalesAlerts, you can be notified of activities as well as changes that occur in other designated fields. For example, you might want to receive notification when a Leads record changes to an Accounts record, or of an upcoming event, such as a birthday or expected closing date.

SalesAlerts also includes a desktop application that further expands Sugar's native functionality. Sales managers can opt to receive alerts for their sales force — or access the desktop application to see all their alerts in one central location. End users can use SalesAlerts to quickly search for information scattered throughout Sugar without having to go directly into Sugar to initiate the search.

Chapter 19

Ten Ways to Become a Master Sugar Chef

*W*e all learn differently. Some of you are visual learners and rely on documentation to help you. Others of you may take a more hands-on approach and prefer to tinker with a program as a way to learn. Still others of you require a bit more handholding, and prefer to have someone directly show you the ropes. I hope this chapter helps you find the answers to your sugary questions — no matter what your learning style!

Read this Book!

My editor advised me when I wrote my first *For Dummies* book that I was not writing the Great American novel — and that very few people would read my book from cover-to-cover. That said, I'm really hoping that *eventually* you will read the book from cover-to-cover.

Although this book comes complete with a cover in a very tasteful shade of yellow that may enhance your office décor, it's not going to do you a whole lot of good sitting on your bookshelf. Feel free to use the Index (conveniently located in the back of the book) to help you find an answer in the flip of a page.

If you happen to be embarrassed to be seen reading a *For Dummies* title, try pasting the cover of your favorite computer magazine over the book — and remember just which Dummy will have the last laugh!

Visit the Help Menus

In addition to the information that I provide in this book, SugarCRM comes with a very good — and quite extensive — online Help system that supplies step-by-step instructions for just about any sweet feature that you might want to explore. For example, if you're attempting to create a new Contacts record, clicking Help displays a listing of all the Contacts record's fields and what they mean. If you're configuring your e-mail account, clicking Help gives you step-by-step instructions for the configuration process.

You can access the Sugar context-sensitive online Help system by clicking the Help icon displayed in Figure 19-1. Help arrives in the shape of a new window.

Figure 19-1:
The Sugar
Help icon.

? Help

To make life even sweeter, the Help window gives you three options at the top of the window:

- **Print:** Click this option to create a hard copy of the Help window.

- **Email:** Choose this option if you want to send a link to the Help system or to one or twenty of your closest Sugar users.

- **Bookmark this page:** You can save the Help page to your Internet browser if you'd like a repeat performance sometime down the road.

Download a Bit of Documentation

A picture may be worth a thousand words but I'd rather have the thousand words when it comes to researching a problem. And way more than a thousand words are available to you on the SugarCRM Web site. Simply go to the Support & Training menu on Sugar's Home page and choose Documentation.

The Documentation page breaks down the documentation into three sections: Enterprise, Professional, and Community Edition. Click the section that corresponds to your version and you'll see a nice assortment of User Guides. And, as you see in Figure 19-2, additional tabs allow you easy access to the documentation from previous versions of Sugar.

You can choose to see the documentation in either HTML or PDF format; if you choose the PDF format, you have the option of either viewing or saving the document.

For those of you who might not be familiar with Adobe Reader, it includes a couple of really great searching tools that will prove helpful when looking for an answer to your question. In Reader, choose Edit➪Find to produce a simple search window that allows you to search by a single word or phrase. If that doesn't provide what you're looking for, choose Edit➪Search, which will give you more advanced search options.

Although I'm not an advocate of sacrificing more trees in the rain forest, at times you might find it easier to print the documentation — particularly if you want to give your entire office easy access to the manual. Choose File➪Print to print any of the PDF files. You might also consider printing on three-hole punched paper to make it easy to place into a binder.

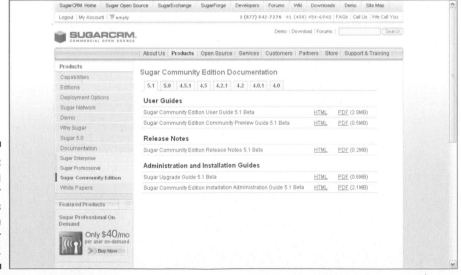

Figure 19-2:
A sampling of the User Guides available on the Sugar Web site.

Adopting a New Sugar Baby

I've spent the last ten years implementing CRM for small to mid-sized businesses, and I've learned that a CRM implementation is not something you enter into without plenty of prior planning.

Sugar designed the Sugar Adoption Program to help keep you organized during the CRM transition. The Sugar Adoption Program Web page features three important links:

- ✔ **List of resources:** Here's where you find links to virtually every little detail to make your Sugar implementation painless — and then some. In addition to common sites, such as the Sugar Wiki, Documentation, Forum, and Training, you find links to a sample Intranet launch page that you can use to help transition your staff into using Sugar. There's also a neat Adoption Checklist spreadsheet that can help you organize your implementation.

- ✔ **Roles and Responsibilities:** Everyone wants to claim credit for when things go right; no one, however, wants to take the blame for when things don't go so right. Here's where you see a clear description of the duties you assign to the members of your implementation team, from the IT manager to the database administrator.

- ✔ **Sugar Adoption Checklist:** Here's where you find a list of the critical checkpoints of a CRM installation, as well as links to corresponding documentation.

  You can access the Sugar Adoption Program materials by clicking the Support and Training menu on the SugarCRM Web site and then choosing Sugar Adoption Program.

Attending Sugar University

Although it doesn't offer a tree-lined campus and a great football team like my alma mater (Go, Gators!), the Sugar University offers a great curriculum of courses designed to increase your knowledge of SugarCRM at a very rapid pace. And, unlike other universities, 80 percent of the Sugar University content is free — as in no tuition!

You find Sugar University by choosing Support & Training on the SugarCRM Home page and then clicking Training. Sugar University offers several options:

- **Online Library:** Every university has a library, and Sugar U is no exception. Here's where you find *How Do I* learning guides with step-by-step instructions for the most common tasks and *Show Me* videos for a visual guide to many of the main Sugar functions.

- **Learning Session:** Think of this as your course catalog because here's where you find all kinds of classes. Many of the classes come in the form of free, pre-recorded Webinars that you can "attend" at your leisure. Others, although free, require prior registration. A few of the courses require "learning credits," which either you purchase or they might be included with your Sugar subscription.

- **Sugar University Offerings:** Here's where you can view all the Sugar training options — and, believe me, there are a bunch. In addition to the *How Do I* guides and *Show Me* videos mentioned earlier, you find links to hands-on workshops and classroom training.

Who knows? Maybe in a few years, there'll be a Sugar University Alumni Association!

Sharing Sweet Words of Love

It amazes me to think of the vast amount of information that the Internet contains. Whether you have a medical ailment or you're looking to purchase a new car, chances are good that the Internet will be one of your primary sources of information. SugarCRM has helped close the gap between users in various locations by creating a couple of sites that allow for virtual, interactive communication. Although you need to take some of the information found there with several grains of salt, these sites allow you to see what other users are thinking — and even post a few thoughts of your own.

Watching the Wiki

Although *Wiki* means "quick" in Hawaiian, *wiki* is more commonly used to describe a collaborative Web site that allows anyone to edit, delete, or modify informational content that has been placed on a Web site. There are actually two Sugar wikis — one for Support and one for Developers. And, because Sugar is Open Source software, Sugar users are constantly editing the wikis. You'll find them to be a great source for issues that might not be covered with the more traditional learning materials.

You can find the Sugar wikis by selecting Support & Training from Sugar's Web site and then choosing Wiki.

Thinking fondly of the Forums

In computer-speak, a *forum* is an online discussion group. In Sugar-speak, the Forums are a great way to post questions you might have about Sugar. Although the sweet folks at Sugar monitor the Forums, you often find that other users supply great answers.

You can get to the Sugar Forums by clicking the Forums link on the Sugar Home page. Here you find links to discussions on everything from general help to issues faced by Sugar developers.

Finding Bugs in the Sugar bowl

Software can be frustrating even for the most seasoned of users. You might spend hours trying to figure something out to no avail only to find that the fault lies not with something *you* are doing but rather in something that the *software* isn't doing.

A software *bug* is an error or defect in your software that causes it not to work correctly. I've heard the term originated years ago when a couple of moths wreaked major havoc when they were French-fried in a super computer. Personally, I think the term originated because bugs can really bug you!

In any event, Sugar has a Web page devoted to those annoying insects. You can access that buggy Web site by going to www.sugarcrm.com/crm/sugarbugs.html. You can submit any bugs that you might stumble across — and discover what is bugging other Sugar users!

Taking a Honeymoon

SugarCRM holds a number of conferences designed to let Sugar end-users learn first-hand about new features that might be coming down the Turnpike as well as to achieve an even higher mastery of their current version of Sugar. You can find the exact date and location of these events by clicking About Us and then choosing Events from www.sugarcrm.com.

Taking a trip to Silicon Valley

The SugarCRM headquarters is located in the heart of Silicon Valley in Cupertino, California. This is where the folks at Sugar hold their yearly bash, SugarCon. In keeping with the spirit of Open Source software, SugarCon is open to vendors, consultants, end-users, and prospects. I guess a lot of people are looking for an excuse to visit California in February!

The three-day event features a number of simultaneous learning tracks as well as the opportunity to network with other Sugar users. Participants can select and attend the tracks that they find the most useful. And, from what my sources tell me, a good time is had by all!

Coming soon to a location near you

If you can't make the trip out to sunny California, you might want to check out CRM Acceleration. CRM Acceleration events take place virtually all over the world and are designed to help companies understand and succeed with SugarCRM. These one-day workshops include sessions on marketing, sales, and customer support and are geared towards both existing and potential Sugar users.

Developing a Love for the Developers Page

Not content with merely *using* Sugar, developers are a weird bunch of people who want to *change* Sugar to take it to its next level. Chapter 15 shows you how to make modifications from within Sugar, and Chapter 18 shows you some of the neat products that some SugarCRM users have developed to work with Sugar. However, if you want to be one of those people that develop neat products yourself, then you want to visit the Sugar Developers Web site. You can access the site by clicking Developers from the SugarCRM Web site.

If you're a developer, you can find a wealth of information on the Sugar Developers Web site, including:

- ✔ A blog.

- ✔ Podcasts that you can download to have with you where your travels may take you.

- ✔ Help on more advanced areas including Oracle, PHP, Apache, and IIS.

- ✔ A toolbox containing snippets of code, tutorials, documentation, and other tools of interest to developers.

- ✔ Links to chat sites and developer user groups.

Using a Portal Instead of a Door

I often wonder how many new words and phrases have been added to the dictionary since the advent of the computer. Interestingly enough, Sugar must have a great vocabulary because they've incorporated so many of these new concepts into their software and Web site. Unfortunately, because the Sugar Web site holds so much information, you might find it a bit difficult to navigate. Enter your portal.

A *portal* is a Web site or service that offers all kinds of resources and services. In the case of SugarCRM, your portal offers you links to everything from support resources and news about upcoming classes to answers to your frequently asked questions.

You can access your personalized support portal in two ways:

- ✔ Click Admin from your SugarCRM Home page and then choose Sugar Support Portal in the Sugar Network subpanel of the Administration Home page.

- ✔ Click Support & Training from the SugarCRM Web site and choose Support Portal.

You need to login to the portal if you haven't done so already. If this is your first time logging in, you'll be asked to provide a username and password.

If you're using the Professional or Enterprise version of SugarCRM, you can activate a more specialized version of the Support Portal (shown in Figure 19-3) that will allow you to submit support questions to the technical support staff directly from your Web site.

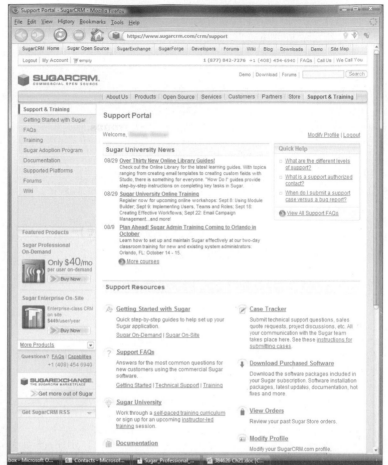

Figure 19-3:
The
SugarCRM
Support
Portal.

Hire a Consultant

Many years ago, I decided to wallpaper my living room. I chose very expensive (and thin!) paper. Not wanting to drip paste on my carpet, I set up a table in my garage for the pasting process, smeared on the paste, and carted it into the dining room. Those of you who have ever tried their luck at wallpapering can imagine the results. For the rest of you, picture a mummy wrapped in a lovely print and you'll get the drift. After I removed the paper and paste from various parts of my anatomy, I sheepishly called in an expert. Mr. Expert gave me a few strange looks, muttered about the table in the garage, and had my dining room done in no time.

You might find yourself in a similar situation when learning Sugar. Perhaps you don't have the time — or patience — to attend a class or read documentation. Maybe you have specific questions about functionality as it applies to your business. For whatever reason, you might want to hire an expert to help you with some — or all — of your installation.

SugarCRM Partners are folks who earn their living helping folks implement Sugar. These partners come in three flavors (gold, silver, and bronze) depending on how large an ad the consultant wants to appear on Sugar's website and how much money they want to commit to be listed as a partner. You can find a complete listing of SugarCRM Partners at www.sugarcrm. com/crm/partners/partnerfinder.html.

Index